CONDUCTING BUSINESS

CONDUCTING BUSINESS

Unveiling the Mystery
Behind the Maestro

Leonard Slatkin

**AMADEUS
PRESS**

An Imprint of Hal Leonard Corporation

JUL 2012

Published in 2012 by Amadeus Press
An Imprint of Hal Leonard Corporation
7777 West Bluemound Road
Milwaukee, WI 53213

Trade Book Division Editorial Offices
33 Plymouth St., Montclair, NJ 07042

Printed in the United States of America
Book design by Mark Lerner

Photographs in this book are courtesy of the Slatkin family.

Every reasonable effort has been made to find copyright holders and secure permission. Any omissions brought to our attention will be remedied in future editions.

Library of Congress Cataloging-in-Publication Data

Slatkin, Leonard.
 Conducting business : unveiling the mystery behind the maestro / Leonard Slatkin. -- 1st hardcover ed.
    p. cm.
 Includes index.
 ISBN 978-1-57467-204-6
 1. Conducting. I. Title.
 MT85.S56 2012
 781.45--dc23
                    2012016970

www.amadeuspress.com

For Cindy

My companion and inspiration

The aim and final end of all music should be none other than the glory of God and the refreshment of the soul.

— JOHANN SEBASTIAN BACH

Music is the divine way to tell beautiful, poetic things to the heart.

— PABLO CASALS

To be a true artist you have to play the way you feel—not the way others think you should feel.

— DON ELLIS

Show me an orchestra that likes its conductor and I'll show you a lousy conductor.

— GODDARD LIEBERSON

Contents

Praeludium

There will come a time when you believe everything is finished.
That will be the beginning.

— LOUIS L'AMOUR

There is an old joke about the audience member who comes up to the conductor after a performance. Having heard a full program, she says, "That was lovely. What do you do for a living?"

At one time, this question would have hardly surprised him. Conducting an orchestra or playing in one was a part-time job. And, back then, it was a him. These days, salaries for musicians at the higher levels are not only competitive with other fields, the income may even exceed some people's wildest dreams. A simpler way to pose the question is, "So, what do you do?"—period!

The orchestral conductor is a relatively new species, having originated in the nineteenth century. In just under two hundred years, conducting has evolved into an extremely complicated profession. It requires much more than wielding the baton, score reading and the ability to listen. The conductor also serves as father, mother, psychologist, teacher, referee and many other roles to his hundred-plus orchestra members. He or she operates as a CEO, a visiting team leader, a production supervisor and a social butterfly. The willingness to participate in fund-raising and a knack for those activities have become necessary duties in today's musical marketplace.

Conducting Business answers the question of what we do. The book is essentially about the profession; it is not a manual on how to conduct. Numerous volumes have been written about conducting technique. The profession's history, likewise, has been well documented. Biographies abound in print, but not much exists to explain what the conductor actually does on an everyday basis. How do we study? Do we need a stick? What is our relationship to the composer? Where is the stage door? I try to unravel the mysteries of a most misunderstood profession. And, I have tried to remove some barriers that stand in the way of those who are attempting to unlock the secrets of the baton in pursuit of a conducting career.

It was not my intention to write an autobiography, but when I began the book and its ideas developed, I realized that stories about my own life and the people who helped shape my career would provide a more thorough understanding of how a conductor comes into being.

So, in the first of the book's three parts, I tell about my background, education and experience, my personal path to the podium. As my dreaming shifts to becoming, the second part gradually moves away from my chronological life story and into greater detail about the challenges every podium minder faces. The final section offers answers to questions I often am asked. Another chapter shows ten problematic musical examples and illustrates how the conductor figures out and solves them.

Part One

In many ways, I was just a normal kid, going to public schools, playing ball with the guys and blaming my brother for everything. Most of my friends were in the school band and orchestra. The big difference between them and me was that when I got home, it was practice, practice, practice. Once, when my pals wanted me to come outside and play, I actually stopped pounding on the keyboard and brought my baseball glove to the front door. My mother threatened to lock up the piano if I did not finish my Czerny. I did not believe her, and out the door I went. Upon returning home, sure enough, she had secured the lid of the keyboard and it could not be opened.

I was in heaven. No more scales, arpeggios or exercises in thirds. After a few days passed, I started to feel lonely. Beethoven and I were just getting acquainted with each other and I missed him. My mom would not budge. Screaming, kicking and yelling did me no good. Only when I finally agreed that practicing came first was the lid unlocked and a newfound lifestyle kicked in.

With virtually everyone in my family a part of the music industry, I had a front-row seat to witness the degree of discipline these music professionals applied to their work. My parents, devoted to film industry soundtracks, chamber music, popular recording and freelance classical performance, certainly packed a lot into their lives. Sadly, as much as they might have tried, raising a couple of children did not come so naturally. My brother and I grew up as independents, struggling to fathom the perpetual stress that seemed to surround us. Eventually, we managed to figure it out, and despite the obstacles, both of us have done well in our chosen musical careers.

The book's second chapter elaborates on our family's rich musical history. My mother came from a musical dynasty which originated in the Ukraine and my father, likewise of Russian heritage, possessed musical gifts so prodigious that he more than compensated for the fact that he was the sole talent on that side of the family. To grow up in Los Angeles with parents who were "stars in the musical firmament" enabled us to get to know practically every prominent musician on the West Coast. Imagine the likes of Frank Sinatra, Arnold Schoenberg, John Williams, Art Tatum, André Previn and Jascha Heifetz visiting your home! These acquaintances led to a variety of wonderful anecdotes, a number of which I recount in Part One.

Living in a household filled with musical talent should have given me a strong head start in the field and an easy transition into the profession. But this was hardly the case. Personal tragedy also made things very difficult. My father died at the age of forty-seven and his passing dramatically altered life for me. I left the musical fold for a little while, but with encouragement from friends and family, decided to pursue the path my dad had begun to forge for himself, that of conducting symphonic ensembles.

It was my good fortune to learn from two of the finest, Walter Susskind and Jean Morel. These two opposite personalities, plus the disparate disciplines of Aspen and Juilliard, provided the necessary technical skills I needed to make progress on the path to professional conducting. However, as this book repeatedly demonstrates, conducting is about so much more than just waving a stick.

Part Two

Conducting Business continues with my entry into the workforce, which started after I pursued the typical opportunities available to aspiring conductors, with student, amateur or community ensembles. In October of 1968, I took the podium of a professional symphony orchestra for the first time. I was standing in front of dozens of experienced musicians who possessed a lot more knowledge, individually and collectively, than I did. What could I possibly say that they did not already know?

My professional career began as assistant conductor of the Saint Louis Symphony. In this capacity as assistant, or as a répétiteur or coach, the would-be maestro poises him- or herself for a professional career. Most conductors spend their apprentice period watching and waiting, sometimes seeing the very best conductors and sometimes merely observing what does not work. From learning patience to walking on stage for the first time, these early forays are critical for meaningful musical development.

After six years in various secondary capacities, I was catapulted into the international spotlight with three major debuts in one season, New York, Chicago and London. My top priority, then, was to seek the career advice of two men who would become mentors to me, John Edwards and David Hyslop. Mentors are vital: no conductor can do this job alone.

Through a focus on my experiences in Saint Louis, Washington DC, Detroit and London, the book proceeds to examine rehearsal technique, hiring and dismissing musicians, and the position of music director. I discuss at length the art of score study, every nuance of which a conductor must master, and the learning of various tricks to enhance visual and aural acuity. This part of the book provides guidance on matters as diverse as effective communication with members of the board of directors, fund-raising, public speaking, choosing musical editions and even concert attire. The conductor is the voice of a community's musical education: leading local young people's concerts, working with student orchestras or passing along whatever wisdom he or she has acquired as mentor to the next generation of podium talent.

This section covers practical matters conductors often skip when discussing their work. These include managerial skills for successful dealings with artistic committees, executive directors and journalists, as well as organizational skills required to make recordings, arrange tours and conduct alfresco performances in the summer. Although my own visits to the world of opera were infrequent, the subject matter is important. In earlier eras, the opera house was the starting

point for most conductors; later, they climbed out of the pit and onto the podium. Whether at home, on tour or in the recording studio, the conductor must
learn the art of creative multi-tasking.

Sometimes it seems that controversy accompanies the job description, and
as an example, this chapter addresses one such unpleasantness in my musical life. It occurred during an engagement at the Metropolitan Opera, and
I happened to be writing about those appearances, contemporaneously, for
my website. That act in itself seemed to generate a buzz, just because I told
the truth. Though circumstances prevented me from continuing the narrative
on my blog, the entire story is contained in these pages, exactly as I wrote it
in March 2010.

Another area terribly neglected in print is how conductors react, or do not
react, in the event of labor strife. I have endured three such times of turmoil,
the most recent being a horrendous half-year work stoppage in Detroit. A
would-be music director must know every aspect of the union contract, as
almost every word in the document will affect the future of his or her orchestra
members. On the brighter side, I have included some personal reminiscences
of significant people and milestones in my own life on the podium. Leonard
Bernstein was the very model of the American conductor, both in life and
in death. His profound impact on the American musical scene can never be
minimized. Even though he and I did not know each other well, there is no
question that he influenced my musical persona, mine along with the majority
of American conductors.

One can never know if fate plays a hand, but sometimes, being in the right
place can transform a conductor's life. For me, two premieres in Chicago were
particular turning points, with works by Carter and Del Tredici. Fast-forward
to London, just four days after the attacks of September 11, where unexpectedly
I was summoned to lead what had to be the most difficult and emotion-laden
concert of my career. The video of that evening's performance of the Barber
Adagio for Strings has become a much-viewed hit on YouTube. A conductor
simply needs to be prepared for anything, and it is not always so simple.

Legend has it that conductors are among the most long-lived of professionals,
but there are health perils aplenty. Although I have rarely been forced to cancel

an engagement, a heart attack put me out of commission for three months. In this section, I describe why and how the conductor must maintain physical, as well as emotional, strength.

Part Three

Although this volume is not about conducting technique, I decided to show the reader some musical challenges, passages from symphonic works with problems in common with many other pieces in the repertoire. These excerpts present musical puzzles that the conductor must solve before rehearsal. To understand the challenges, the ability to read a score is unnecessary. This book is intended for all music lovers.

Finally, I close with some thoughts and observations about the conducting profession and music in general. Some comments are lighthearted and some are of serious import.

So far, I have had a wonderful life creating and recreating the musical experience. For those readers who have spent a good deal of time developing their own lives as conductors, some of what these pages contain will be old news. But for readers just setting out on the path or those who are curious about this most mysterious of occupations, I hope you will find the observations and advice helpful.

And entertaining: there are some good stories along the way.

PART
ONE

A story should have a beginning, a middle, and an end . . . but not necessarily in that order.
— JEAN-LUC GODARD

1

The Bug Bites

*Music is the one incorporeal entrance into the higher world of
knowledge which comprehends mankind but which mankind
cannot comprehend.*

— LUDWIG VAN BEETHOVEN, QUOTED BY
BETTINA VON ARNIM, LETTER TO GOETHE, 1810

Conducting is a truly mysterious art and job. You work alone but also with more than a hundred people. Most of the time, you turn your back to the people you are supposed to be entertaining. You are consumed by a feeling of power and simultaneous helplessness. Talent cannot be measured until you gain experience. The profession is fraught with peril. Why go into it?

How do you know that the podium is for you?

For conductors this is perhaps the most difficult question to answer. Whether practicing alone or playing with others, singers or instrumentalists are capable of translating music notation into sound. During the study process, however, the conductor cannot produce musical sounds by waving a stick. There is no ensemble to practice with. And who wants an orchestra in the living room, anyway?

Some would label it a calling, as a result of waking up one day and saying, "I can do this!" But there are certainly a lot of closet conductors out there too. Nearly all have envisioned themselves in front of a hundred people, moving their arms and producing a massive force of musical sound from those gestures. People tend to do this in private, but a few manage to take it to the public level.

The majority of conductors begin their musical journey as instrumentalists, some as vocalists. Almost no one simply declares he or she is going to conduct as the first step in the musical process. Those who play piano, violin, clarinet or anything else have a solid degree of proficiency on their chosen instrument before stepping onto the podium. Many, in fact, achieve outstanding performing careers beforehand.

Felix Mendelssohn was the first "conductor" in the modern sense. Prior to him, the person leading the orchestra was usually the concertmaster, sometimes the soloist or, of course, the church organist. We do not know what kind of performances those early exponents of conducting produced, but we are well aware of the types of problems they encountered.

Beethoven, by the end of his life profoundly deaf, led the premiere of his Ninth Symphony, unable to hear the orchestra and chorus. Rachmaninov sank into a massive depression over the first performance of his First Symphony, which was directed by a highly unsympathetic Alexander Glazunov. Hector Berlioz took up the baton merely because he grew dissatisfied with the feeble attempts of others.

For the most part, composers and conductors of newish pieces were one in the same. Whether Brahms, Dvořák, Mahler, Tchaikovsky or so many others, the establishment of musical tradition was handed to us by the creators of the music. It was left to the twentieth century to separate the composer from the interpreter. This applied to the field of instrumental performance as well as conducting. When we think of Paganini, Liszt, Chopin or Schumann, our impressions are of composers of great music, and equally of great performers.

The operatic realm was a bit different. During the romantic era, Wagner was likely the only composer who could both write for the stage and also deliver a fine performance on the podium. But even he left most of the premieres to others. We certainly do not think of Verdi, Puccini, Gounod or Bizet as baton wielders.

Richard Strauss and Gustav Mahler were accomplished instrumentalists, but neither is remembered for that aspect of their careers. Both served as figureheads to at least two generations of conductors who would raise the profession to greater prominence.

At the beginning of the twentieth century, Weingartner, Furtwängler, Toscanini as well as many others, all from solid instrumental and compositional backgrounds, dropped those components of their careers to concentrate exclusively on conducting. No longer were the instrumentalist/composer and conductor the same person. However, they were several generations removed from personally knowing Mozart, Beethoven or Schubert. Hearing those incomparable composers perform would have been extraordinary, but it likely would have made it difficult for a conductor to interpret the music in his own way. Freed from this possible constraint, musicians now had the leeway to realize the vision of the composer with new and original perspectives.

There is a story about the late pianist Sheldon Skolnick, in which he recounts a lesson with his teacher, the eminent pianist and conductor Rudolph Ganz. Shelly was playing a Brahms rhapsody at that lesson when Ganz jumped up and said, "No, no. That is not how Brahms played it," and the teacher proceeded to play through the piece, having known Brahms well. When he finished, Ganz then remarked, "Now, this is how the composer performed it. If you want to know how Bach played, you have to ask Landowska," the famous English harpsichordist, who specialized in Bach but actually lived about two hundred years after Bach died.

The enmity between Furtwängler and Toscanini is notorious, although evidence suggests that the men had mutual respect for each other. When I was young, this was a hotly argued topic among students who were considering entering the conducting profession. Who was right? Which one carried the interpretive mantle of the past masters and whose path would we choose to follow? It seemed there was one camp or the other, no in between. The dilemma was similar to pianists deciding if they would emulate Horowitz or Schnabel, violinists contemplating Kreisler over Heifetz, and even composers adhering to the schools of Stravinsky or Schoenberg.

The mid-twentieth century was a time of tremendous change and musical challenges. Certainly the age of the maestro had begun, spawning podium figures larger than life. Whether von Karajan, Bernstein, Solti, Walter, Reiner or Szell, to name only a few, the international stage saw the conductor as the dominant figure of the concert hall. They, along with their successors, became the arbiters of musical taste worldwide. Recordings further enhanced the mystique and gave musicians an audio clue as to how these masters regarded the great works. In addition, they were responsible for bringing to life new compositions through performance and commissions. With the performer and composer now separated, necessity demanded that the conductor keep new music in front of the public.

Several composers turned to conducting in the latter part of their lives. Copland, Stravinsky, Britten and Hindemith were among those to commit a vast number of their works to disc. Usually you went to their concerts with a degree of reverence for the composer, but not so much conviction as to their conducting prowess. The next generation would be rather different. Boulez and Bernstein would exemplify the composer turned conductor in a positive light, although their compositional outputs diminished.

As we moved into the twenty-first century, the conductor lost a bit of the glamour associated with the greats of the past. A few maestros brought individuality to their performances, but most who followed a traditional symphonic path could not duplicate the special qualities of the great conductors from previous eras.

Specialization provided another way for conductors and instrumentalists to find new interpretive ideas. Historically informed performance practice made for some very literal concerts, but in many cases it became difficult to distinguish one Beethoven symphony cycle from another. Trying to duplicate what the composer might have heard is certainly valid, but the rules governing this practice have actually caused more than a few conductors to shy away from this repertoire.

But can today's listener hear music in the same way that it was heard in the past? Of course not. We cannot walk into a museum and see a Van Gogh without an awareness that we have also seen Monet. And modern ears that hear Bach and Haydn have also heard Bartók and Lloyd Webber. This knowledge influences how we listen today. Music is never static; it always moves forward.

So how do the conductors get started? By listening, seeing, learning and drawing on that unspoken inspiration that guided them into music in the first place. Sometimes a single performance transforms your life; sometimes you just feel that this is what you were born to do. In any event, the decision to pursue a career on the podium is only the first step in a profession that will take a lifetime to master.

When I was nine years old, I had a record player in my bedroom. That phonograph transported me to all kinds of sonic wonderlands. At that time, I had given up the violin and was venturing into the world of keyboard studies. My record library now included albums from Horowitz rather than Heifetz.

About five blocks away from our family home were the studios of KFAC, the only classical music radio station in Los Angeles. Even at that young age, I would walk down Wilshire Boulevard to hang out with the men who spun the records, in particular an announcer named Thomas Cassidy. He had a two-hour show sponsored by the local gas company. The opening strains of Tchaikovsky's First Piano Concerto would introduce the program and it would conclude with the beginning of that work's slow movement.

Tom also served as the voice of the Hollywood Bowl. Back in the '50s, a reflecting pool of water separated the stage from the audience. At intermission, we were treated to a magical fountain show, seemingly choreographed with multicolored floodlights and piped-in music, and then Tom would step to the microphone to inform us about upcoming concerts. Some nights this was the highlight, far outclassing the orchestral program.

It was at this station where I first began to think about conducting. The DJs—in those days, they played the records and tried to avoid scratching them—would let me borrow records for listening pleasure in my bedroom. I would set up a lamp so that the light shone onto a gray wall. Then I would put on a disc and stand between the lamp and wall so I could see myself on what almost looked like a movie screen. The shadow image projected showed that I was at least as good as anyone I saw either downtown or at the Bowl. Or so I thought.

Of course I never told my parents what I was up to, though they must have suspected something.

At that time, my father had just begun to lead recording sessions as a conductor. His main work, primarily as a violinist, revolved around the movie studios, his string quartet and Capitol Records. But in the early '50s, he was given the opportunity to conduct some sessions for Capitol. Each record label had a pickup group that was given a name like RCA Symphony or Columbia Symphony. Concert Arts was the pseudonym for Capitol. Later, my dad would lead recordings for the same label with the Hollywood Bowl Orchestra.

I had already quit the violin because I recognized that I would not become my father's equal, so it was logical to suppose that I would shy away from conducting. For the most part, I kept quiet. It was only when I reached high school that I went public and did some arranging and conducting for the holiday and spring musicals.

I am not sure who was the first orchestral conductor I ever saw, but I definitely remember who made a lasting impression on me. Toscanini. This name was legendary in our household. When the radio announced that the maestro and the NBC Symphony would be coming to Los Angeles on a tour in 1952, the family grabbed tickets, and my life changed. *Pictures at an Exhibition* was on the program, a work I knew from several different recordings. Here was a man, minimal in his gestures, producing the most amazing sounds I had ever heard from an orchestra. From that point, every penny of my allowance went toward buying his recordings, and of course, I conducted along with them in my bedroom.

In the 1950s, the Los Angeles Philharmonic was hardly the orchestra it is today. In fact, other orchestras in the area, notably in Glendale and Pasadena, were considered far superior. However, a couple of times a season, I would take the bus downtown and hear the orchestra in its home, Philharmonic Auditorium, a truly bleak hall with unfortunate acoustics. Still, I marveled at the wizardry of the remarkable artists who came to play or conduct: Heifetz, Ormandy, Rubinstein and Barbirolli.

Another transformational concert experience for me took place when Fritz Reiner stood before my hometown band. With the tiniest flick of the wrist, he coaxed a degree of precision and finesse out of the instrumentalists that I had never before experienced. All of a sudden, the LA Phil sounded like a great orchestra, at least to my young ears. Once again, I bought recordings and watched the shadow on the wall in my room.

My friends at this time were all kids in the neighborhood, and we seemed to share musical interests. Usually two or three of us would go to the concerts together. A few times a week, we walked to the Bowl, kicking a rock to see if we could keep it in play over the three-mile distance. After the performances, we would go to a diner and have a bite, discussing the merits or horrors of what we had heard. When I arrived home, my parents showed an interest in my opinions. They rarely attended these concerts, as their workload was prohibitive. I really doubt they were equally intrigued by the orchestra, as their own circle of musical colleagues was extraordinary; perhaps to them, the Philharmonic was merely ordinary.

Along with piano, I took up the viola. It was the string instrument that no one else in the family played. It was also the instrument that nobody at either my junior high or high school attempted to master. There exists a truly appalling recording from one of our spring concerts, where the first movement of the "Unfinished" Symphony was on the program. At one point, after a glorious buildup, the orchestra stops and the viola part is exposed, playing a little rhythmic figure. I was the lone violist. If anyone ever finds that recording, it might be used against me, as my pathetic, tinny sound is surprisingly audible.

I also participated in the California Youth Symphony Orchestra led by a Russian conductor, Peter Meremblum. Almost every talented young instrumentalist in LA played in this group, and amazingly, I was placed on the first stand. One day, the conductor was called away to the phone during rehearsal. He looked down at me and said, "Slatkin. You wish to conduct?" I did not know what to say, but before I could summon a response, he threw the score of the overture to La forza del destino at me. All of a sudden, at age sixteen, I was allowed to stand on the podium for a few minutes.

I have no recollection of how well the music went. All I remember is the overwhelming feeling that swept over me that morning. I knew then and there that this is what I wanted to do. There was no turning back.

2

Life Before Life

Insanity is hereditary. You get it from your children.

—SAM LEVENSON

Where does it come from? How can talent be measured and is it inherited or learned?

I never gave it much thought. In my household, I was surrounded by music round the clock—my parents practicing individually, musical colleagues joining

Modest Altschuler

in to play chamber music, or just a visiting student stopping by for a lesson and chat. If children were guests at the house, they usually exhibited the same talents as their parents, almost always musical.

There have been so many dynasties in the music world—Bach, Mozart, Mendelssohn, Schumann, Altschuler.

Who?

Modest Altschuler (February 15, 1873–September 12, 1963) was just one member of an extraordinary Russian family who had immigrated to the United States near the end of the nineteenth century. A cellist, conductor and composer, he carved out a unique niche and made an indelible mark on the American musical scene.

He was also my great-uncle.

Modest was born in Mogilev, near Kiev, when it was then a part of Russia, later part of the USSR. Today it is Belarus. It was also the birthplace of other distinguished musicians including Irving Berlin. That region, throughout history, has been claimed by several countries, and when Altschuler was thirteen, it was part of Poland.

He studied cello at the Warsaw Conservatory, and following graduation, moved to Moscow where he continued his studies, adding composition with Arensky and Tanyev. Altschuler had a flourishing career when the seeds of revolution were being planted. Like many of his compatriots, he fled the confines of Russia and came to an unknown future in the United States. This was a bold move in 1893.

His early years in America are not well documented. Most likely he landed jobs as a cellist, playing in vaudeville houses and later, cinemas, when grand theaters offered silent films with full orchestral accompaniment. Of political necessity, the Russian community was growing in New York. Many musicians would follow, primarily of Jewish heritage. To provide a performing outlet for many of the new arrivals, Altschuler formed the Russian Symphony Orchestra Society in 1903.

He was aided by one of his cellist brothers as well as the distinguished violinist Alexander Sazlawsky. Together they worked to establish the orchestra, and Altschuler conducted the new ensemble's debut concert at Cooper Union Hall on January 7, 1904. The program emphasized the players' heritage, with works by Glinka, Tchaikovsky, Wieniawski and Rachmaninov. The latter turned out to be the US premiere of *The Rock*. It made sense for Modest to promote this young composer, as they had shared teachers, and he and Rachmaninov were in the same class in Moscow.

In his autobiography, the young Andre Kostelanetz relates a story about the time he was taken to visit the maestro, in hopes of getting encouragement to enter the conducting profession. After telling Altschuler of his aspirations, this is what he received in response.

"In my travels in this country I have seen that there is one profession that has a great need for people . . . Why don't you become a dentist?"

For fifteen years, the Russian Symphony Orchestra played music written principally by Russian composers, with only a few exceptions, most notably, a premiere of the Third Symphony of Sibelius. The orchestra personnel, newly arrived and willing to work for little compensation, were eager to introduce their music to the New World. Altschuler brought many unknown works to American audiences, some of which would become familiar staples of the symphonic repertoire. Among those composers were Rimsky-Korsakov, Tchaikovsky, Ippolitov-Ivanov, Mussorgsky and Glazunov. In 1908, Modest presented the American premiere of Rachmaninov's Second Symphony. And in 1910, he played *Fireworks* by Igor Stravinsky, giving the renowned composer his first hearing in the United States.

In addition to many composers, Altschuler also introduced a number of prominent artists to American listeners: the violinist Mischa Elman, the pianist Josef Lhévinne, as well as Sergei Prokofiev, playing his First Piano Concerto. Scriabin was invited to guest conduct the orchestra.

The orchestra also made a number of recordings for the Columbia label. Altschuler did not commit any of his own compositions to disc, but coincidentally, one of his pieces, *Russian Sailor's Dance*, was recorded with the Detroit Symphony, led by its music director at the time, Ossip Gabrilovitch. I would become music director of that orchestra almost a century later.

The Russian Symphony Society with Modest Altschuler

Altschuler did not perform much music from his adopted country, with only a handful of works represented in the fifteen-year existence of the orchestra. But he realized, as Dvořák had, a potential that would come to life just a few years after the Russian Symphony disbanded. The following is from a 1913 interview he had with Victor Talking Machine Recordings.

> It should be very interesting for Americans who are studying with the hope of becoming composers to review the astonishing progress of the Russias in seventy-five years. Glinka was born in 1804, and did not commence to write as a real master until about 1834. Prior to that time Russia imported its music from other lands, but neglected the riches at its own threshold. The succeeding masters made themselves familiar with the music of other lands, but did not lose sight of their Russian heritage. In less than a century the land of his Imperial Majesty the Czar has emerged from musical obscurity to foremost rank among the musical nations of the world. America may have no century-old mine of folk-melody of its own, but are not the folk melodies of all the world the common possession of the nation which has held its arms so wide open to the liberty-loving people of all lands? Perhaps in the melting pot there may come a new art that shall be even closer in touch with the heartbeats of mankind. The compositions of MacDowell and others have shown us that this prophecy is very likely to be realized.

Eventually the need for this musical outlet disappeared, as New York now hosted a variety of symphonic ensembles playing a wide range of music welcoming the burgeoning immigrant population. Modest packed his bags and traveled west, stopping in Indianapolis to head a music theater organization.

Meanwhile, one of his brothers, Gregory, remained busy in New York City. Another outstanding cellist, he secured his first job playing in a vaudeville house. He was so grateful to the conductor that he decided to name his two sons after the music director. Consequently my two uncles were Victor and Herbert.

Into this family, my mother, Eleanor, was born in May 1917. By then, frictions had developed between the Altschuler siblings. And as a result, some, including Gregory, simplified their surname to Aller. My grandfather began to accept students and among them, his own daughter. She exhibited extraordinary musical

Gregory Aller, 1950s

talent, as did her brother Victor, who studied piano. Unfortunately, Herbert turned out to be tone deaf and would become a lawyer. In the late '20s, Gregory, at the invitation of Modest, brought the family to Los Angeles. The inexorable westward movement held promise of a better life for an inordinate number of Americans, envisioning musical life in the region as full of opportunity. A tragedy, the death of Gregory's wife, Fanny, in an automobile accident a few years before, possibly made the decision to pull up stakes more bearable. Gregory continued to flourish in Los Angeles as a teacher, eventually becoming the go-to person for talented cellists. Eleanor received a scholarship to study at the Juilliard School in New York with Felix Salmond, the eminent British cellist. This class included Leonard Rose, Harvey Shapiro, Bernard Greenhouse and others, all of whom would have distinguished careers in the music field.

Another family would also leave Russia, but several years after the Altschulers. From Odessa, the Zlotkins arrived at Ellis Island in 1913. When they gave

Eleanor Aller, 1926

their name to the immigration officer, he wrote down a phonetic version of what he heard, as was commonly the case for so many new arrivals.

When I would ask my grandmother about the origins of the family name, she would say, "Our life did not begin until we arrived here. We are Slatkin!" Neither of my grandparents spoke of their lives in Russia.

My brother found evidence on a tombstone in Saint Louis that the transliteration was actually "Zlotkin," and that is how he has spelled his last name since the late 1970s.

Compared to the Altschulers, the Zlotkin clan had very little inclination toward music.

There were no instrumentalists or singers to be found in the family tree. After coming to New York, they transferred to Saint Louis, Missouri, where other relatives had settled. Herman Slatkin set up a barbershop, a profession passed down for several generations. His wife, Bertha, filled the role of traditional Russian housewife.

My father, Felix, was born on December 22, 1915. He would have one sister, Libby, born a few years later. Felix showed genuine talent for the violin at a very early age. In spite of Herman's complete lack of training, he spotted his son's ability and quickly got him an instrument and lessons. Decades later, when I assumed my post as assistant conductor in Saint Louis, about half that city's older population claimed that they could hear young Felix practicing from the window of the Slatkin apartment located on Washington Boulevard.

At the age of sixteen, Felix was accepted as a student at Philadelphia's Curtis Institute of Music, and he was the youngest person ever to enter that conservatory. His teacher was the great violinist and pedagogue Efrem Zimbalist. Like my mother's teacher, Salmond, Zimbalist had an extraordinary class of students. Since its founding, Curtis has described itself as an all-scholarship institution, but my grandfather had to pay part of the costs. To supplement his income, he worked daily in a hardware store, as well as his own barbershop, toiling between the two jobs for sixteen or more hours a day.

Felix demonstrated remarkable gifts which got him in trouble once in a while. Because he was such a prodigious sight-reader, Zimbalist suspected that he was not practicing. In the middle of one lesson,

Felix Slatkin

he sent his student out of the studio to bring him a glass of water. During the time when Master Slatkin was away, Zimbalist altered some of the sharps and flats in the piece of music in progress. When Felix returned and resumed his lesson, he played the changes as if he had practiced them this way. Zimbalist threw him out of his studio for two weeks.

The conductor of the Curtis orchestra was no less than Fritz Reiner. Of course all of the students needed to audition on their instruments for the maestro, but Reiner also insisted they sing a bit, perhaps to show solfège skills. Felix was not so good at this, and Reiner quipped, "He will not be on the stage of the Metropolitan Opera."

By his third year, Felix needed a better violin to play in performance. Curtis wanted to charge my grandfather for the use of one of the school's fine instruments, and he simply could not afford either this or the school's increasing fees. So Felix returned home, and at the age of nineteen, he became assistant concertmaster of the Saint Louis Symphony, the youngest person in the orchestra. Three years into his contract, Felix requested a five-dollar raise. The orchestra's music director, Vladimir Golschmann, refused to grant it and the orchestra lost its second-in-command. Several musicians had apparently asked for a salary increase and were all denied, but Golschmann got a significant raise.

The Slatkin family concluded that there were greener musical pastures out west, and like the Altschulers, headed to Los Angeles. Herman established a barbershop and young Felix found employment with the Warner Brothers orchestra. Eleanor had completed her studies in New York, and returned to Los Angeles to rejoin the Aller clan.

There are conflicting stories as to how Felix and Eleanor first met. One version has them meeting at an impromptu chamber music reading. The other resembles a more dramatic, Hollywood-style tale.

The Hollywood Bowl sponsored a competition for string players in 1935. Both Eleanor and Felix entered and the violinist, my father, won. But the word on the streets had it that the contest had been rigged. Eleanor was furious, but her father, Gregory, insisted that they attend the concert anyway, where Felix, the winner, would be playing with pianist/conductor José Iturbi. When it was over, the Allers conceded that the young man actually deserved to win, but that

Eleanor and Felix, 1939

did not appease Eleanor's anger. Felix soon invited her out for coffee and some chamber music. A couple of years later they were married.

By then, Felix had become concertmaster of the 20th Century Fox Studio Orchestra, and Eleanor was principal cellist at Warner Brothers, the first woman to hold any titled position with a studio orchestra. Her brother Victor was also on staff, as a pianist. Together, they built a formidable reputation with plenty of solo work that can still be heard today.

There was a significant interruption in musical life for the Slatkins when Felix was summoned to military service in World War II. A special ensemble with the weighty name, Army–Air Force Tactical Command Orchestra, had been formed in Santa Ana, California, under the auspices of both the army and air force. This was a salvation for numerous musicians who supported the war effort yet had no desire to go overseas and fight. This orchestra was arguably the best in the United States. Such was its quality that the extraordinary violinist Ruggiero Ricci only managed to attain the third stand, inside chair. Felix was both concertmaster and conductor. The orchestra devoted their service primarily to radio broadcasting, airing music to the troops. In addition, the orchestra raised over $100 million in war bonds. Some recordings exist, and the quality of musicianship is apparent in every bar.

Erno Neufeld, Felix, Marshall Sosson and Ruggiero Ricci, 1943

In 1939, Eleanor and Felix decided to form a string quartet. The other members, Joachim Chassman and Paul Robyn, came from the 20th Century Fox orchestra. After much discussion, they selected the name Hollywood String Quartet. Some people questioned this choice, as the world of classical music frowned on anything related to the movies, deeming it lowbrow and not appropriately serious. But because the motion picture industry had provided the economic stability necessary to start a chamber group, the four musicians felt the name was appropriate. Indeed it was slow going at first, but eventually, mainly via their records, the Hollywood became one of the most respected quartets of all time.

Their heyday was from 1949 until 1958. At the outset, the foursome performed in smaller local venues, such as the Assistance League and Los Angeles County Museum. Gradually, as word of the quartet's excellence spread, the group started touring, mostly up the coast to San Francisco. On disc, they recorded both traditional and unfamiliar repertoire. Their debut album paired the first recordings of quartets by Villa-Lobos and Walton.

Perhaps their most famous disc included the premiere recording of the sextet edition of Arnold Schoenberg's *Verklärte Nacht*. Joining the quartet were two studio musicians, violist Alfred Dinkin and cellist Kurt Reher. By this time the

The Hollywood String Quartet, 1948

quartet also had a new second violinist, Paul Shure. Not only was this performance legendary, the story behind it was too.

Capitol Records, the quartet's home label, wanted Schoenberg to write the
liner notes for the album. The composer insisted that he hear the ensemble play
the work before agreeing—not an unreasonable request. On a very hot summer's
day, the six musicians trekked to Schoenberg's house and were greeted by his
wife. The master entered the living room area wearing a heavy, black overcoat
and muffler, oblivious to the outside temperature of over 100 degrees. Naturally,
he had all the windows and doors shut. This predated the age of air-conditioning.

After settling into their chairs, the musicians noticed Schoenberg sitting at a
table with score and pencil. They began, and after no more than two measures,
the composer began offering suggestions. He expounded for about ten minutes
until finally, Felix asked if it would be possible to play through the piece completely before digging in and working on it in rehearsal.

Schoenberg agreed, and at the conclusion of nearly thirty minutes of music
with pools of perspiration dripping from the sextet's bodies, the great man
stood and started to leave.

Felix said, "But Maestro, now we would like to work and listen to your comments."

"There is nothing to say," replied the composer. "You will have your note in the morning. Now it is time for refreshments."

Mrs. Schoenberg came into the room bearing, of all things, bourbon and doughnuts!

The next morning, an envelope appeared under our front door at home. It contained the liner notes as promised.

When the group performed either piano quartets or quintets, Eleanor's brother, Victor, would join in. He was an elegant artist, mostly serious, and the ideal partner in this repertoire. Recordings with him feature works of Brahms, Schumann, Franck and Shostakovich.

Perhaps the finest hours for the group occurred in 1957, when its players were invited to the prestigious Edinburgh Festival to perform the late quartets of Beethoven. It coincided with the quartet's release of these works on disc. The reception was rapturous. The Hollywood String Quartet also played one performance in Royal Festival Hall in London.

Many commentators in those days regarded the Hollywooders as a West Coast equivalent of the New York–based Juilliard Quartet, but this was hardly the case. Despite some overlapping repertoire, the two ensembles played in vastly different styles. The Manhattanites focused on intellectual performance coupled with clarity of line. Out on the Left Coast, more attention was paid to the actual sonority and lyric quality. However, both were great, virtuoso ensembles that elevated music in the United States.

Just after the UK tour, the English company EMI bought Capitol Records. One of their labels, His Master's Voice, had already issued recordings by the Amadeus Quartet. EMI did not want or need a second string quartet. So following a final tour, this one to New Zealand and Australia, the Hollywood Quartet ceased to exist. None of the members felt they could continue without the exposure of the recordings. And they were not about to give up the lucrative, and at that time, artistically satisfying work at the studios. The ensemble disquarteted in 1959. Sadly, the music world would be denied a planned recording project of the Bartók cycle as well as the Ravel and Debussy quartets. They won a Grammy in 1958, the inaugural year of these annual presentations, for their recording of the String Quartet Opus 130 by Beethoven.

It is difficult to recognize greatness when it surrounds you every day. Each night, for almost fifteen years, I heard the sounds of this group. Sometimes I would fall asleep on the staircase and had to be carried to bed. My earliest musical memories were not of Beethoven or Schubert but of Villa-Lobos, whose Sixth Quartet had a particular moment that sounded to me like teddy bears at play. I even had the opportunity, on my seventh birthday, to play the second violin part of a Haydn quartet with the others in the ensemble.

But I am getting ahead of myself.

3

Growing Up Slatkin

If you carry your childhood with you, you never become older.

—ABRAHAM SUTZKEVER

On September 1, 1944, I entered the world. Felix and Eleanor had conceived five times previously, but all ended, sadly, in miscarriage. Now World War II was approaching its victorious conclusion, so optimism had started to sweep the nation, and for the Slatkins, things were looking up, too. I shrieked and it was the sweetest sound the two musicians had ever heard.

At the time of my birth, we lived in Beverly Hills, but our house was hardly one of the glamorous mansions that dotted the western part of the city. One big plus of that location was that the Warner Brothers movie theater was just up the street on Wilshire Boulevard. Every studio had its own cinema. My friends and I joined the Bugs Bunny Club and every Saturday morning at eleven o'clock, we were treated to the most incredible array of visual entertainment any child could hope for. For ten cents (this was 1949) you got five cartoons, a newsreel, previews of coming attractions, a chapter of a cliff-hanger serial, an intermission that usually featured a yo-yo expert who always conveniently set up shop in the lobby after the show to sell his wares, and a feature-length western. I was partial to Hopalong Cassidy and even had a Hoppy outfit. Those were the days.

But by late 1949, the family moved to the Wilshire/La Brea district. With my mother working at Warner's and my father at 20th Century Fox, this proved a good compromise in terms of the commuting distance between the two studios. My brother, Fred, and I did not get to see our folks that often. By day they were working in the film world and by night they rehearsed at home with the other two members of the quartet. Dinnertime was pretty much the only time we were able to interact with our parents.

A succession of housekeepers handled most of our upbringing. They lived with us in a small room just off the main bedroom area. Several of them were quite memorable. Bertha was a large woman with a smile that lit up the whole neighborhood. And boy, could she cook! Her pecan pie had become so popular that musician colleagues would ask our parents when she intended to bake the next one. There seemed to be a waiting list, and some fans would show up at exactly the moment the pie came out of the oven.

Annie was also a good cook, but possibly the most eccentric of the lot. She kept the radio on incessantly, listening to preachers and gospel music. We had a basset hound named Jeeves. Annie was convinced that the dog was actually called Jesus. Whenever the dog escaped out the front door, Annie would go running down the street, yelling, "Come home, Jesus!" You would have thought that the Slatkins had converted.

Religion was not a very strong part of my upbringing. For one mercifully brief semester, I was sent to a Hebrew kindergarten. I hated it, especially when asked to play the role of Hamen, the bad guy, for the school's Purim play. One night at dinner, my parents asked me if I wanted to go to study for bar mitzvah. I said no. End of discussion and end of Talmudic scholarship.

While I was struggling with childhood academia, the world around me was bursting with artistic talent. Los Angeles boasted one of the most sophisticated communities imaginable. It was the land of opportunity for musicians, writers and painters. Many came to escape the ravages of the war-torn continent. Some came to take advantage of the hospitable climate. And some simply came to make money.

In Los Angeles, the motion picture industry was the chief beneficiary of these émigrés, but they very much enriched the general musical community, too. It is hard to believe that both Stravinsky and Schoenberg lived there at the same time. Rachmaninov settled in LA as well. The wave of new émigrés included Miklos Rosza, Max Steiner, Mario Castelnuovo-Tedesco, Bernard Hermann, Dimitri Tiompkin and Erich Wolfgang Korngold. When added to the already illustrious roster of homegrown talents, such as Alfred Newman, Victor Young and Alex North, Hollywood was indeed in a golden age.

However, a new force was at work in 1950s America. As the recently won
peace was truly settling in, the country became frightened by the specter of
rampant communism and an intense campaign to eradicate this ideology from
the collective conscience began. This movement reached its tragic climax with
a notorious series of hearings led by Senator Joseph McCarthy. The House
Un-American Activities Committee went after thousands of citizens, accusing
them of either being communists or at least sympathizing with them. The arts,
traditionally seen as liberal, were particularly vulnerable.

Our house was always a hotbed of activity, and a large number of people
from the arts community were entertained in our living room on a regular basis. The anti-communist fever extended to the opposition of unions and other
liberal concepts. One of the issues that struck Hollywood during this period of
uncertainty was the film studios' policy on hiring practices. There were eleven
major motion picture companies, each with its own permanent stable of actors, writers, composers and other artists. Six hundred and fifty musicians were
employed full time and had secure jobs, health plans and pension programs.
The American Federation of Musicians, fearing backlash from the McCarthy
commission, claimed that the studios were "closed shops" with policies that
prevented all musicians from having equal opportunities to get work. Therefore,
the AFM ruled that individual contracts were to be abolished, with players hired
on a film-by-film basis. It was the union's contention that this would increase
the opportunities for a larger number of musicians.

Performers opposed to the open shop philosophy established the Musician's
Guild. Cecil Reed, who headed the group, would have to go up against the
strong-willed union boss, James Petrillo. This was serious work, truly dangerous,
as some viewed it as anti-McCarthy, potentially anti-American and therefore
pro-communist. Many of the guild's meetings were held at the Slatkin home,
usually late at night. Our parents instructed my brother and me not to breathe
a word about these gatherings. Not that we understood what was going on,
but we certainly knew the people who attended. If anybody asked, we were to
answer that our dad was just having another of his poker games.

The guild did not prevail. Studios were forced to abandon the contract system
and it was every musician for him- or herself. The result was exactly the opposite of what was intended. Instead of job creation, the same limited number

of musicians would work at multiple studios. Only about two hundred musicians became the regulars throughout the entire film industry. Many wound up without a job and had to leave for other cities, including Las Vegas, which was growing rapidly and needed good players in the orchestra pits of its show palaces. I don't know if the public ever learned that the clandestine meetings happened at the Slatkin house, but I do remember a distinct pall that came over our home when the cause was obviously lost. Now my parents would have to work harder than ever, as those musicians who were among the elite working class could not afford to turn down jobs for fear of not being hired in the future.

An almost endless parade of the most interesting people continued to stream through our door—studio contacts, friends in the recording business and other musicians. All of the composers my parents were working with would listen to the quartet rehearse, especially if there was a recording or performance coming up. The film community musicians were frequent guests as they increasingly relied on my father for advice. The highly successful popular recording industry would have its share of personalities visiting the homestead as well.

A cavalcade of stars would appear almost daily. They would range from Igor Stravinsky to Danny Kaye, Arnold Schoenberg to Frank Sinatra, and Erich Wolfgang Korngold to Nat King Cole. The list was endless. I was still quite young at the time, so these people seemed nothing more than ordinary grown-ups who chatted with my mom and dad. Except one. I adored a Doris Day song, "Secret Love." After one of my parents' recording sessions, we went to a nearby Italian restaurant for a bite to eat. At the next table sat my heartthrob. Even though she worked for a different studio, my parents somehow managed to have her join us for a few minutes. I was speechless. I was six years old. In retrospect, it seems funny that I would not hesitate to say hello to Stravinsky, but Miss Day's presence rendered me incapable of saying a word.

Most of my childhood friends lived in the immediate area. Only a few of them were musically inclined. We did normal kid things—traded baseball cards, teased our classmates, complained about our parents—and I didn't think about academic matters. School was boring and at that level, not so difficult. It was fortunate that I was a product of the California public schools. At the time, it was held up as the model educational system on which other schools should have been based.

At Wilshire Crest Elementary School, Mrs. Otto came twice a week to teach music. We learned singing, how to play the Autoharp and other rudimentary instruments. Whenever I return to conduct in Los Angeles, well-wishers will come backstage and tell me how much Mrs. Otto affected their lives, regardless of their pursuit of non-musical careers. Every child had access to the arts. The same held true at John Burroughs Junior High. I played violin in the orchestra. Eileen Wingard was the teacher, and although we adored her, one time we locked her in the double bass closet. At Los Angeles High there were three choruses, two bands and an orchestra. Peter Schickele was the composer in residence under a Ford Foundation grant. Sadly, those days are long gone, but the memory of this time would prove useful almost a half century later.

I played glockenspiel in the band. Throughout the winter semester, we performed at the football games. It was my job to march down the forty-yard line, make a right turn and form the tip of the L, for LA. During the following semester, the ensemble morphed into a concert band.

The music director, Raymond Wurfl, cut us a lot of slack. One of the perks of playing in the band was that we were excused from physical education classes. Being on the football field constituted exercise. Somehow, the administration must have thought that we were marching all year long when, in fact, we only did so during football season.

My brother had begun cello lessons and I was switching from violin to piano. He did not study with our mother, but rather, with our grandfather, Gregory, who was surprisingly patient. Eleanor mainly stayed out of the way, as she probably should have. I began piano lessons with Gregory after realizing that I would not be nearly as good a violinist as my father. When it appeared that I had some aptitude for this instrument, Gregory sent me to study with his son, my uncle Victor.

By the mid-'50s, my brother and I were progressing relatively well on our respective instruments. Victor's daughter, Judy Aller, had started violin lessons with my father, and on Sundays, the household resembled an unusual conservatory. In the living room I would have a piano lesson with Victor. Fred, in his room, would take a cello lesson with Gregory and Judy would have violin instruction with Felix in the master bedroom. After an hour we would gathered in the living room for chamber music coaching as a piano trio. For this my mother

would join the three teachers. At one
end of the room were the three of us
fledglings and at the opposite end,
all four elders sat on the same couch.

A coaching session would go
something like this:

We would play about two bars of
a Haydn trio.

Eleanor: "The piano's too loud."

Victor: "It's fine. The cello has to
play stronger."

Gregory: "It won't matter because
the violin will still cover the cello."

Felix, Fred and me playing trios, 1956

Felix: "Judy never plays too loud."

And on and on they went, arguing about balance, intonation and phrasing.
I'm positive our trio never got through a whole piece without interruption. We
definitely never played as a group in public.

Fred and I would do some playing together occasionally. For the most part it
took place within the confines of the house, but once in a while we ventured out
to the small halls that dotted the Los Angeles region. We frequently played the
Lalo Cello Concerto. It had a nice piano part that, to some degree, sounds better
on that instrument than in the orchestral version. We would read through a lot
of pieces. One day, Fred came home with the Shostakovich Cello Sonata which
he had just purchased and wanted to play through. Although I was not a great
pianist, I could sight-read decently, and rarely looked ahead in the music to see
what passages were coming up. We began, and most of the sonata was going just
fine. There were a couple of tricky spots in the second movement, but nothing
that I couldn't approximate. The finale also appeared straightforward. A couple of
simple chords came at the end of the page about halfway through the movement,
and then I hit page thirty-five. I had never encountered so many sixteenth notes in
my life! I kept at it, and then Fred just broke out laughing. It was such a mess that I
vowed to always locate the hard parts before agreeing to play anything ever again.

Meanwhile, the family enjoyed one other passion we could share in a meaningful way: baseball. There were two minor-league clubs in the Los Angeles area,

the LA Angels and the Hollywood Stars. The teams played in wonderful old, small ballparks, with the Angels in Wrigley Field downtown and the Stars at Gilmore Field, about a five-minute drive from our house. My father had grown up with the Saint Louis Cardinals and would regale us with stories of the greats from his era —Stan Musial, Dizzy Dean and so on. He would also explain to us the National League's superiority over the American League. Both clubs were part of the major leagues' farm system so we had an opportunity to see the up-and-comers as well as the has-beens.

At night, I listened to games on the radio. When the team was playing out of town, the broadcasts were done as "re-creations" of the game, delayed by a few minutes while the announcer received the information of the actual events via ticker tape. The radio engineer would add recordings of crowd noises and if something spectacular happened, the broadcaster hit a piece of wood to simulate the sound of a bat hitting the ball, then raised the volume of the invisible crowd reacting to the event. It sure seemed real to a little kid. When we first acquired a television, I would turn the sound off and pretend to call the games. I was quite certain that when I grew up, my career would be that of a play-by-play man. When I was grown up and working in Saint Louis, I had the opportunity on several occasions to fulfill that fantasy. Sitting next to the Hall of Fame broadcaster Jack Buck, I was allowed to announce an inning or two. One time, Jack stepped out of the booth and told me to go it alone. The sports world should be glad I kept my day job.

In 1955, I got my first paying job. No, it wasn't in music; it was delivering the afternoon paper. I would wait on a street corner for the man in the newspaper truck to throw a bundle out the door. Then I would remove each paper, carefully fold it, and stick it in a sack over the back wheels of my bicycle. When really big news occurred, the front page would be green. The best green day I remember was when the headline informed us of Jonas Salk's discovery of a vaccine for polio.

I had about forty-five newspapers to deliver on my route. I think my parents encouraged me to do this job so I would understand the meaning of responsibility. Not only did I deliver the papers, I also collected the monthly fee from each subscriber. I tried not to throw the papers into the bushes, and with practice developed a sidearm technique that was fairly accurate. Unfortunately, I grew rather bored after two months and attempted to see how fast I could finish the whole paper route. This resulted in several mangled editions and the newspaper landing in puddles of water. It also resulted in getting me fired.

By the time I started attending John Burroughs Junior High, my violin playing was going south. It was still important for me to be involved in the school's music program, so I took up the viola. My playing skills were somewhat limited, as was the case for many of the kids in the ensemble. But we forged solid friendships and in some ways, that was even more important than the music-making. We hung out together, went to concerts and seemed like an inseparable unit.

Most of the students from Burroughs funneled into Los Angeles High School. The mix of race and ethnicity among the students made this time remarkable. We all seemed to get along and were oblivious to the racial tensions that existed in the real world. One night during the summer of 1961, I would learn that our idyllic, care-free way of life at school did not mirror reality. I took a classmate, who was black, to the Hollywood Bowl. Since I knew most of the musicians in the orchestra, it seemed like I could make a good impression by introducing the young lady to some of them.

When we arrived at the backstage door, one of the musicians took a look at us and spit on the girl. I was shocked!

My date gave me a lesson in social studies that the school did not teach. Listening to her tell me about injustice and intolerance was eye-opening. I had never dreamed that the world could be so cruel. The next year at school was not quite the same.

For reasons that remain unclear, I decided to run for class vice president. I beat my friend, Steve Lee, and another friend, Ed Buckley, was elected president.

My connections to the music and film world likely led to my victory. The main responsibility of the vice president was to organize the senior prom. With assistance from my parents, I was given access to a prop studio where we would get the decorations for that auspicious evening. Instead of the school's traditional four-piece combo, I secured a group of eight musicians to play. Everyone seemed happy with the dance. As for me, I was so exhausted from lugging scenery around that I spent prom night fast asleep in a back room.

Twenty-five years later, I was scheduled to guest conduct in Wichita, but that orchestra went on strike. So I hopped on a plane and showed up at the high school class reunion. A board there displayed photos of classmates who had been killed in Vietnam. Thankfully, only a few had been lost, but some peers, including a very talented violinist, Bill Henry, had also died from other causes. The reunion was a sober reminder of reality, but we shared a good deal of the evening lost in the wondrous time that was our age of innocence.

One person came up to me, read my nametag and asked, "Are you the Leonard Slatkin who is a conductor?"

"Yes," I replied with a sense of pride.

"Oh. I knew that we had someone by that name who has a good career, but I never thought it would be you."

My family did not really pay much attention to either my brother's or my academic achievements. We did manage to do well enough, but our grades weren't great. I had to go to summer school and retake industrial drawing, which, along with electric shop and woodworking, would be of no benefit later on. When I expressed a pragmatic interest in home economics—cooking—my friends made the predictable unpleasant remarks. Today, no one would bat an eyelash.

Despite the baseball announcing phase, never did I doubt that music would be my chosen profession. Neither did anyone else. After graduation, my classmates pretty much knew where they were headed. And to this day, we credit much of our success to those amazing years of growth in that building on Olympic Boulevard.

4

Some of That Jazz

We never play anything the same way once.

—SHELLY MANNE

As a kid, I listened to everything, even country and western music. I have since learned that there is a big difference between this genre and plain old country music. Thank you, Nashville. On a radio station in Los Angeles, KGER, at eight P.M., bedtime for this six-year-old, the "Squeakin' Deacon" was my go-to-sleep voice. The DJ would spin three discs just for kids and then tell them it was time for bed. "Ghost Riders in the Sky," a Vaughn Monroe hit, was my most cherished record.

When I was quite young, I brought home my first Elvis Presley album. Given my parents' eclectic tastes, it came as a surprise that they did not welcome this music into the house. After all, Capitol Records had kept them very busy in the studios with other popular artists of the day. The late '50s and early '60s was a transitional period in popular culture. Big bands had died off and were being replaced with a different kind of sound. Like most parents, my folks thought Elvis' music was inappropriate for children, but a couple years later they would do some recordings with the King.

A frequent guest in our home was Frank Sinatra. "Uncle Frank," as my brother and I referred to him, used to take Fred and me upstairs and sing us to sleep. He always insisted on having our parents as the first-call musicians for his every recording session. Whenever possible, Capitol would try to send Nelson Riddle, Sinatra's top arranger, out of town. His charts may have been the best in the business, but Nelson was not a particularly good conductor. Under him, Capitol was lucky if they could squeeze out two songs per session. So when you see a Sinatra album that reads "arranged and conducted by Nelson Riddle," the first part is true, but sometimes it was actually my father who was conducting.

One day, my father notified Frank that he had the flu and could not play a session. Sinatra told the orchestra that he would not record without Felix, paid them, and everyone went home. The public has mostly forgotten that Sinatra himself conducted a few albums. His largest-scale recording was *Tone Poems of Color*. My father was Frank's conducting coach for this and several other later albums.

We also spent time at his residences—not only the Los Angeles home, but also in Palm Springs and Las Vegas. At the glamorous Desert Inn, the two young Slatkins would hang out by the swimming pool, and every so often would hear a page over the PA system announcing that we were wanted in Mr. Sinatra's quarters. In Palm Springs, we had full run of the house. This is where I discovered some nude photos of Marilyn Monroe stashed away in a drawer.

One day, Frank informed Capitol that he wanted to record an album, and feature the Hollywood String Quartet with the ensemble's name on the cover. The company dismissed the idea, certain that fans would not buy a recording combining Sinatra's singing with a highbrow classical group. This was decades before crossover. Sinatra threatened to leave the label and they conceded. *Close to You*, as its title implies, was a very intimate album. Capitol was correct; the release did not sell well at all, but it became something of a cult phenomenon, garnering high praise from critics and Sinatra-philes.

When Frank finally left Capitol to found Reprise Records, he brought my dad with him. Together they helped start the company, and my father produced a number of albums there. The family got to meet the members of the Rat Pack, who also came to our house.

After that, Felix was wooed away by Sy Waronker, an astute businessman and record producer. Sy had bought Liberty Records and was about to turn the company into a major force in the recording industry. His son, Lenny, inherited the producer gene and became the head of Warner Records. Liberty had a few famous artists, Martin Denny, Julie London and Bobby Troup among them. But with my father, the upstart label added a whole new dimension and a new career was born.

Although the first albums my dad did as an arranger were titled *Fantastic Percussion* and *Fantastic Brass*, it would be the *Fantastic Strings of Felix Slatkin* that best showcased his newfound talents. These albums, featuring the top studio musicians in Los Angeles, were inventive, witty and superbly recorded. They would become staples of almost every light music radio station's repertoire. Today, if you can find them at all, they reside in a section of the CD and LP bins devoted to "lounge" music. My father would be pissed off to know this. One musical world in which my parents did not work was that of jazz. But they loved this musical form and brought it into the home. Art Tatum came by to play our piano, as did George Shearing and Nat King Cole. Many of the studio greats were outstanding jazz performers as well, including the sax-playing Nash Brothers, Ted and Dick; trumpeter Conrad Gozzo; bassist Ray Brown, who my mother taught how to use a bow; and the legendary drummer Shelly Manne.

Shelly had a club located on Cahuenga Boulevard, close to the Capitol Records building in Hollywood. When I was old enough, I would drop in to hear some of the finest musicians on earth. West Coast jazz was decidedly different from its eastern counterpart. We heard Stan Kenton, Bud Shank, Cal Tjader, Gerald Wilson, Armando Peraza—the list could fill a dozen pages. And when the public nightlife shut down, at about one in the morning, musicians would come into the Manne Hole and jam until the wee hours. I was privy to some of these exclusive, private sessions. Imagine Dave Brubeck playing with Miles Davis. Shorty Rogers jamming with Maynard Ferguson. You get the idea.

Although I never considered myself a true jazz pianist, I did have some forays into the late night entertainment world. It all started for me in 1961, at age sixteen, when I asked my parents if I could look for a summer job. As it turned out, my father happened to know a few people who were in the market for a pianist.

Even though my extemporaneous skills were somewhat limited, I could improvise and play from a fake book. These collections of songs have been around for some seven decades. They contain popular tunes, most still under copyright, with just the melody line, lyrics and chord symbols. A lot of musicians used the anthologies to learn the latest hits. The fake book was a kind of status symbol, as it indicated that somehow you were cool. Probably because it was also illegal.

I would be paid under the table since I had not reached the legal age for working in a drinking establishment. The one stipulation was that I couldn't tell a soul that I was doing this. I secretly practiced with the book for about three weeks before the first night of my barroom debut.

And what a night!

Upon arriving, I headed straight to the bartender.

"You play the piano. Someone asks for a song, you play it. Do not talk to the customers. If anyone strikes up a conversation, send them to me. Tips are all yours."

That was about it. I went to the piano and placed a few dollars in the brandy snifter on the rack to encourage patrons to add to the small collection.

For a while, nobody came in. Customers already present were seated at the bar. Finally, a man walked over and sat down near the keyboard. He requested "Moonglow," a popular song from the '30s that had been recorded many times. I flipped to the page in my trusted fake book, played the tune, and thought I was done.

The gentleman slid a twenty-dollar bill in the snifter, my first tip, and asked me to play it again. This surprised me, but I gladly obeyed. Next, a fifty-dollar bill was put in the glass bank. Perhaps he was a little drunk, but once more, he wanted to hear "Moonglow."

Then he said something as I was playing. "That was the song that was playing on the radio when I met the woman who would become my wife."

I nodded and smiled but said nothing, as per the bartender's instruction.

"It was our song, at least until tonight."

"She left me this evening."

Okay, that much I understood. My head nodded sadly back and forth as I continued the song.

"She is going to live with another woman."

I thought to myself, "Okay, she has a roommate." My fingers remained on the keys. You have to understand that I was an especially naïve young person and knew nothing about matters of sex and sexuality.

"So I wanted to hear this song for the last time before I drive down to Santa Monica Pier and kill myself."

Lots of wrong notes now.

The man got up while I was still playing, placed a hundred dollars in the snifter, and walked out.

I dashed over to the bartender, exhorting him to stop the patron.

"Why?"

"Because he is going to commit suicide!"

"Did you play what he wanted?"

"Yes."

"Then what he does next is his business. Get back to the piano."

For the next two weeks, I scoured the *LA Times*, expecting to read about a body that washed up on the beach.

To this day, I remain passionate about listening to jazz. I have worked with some of the greats, for example, Brubeck, Ella Fitzgerald, Doc Severinsen, Nancy Wilson and Wynton Marsalis, and each one had charts made with orchestral accompaniment.

I have heard others in international venues: Oscar Peterson in Tokyo, Michel Camilo in the Dominican Republic, John McLaughlin in London and Dizzy Gillespie in Paris.

Not that I ignore the other idioms. These days it is so easy to access any style of music. Between the Internet, discs and satellite, the choices are endless. One difference between the younger generation of musicians and those from my earlier years is that today's performers tend to embrace more diverse kinds of music. I was lucky to grow up in an environment that encouraged variety. Even though Elvis was verboten, the Beatles were accepted, as was Dolly Parton, Barbra Streisand and Buddy Holly.

One year, I was a presenter at the Grammy Awards in Los Angeles. My challenge was to correctly pronounce the nominees in all classical categories. This part of the ceremony occurs in the afternoon, with only a handful of people in the audience, and certainly not shown on the telecast.

The same is true for the majority of the awards. This made the time in the green room extraordinary, as I mingled with recording artists from all walks of musical life. For a few minutes, I was in conversation with Lyle Lovett, Mary Chapin Carpenter, Run DMC and Gloria Estefan, all at the same time! And our similarities far outweighed our differences; although our music employed a wide variety of musical languages, we understood each other perfectly.

Perhaps what Duke Ellington, among others, said is really true: "There are only two kinds of music. Good music and the other stuff."

5

The Turning Point

That's life. Whichever way you turn, fate sticks out a foot to trip you.

—MARTIN GOLDSMITH

Everything seemed fine. High school was behind me. I was headed off to college with a scholarship. How was I to know what the next couple of years would hold?

In the early '60s, Indiana University emerged as a major player in the musical/academic world. It boasted one of the strongest faculties in the United States and had the financial backing of several major donors.

During this phase, my chief interest lay in composition. With a handful of musicals and concerts behind me, and studies with notable teachers in Los Angeles fresh in my mind, I packed up and traveled halfway across the country.

Much was new for me: living in a dormitory, going to classes with such a large number of students in attendance, and snow. In many ways, I was glad to be away from home. Our father was an alcoholic, not abusive physically, but so distant from my brother and me that it bordered on neglect. My mother obsessed over her work, but she at least attempted to hold the family together. By the time I graduated from high school, my parents were busier than ever before. The result was that my brother and I were prepared for a life of independence, as we had learned to thrive on our own. The most difficult part of leaving home was saying good-bye to my dog.

When I arrived in Bloomington, there was the matter of accommodations. I was placed in Foster Quadrangle, where I was the only student studying fine arts. At first it seemed like a huge adventure. Everything was new and I had no idea what would happen next.

The first day at the music school proved instructive. We were given an orientation, shown around the buildings, and assigned classroom studies. Harmony and theory classes ran five days a week, two held with the entire freshman class.

Composition lessons were with Bernard Heiden, a fine academic and teacher. I studied piano with Menahem Pressler of the Beaux Arts Trio. Other distinguished faculty included the legendary violinist Joseph Gingold and cellist János Starker, with whom I would later make several recordings.

I played viola in one of the opera orchestras led by an old-fashioned tyrant, Tibor Kozma. He would get worked up over some detail and then pick some poor girl in the ensemble to blame, usually sending her out of the rehearsal in tears. I vowed that if I ever conducted, I would never behave so rudely.

In late October of 1962, most of the men in the dorm gathered around the television in the basement. President Kennedy was addressing the nation about a conflict over missiles in Cuba. Each of us was eligible to be conscripted into the armed services, and we were convinced that the next day, we would be shipped out.

All male students at IU were required to take Reserve Officers Training Corps (ROTC). Freshmen and sophomores had to participate twice a week under a mandate from the school's land grant. Graduation depended on completion of this part of the curriculum. Established in 1916, ROTC was a program originally designed to indoctrinate college-age men into the ways of military thinking so they would be prepared as officers when they graduated.

My only contact with this facet of the school's agenda occurred over Thanksgiving. Indiana University, as a state school, enrolled students primarily from the region. Those from distant states did not travel home for the four-day holiday. Foster Quadrangle shut down, and the remaining students were housed in the air force ROTC barracks. Two years earlier, a US pilot, Francis Gary Powers, had been shot down over Russian territory. Training for this mission had occurred at IU. On the bulletin boards were copies of documents marked CLASSIFIED. Of course I felt compelled to read them all.

To a large extent, my eventual departure from the school had to do with this aspect of campus life.

On the first day of the ROTC class I had a severe cold, so I did not attend. It was the same story for the next session. Seemingly, skipping at the start did not seem to matter, as the main activity was the handing out of uniforms. At that time in my life, I had no political leanings but I chose to wait a year to start this class. Two months passed and some administrator noticed that I had never once shown up. I was quickly summoned to the ROTC command center.

After instructions on how to salute, I was sent in to report to the commanding officer.

"Cadet Slatkin reporting, sir!" I exclaimed.

"Why haven't you come to the drills?" he inquired.

"I thought I would wait until next year."

"You realize that if you do not go, you cannot graduate. Plus, the discipline is good for all young men."

I sarcastically replied, "Have you been to the music school?"

The commander invited me to observe the drills the next day so I would see how it all worked. Due to a heavy snowfall overnight, the maneuvers were moved into the massive field house, which had some of the most resonant acoustics imaginable. I watched in amazement as troops were marched into a wall due to hearing the wrong set of orders barked at them.

"This was not our best day," said the officer, "but you really cannot graduate until ROTC is completed."

By that time, I already knew that my stint at IU would not last much longer. The lack of individual lessons was also grating on me. I did not care for campus life at a big university. My activities outside of classes were limited to bowling and playing euchre late into the night.

I left for the Christmas holiday and did not return. ROTC was eventually dropped as a compulsory class and made voluntary. Forty-five years later, I would join the faculty at IU.

Since it was too late in the semester to enroll in another music program, I elected to attend Los Angeles City College to finish out the school year. There was no particular goal except to keep myself busy. I played viola in the orchestra, and on one memorable occasion, my father actually conducted for me when I was soloist in the Bach D Minor Keyboard Concerto.

The week of March 4, 1963, would prove to be one of the most dramatic and challenging in my life. To start with, my dad was working on his latest album for Liberty Records. Recording sessions were scheduled to begin on Saturday, and so a good amount of touching up needed to be done on the arrangements.

And on Saturday night, there was to be a performance of the Brahms Double Concerto, a work my parents would play in public for the first time. The pair had been practicing at home for a few weeks, and the dress rehearsal was on Wednesday evening. Accompanying them was the outstanding Glendale Symphony, of which my dad had also served as the music director. I am certain that if the work in the recording industry had been less lucrative, he would have dropped everything to take on a permanent conducting position. In fact, he had been offered one in Tucson, Arizona, but turned it down.

Everyone present that midweek night described theirs as a Brahms like few others. All the struggles of domestic life disappeared in the music-making.

On Friday, my brother had a performance of the Hindemith Octet with other instrumentalists from the Young Musicians Foundation. The whole family had planned to attend, but late in the afternoon, our father lay on the couch, having passed out from one too many Scotch and sodas. We tried to wake him, but he was sawing away. Besides, it would do little good for him to be seen in such a stupor.

The concert was splendid and we were excited to tell Dad about it when we returned home around ten thirty. Upon entering the house, he was not to be found, at least downstairs. My mother went up to the bedroom, and screamed. I rushed up only to find my father on the bathroom floor, not breathing and completely pale. I tried to administer mouth-to-mouth resuscitation but it did nothing.

Our mother phoned the physician who arrived in fifteen minutes. He asked us all to wait downstairs. A few minutes later, the doctor came into the living room and said, "He's gone." Dad was forty-seven years old and I was nineteen. The cause of death was listed as a heart attack, but most of us knew that there was much more to it. The drinking, smoking more than three packs of cigarettes a day, being overweight and being a workaholic all contributed.

Somehow I had the presence of mind to call our uncles. My mother was in shock, and the doctor had given her a sedative. Between the relatives and friends who now knew, we managed to arrange everything for a memorial. At some point, I went up to my room, not sleeping but not crying either.

The next day, my own friends came over and suggested that we go to a movie. I thought this an outlandish idea, but my mother believed it would be good for me. It was a schlock horror movie, based on "The Raven" by Edgar Allan Poe. And it turned out to be exactly what I needed. About ten years later, I would write a piece of music for narrator and orchestra, incorporating Poe's text and utilizing the talents of one of the stars of the film, Vincent Price.

The service was held at the Hollywood Memorial Park Cemetery two days later. Felix's father was interred there, and it is the final resting place for numerous luminaries, including Charlie Chaplin, Douglas Fairbanks, Cecil B. DeMille and Erich Wolfgang Korngold. Frank Sinatra was one of the eulogists. About fifteen hundred people attended, attesting to my dad's stature in the field as well as his popularity as a person. My mother had selected two recordings by the Hollywood String Quartet to serve as musical interludes: the slow movements of the Schubert Quintet and Brahms' Third Piano Quartet.

A reception took place at our house. I hardly remember the event, as after three days of emotional detachment, I spent the afternoon in my room, crying. From that day forward, I started to block out most of the memories from my youth. It would take intensive therapy to bring them back.

For the remainder of the school year, I shifted away from music completely. I had decided that this kind of life was too demanding. For the time being, I focused on becoming an English teacher, taking classes at Los Angeles City College. Apparently other people had different plans for me. The head of the music department, Dominic De Sarro, asked me if I wanted to conduct a piece or two at the college's upcoming concert. I agreed, somewhat reluctantly.

The next year, I opted to stay at City College. Still not sure about returning to music, I immersed myself in all manner of literature, but in the back of my mind a new thought was taking shape. It took a long time, but eventually I realized that my father's death meant that I no longer had to compete with him.

I understand how harsh this reality sounds, and to say that I would not be conducting today had my father lived longer might be a stretch. But it is likely true. There was no question that I would spend many years wrestling with this emotional issue if I intended to pursue a path to the podium. As I gained experience at school, I started to believe that this is what I was meant to do.

JFK was assassinated that November. We were between classes and the PA system delivered the news. Students and faculty openly wept. My own political and social beliefs had come into focus, and this announcement put me into a state of shock.

As the semester wound down, I had established a musical course of action; the Aspen Music School would be a good place for me to find out if I was equipped to enter the highly competitive world of the conductor. The last thing I wanted was for the profession to exact the same toll on me as it had on my dad.

Little did I know that other fathers would be waiting in the wings.

6

Listening with Your Eyes

Study the past if you would define the future.

—CONFUCIUS

The conductor sits alone, score on the desk, no musicians in sight. The communication is between him and the composer, without benefit of words. Somehow, centuries are crossed, ideas tacitly conveyed, and the study of the music begins.

The process is indeed lonely.

One of the first questions aspiring conductors ask me is, "How do you study?" Surprisingly, biographies and memoirs of orchestral leaders seem to avoid discussion of this fundamental aspect of the art. In fact, there are as many responses as there are conductors. Everyone has his or her way of learning.

Most musicians assume that a career in conducting requires proficiency at the piano. Score reading at the keyboard has been mandatory for admission to any conducting course, including the one at Juilliard. Similarly, you are expected to be fluent in solfège, that system of do-re-mi that is so misunderstood. What tools and talents do you really need in order to decipher all those circles and dots, instructions and transpositions?

In the late summer of 1964, I auditioned for Jean Morel's class. Prior to that, a vast majority of my conducting education had consisted of observing other people on the podium. I had a few private lessons with Ingolf Dahl, a fine and underrated composer/conductor, at the University of Southern California. Dahl's approach to teaching primarily focused on baton technique. The actual reading of the score was not discussed.

Another necessary skill on the entrance exam at Juilliard was the ability to read four-part Bach chorales at the piano in four different clefs. A book that seems to have been in print for eons, the *Bach-Riemenschneider*, contains pretty much all of the chorales, but this handy volume does not explain how to go about learning the clefs and transpositions. The two instruments I played in childhood, piano and viola, helped. Piano pieces utilize the treble and bass clefs. The viola is written in alto and treble clefs.

When I decided to study the viola, I had no idea how to read the alto clef. My father suggested that I take the minuets from Haydn quartets and play one a day. My viola skills were not great, but I could get around fairly simple parts. A very helpful piece of advice my dad gave me was, "Even if you make mistakes, keep going. Don't stop for anything."

My father was right. Keep at it long enough until it becomes second nature. As with reading or speaking a foreign language, you must learn without having to think about translating or transposing.

I used to accompany my brother, and a great deal of his printed music was in the tenor clef. Even though I did not play his lines, after a while I could associate the written note with how it sounded in a different clef.

The Juilliard entrance exam required all conductors to be able to read four clefs at the piano, and this included one I had not learned as an instrumentalist, the soprano clef. Composers from the baroque era and even Haydn and Mozart used this, but for the most part, we rarely see it anymore. I struggled to divide my brain into four distinct compartments. The only way to do this was to start with two clefs at a time, adding the others when I felt secure.

Eventually I could get through this part of the audition, but what did it have do with learning how to read a score, especially transposing? What about those horns in F, the clarinet in A, or the trumpet in D? To learn this, I practiced as I had when beginning to play the viola, reading simple parts from the repertoire on the piano as they would sound when rendered by the actual instruments for which they were written.

This task is rather elementary for early music compositions written before the brass instruments had valves. At that time, only a limited number of notes were possible, making transposition less difficult. I found that there was another way to solve the problem using my knowledge of the clef system. For example, in the case of the trumpet in D, all you do is imagine the alto clef and add a couple of sharps. Clarinet in A? Piece of cake, if you have learned the soprano clef. Any instrument in E-flat? Also alto clef, but with the requisite couple of flats.

Confusing? Yes, but with practice and patience, learning the transpositions is not so difficult. Putting everything together is another matter altogether. The four-part chorales now seem like child's play, since the average score of a late nineteenth-century orchestral composition may have eight or nine different transpositions. Learning this aspect of the conductor's craft takes a long time.

For me, reading a score is similar to a film director's envisioning a screenplay. The conductor's language consists of notes instead of words; visual images comprise the director's language. It is the conductor's obligation to create a mental image of what the full score will sound like when the forces are gathered, but learning how to translate the notes into imagined sound can be arduous.

By the time I arrived for the audition in Manhattan, I was fairly secure in my four-clef piano reading. It would serve me well in an unexpected way when I actually matriculated.

There was a wonderful woman, Madame Renée Longy, who taught ear training. Her reputation was as a tough lady who did not tolerate any nonsense. If you could not properly solfège, she would not be afraid to scold you in front of the whole class. I never could do it and still cannot, probably because it is a method for sight-reading, and having perfect pitch made that relatively easy for me.

Conductors and composers at Juilliard were treated somewhat differently than the instrumentalists and singers. We had special courses in ear training as well as in harmony and theory. The class was called "Literature and Materials of Music." When the first day of school arrived, I showed up at Madame Longy's room along with the other first-year students. When it was my turn, she asked, with a heavy French accent, "Slatkeen. I know zis name. Are you related to Felix?"

"I am his son."

"Ah, yes. I taught him at Curtis. He always wore short pants."

Then I sat down, and instead of the two lines of *Bach-Riemenschneider* that she requested, I showed off and played four.

"Why are you here in zee first year? Go away and come back in three years!"

When my senior year rolled around, I returned to the class for the fourth year of ear training.

"Slatkeen. What are you doing here?"

"You told me to come back now."

"But you have been with Morel. You do not need to be with me."

Hallelujah! I never had to sing one do, re or mi to her.

During the summer of '64, I began my studies with Walter Susskind at the Aspen Music School. It is possible that my musical pedigree helped in gaining entrance to the school, but I also had enough, though limited, experience in conducting at that time.

Mr. Susskind proved extremely helpful in preparing me for the Juilliard audition, going through the pieces I was assigned to conduct, and providing both musical and technical pointers. That summer, a friendship began that would last forever, or so I wished.

For the conducting audition at Juilliard, we had to direct four pieces: Haydn's Symphony No. 99, Beethoven's *Eroica,* Debussy's *Afternoon of a Faun,* and the first tableau of Stravinsky's *Petroushka.* I had approximately three months to study them, and this would really be the first opportunity to apply my newfound skills as a score reader.

It was not easy.

All the *Bach-Riemenschneider* in the world really did not help. Playing just a few different clefs on the piano had not adequately prepared me for dealing with all those instruments in the orchestra. There are a number of conductors, past and present, who genuinely abide by the belief that accurate score study must take place at the keyboard. I respectfully disagree. If the sonority of the piano gets stuck in your head, it makes it more, not less, difficult to transfer this to the orchestra in front of you. Breathing, bow strokes and mallets are among the elements you must hear in your head, things the piano cannot reproduce.

Typical score study consists of nothing more than a conversation between the text and the conductor who tries to take as much into the eye and ear as possible. This is not the time to focus on individual lines, but rather on the whole ensemble and the entire composition. The stage or film director analogy applies well here too. That person must peruse a script and imagine what the actors will sound like and what the scenery and costumes will look like. Just as with the conductor, there are no sets in the living room. No orchestra either.

When opening a score for the first time, I look at the instruments the composer employs. There is usually a list of these before the actual music pages begin. Are there any that are out of the ordinary? What keys are they in? Is the score transposed or do the instruments sound as written? What this means is, does the conductor see what the musicians have in front of them, or do the composers make it easy and write all the parts in C, without transpositions. I don't care for the latter very much. For me it is much better to be able to refer, in rehearsal, to the actual notes that are on the stands of those playing the piece. Otherwise you have to tell the musician how the note will sound when played by saying something like, "It is a *concert* F-sharp."

Whether you are studying an old chestnut or a piece receiving its first performance, there are surprising similarities in how you approach these works. A bit later, I will discuss this study process, but for now, let's examine a couple of questions that are frequently asked.

Is it necessary to do a full analysis of the score? I used to do it, but as I became more experienced, I realized that for me, detailed analysis got in the way of understanding the totality of a piece of music. These days I recognize that a bit of dissection does aid in comprehending the formal structure of a given work. Still, in the scores I use now, you will not find annotations about chord changes or the inversion of the tertiary theme. If a piece moves me, the details will reveal themselves through the music, not numbers.

Another question that prospective conductors often bring up is, "Should I listen to recordings of the pieces I am studying?" The party line is, of course, no, but I am going to amend it a bit.

When a cellist, for example, has a lesson, more often than not the teacher will grab the instrument to demonstrate a particular passage, fingering or phrasing. At the very least, the pupil gets feedback from someone, which is something the fledgling conductor does not receive. The best training on earth cannot prepare conductors for the reality that emerges from the first rehearsal. My advice is to learn a piece on your own and borrow only from performances that reside in your memory. When you have thoroughly digested the work, you can then consult a recorded version. By all means, avoid interpretations that you do not like, but if a particular detail strikes you positively, ask yourself why the conductor made that decision. If you have no answer beyond "because he must have felt it that way," then you must look for an alternative solution you can call your own. Every nuance in the score must be understood before commencing on an interpretation.

Once, at my National Conducting Institute in Washington, a budding maestro was rehearsing the Second Suite from Ravel's *Daphnis et Chloé*. The lengthy passage with the flute solo was failing miserably. After a couple days, my teaching partner that year, Murry Sidlin, figured out what was wrong.

He confronted the young man and nonchalantly asked, "Whose recording have you been listening to?"

"Charles Munch."

"You are not Munch and the first flutist here is not Doriot Anthony Dwyer! Use your ears and listen."

You must rely on yourself. If you have truly learned the score, your demeanor will radiate a necessary confidence.

In many ways, your technique will reflect what is beneath the notes, not just the surface.

Meanwhile, back at the Juilliard audition, I thought I knew the pieces pretty well. The Haydn and Beethoven were already friends, but not yet close ones. Debussy remained a bit of a mystery and the Stravinsky, at least to a twenty-year-old, overflowed with technical and musical problems.

But I had reached a level where the music felt like a part of me, and I managed to get through the twenty-minute ordeal. A few weeks later, I was accepted into the class.

Studying can be the most frustrating aspect of the conducting profession. Even years of painstaking and solitary work won't perfectly prepare you for those first occasions when you stand before an orchestra. At the very least, though, you get close to history and at best—well—you get close to history.

7

Walter Susskind

*Never forget that you have a responsibility to the composer,
musicians and audience. The responsibility to yourself comes last.*

—WALTER SUSSKIND

Every musician has one or more teachers who transcend the meaning of the word. That person acts as a surrogate parent, protector and guide. One of mine was Walter Susskind.

The son of a music critic, Susskind was born in Prague and established his career as a pianist before studying conducting with George Szell at the German Opera in the Czech capital.

Conducting engagements took him to Scotland, Australia and Toronto, before he settled in as music director of the Aspen Music Festival in Colorado. This is where we met in 1964, when I embarked on the serious pursuit of a conducting career.

At that time, the festival was relatively small, with just 150 or so students. Today it has grown to about eight hundred. When I attended, only three concerts a week were presented, whereas currently there can be three a day. The festival had no campus, and classes were held wherever ample space was found.

Susskind's residence was built on top of a tree. You had to take a small elevator to reach the place. He taught his conducting lessons in that house. There were eight conducting students during that year, but he did not teach us collectively. Rather than assign pieces for study, Susskind would let us bring to the tree house the music we wanted to work on. We would sit on a couch and spread out the score on a table, where he would take us through the piece bar by bar, pointing out what the orchestra needed at each point along the way.

And of course, as with any great teacher, the stories and anecdotes flowed. Many benefits would result from our relationship over the years.

The conducting students had a weekly opportunity to work with the student orchestra. We each led different repertoire and after the sixth week, Susskind determined who among us was ready to show off our skills in front of an audience. Barber's *Adagio for Strings* was my choice, somewhat surprising to everyone, including Susskind. Most of my peers opted for splashier works, but I really wanted to do the *Adagio*.

The performance went well and a couple of days afterward, when I asked Susskind if I could return the next summer, he smiled and said, "You had better."

Aspen was a phenomenal experience for the young musician. The festival was founded in 1949 by the visionary Walter Paepcke as a place for intellectuals and artists to gather and exchange ideas. He felt the initial Aspen Institute mandated a musical component, and brought the Minneapolis Symphony, with Dimitri Mitropoulos, for several concerts. Soloists included Rubinstein, Milstein and Piatigorsky.

The festival soon formed its own orchestra, with leading players from major orchestras serving as the front-desk masters. These instrumentalists also taught at the school.

By the time I arrived, the program had expanded to nine weeks, and students were encouraged to attend as many performances as possible. Our knowledge of repertoire increased, and I heard countless works for the first time. Tippett's *Child of Our Time*, Dvořák's Sixth Symphony, the Lutosławski Concerto for Orchestra, among others. Susskind gave a performance of Deryck Cooke's completion of Mahler's Tenth Symphony. At the moment when the drum signals the funeral cortège for a fallen firefighter, Susskind instructed the percussionist, "That should sound like a couch, falling." I am still not positive what the maestro meant, but the comment seemed appropriate at the time. All these discoveries were critical in my formative conducting years.

On Sunday afternoons, immediately following the dress rehearsal for the afternoon orchestra performance, there was a softball game organized by Keith Brown, the principal trombonist. I played right field, mostly to avoid having to catch the ball, as very few batters hit it out in that direction. During one game, Norman Carol, concertmaster of the Minnesota Orchestra and later the

Philadelphia, hit a single toward me. I got to it a bit late. Trying to stretch it into a double, Norman slid head first into second base and jammed the index finger of his right hand. He still managed to play the concert two hours later, illustrating just how important the ball games were for all of us.

As the years progressed, I had more and more conducting opportunities. During my third season in Aspen, Susskind was named music director of the Saint Louis Symphony. For my final appearance that year, I led the student orchestra in Hindemith's *Symphonic Metamorphosis on Themes by Carl Maria von Weber*. Backstage, Susskind introduced me to Peter Pastreich, the executive director in Saint Louis. On the spot, Peter offered me the job of assistant conductor.

I did not accept it right away, as I had planned on continuing work on my master's degree at Juilliard. Plus, if I left school, I could be drafted into the military, a prospect I truly feared. After a couple of weeks of contemplation, I realized that this opportunity might not occur again, and I agreed to take the position.

When visiting New York, Susskind would introduce me to various artists. One night, Szell was guest conducting the Cleveland Orchestra at Carnegie Hall. It was Susskind's idea for me to meet his own mentor after the performance. The two of us went up to the dressing room and before exchanging any pleasantries, Szell glared at Susskind and said, "You cannot have any of my players for Aspen any more! We are starting our own music festival." I don't think the man was too keen on meeting me.

Excitement and anticipation filled my final Aspen summer. It would be the last one for Susskind and me in the roles of teacher/student. No, that is not quite right. He would forever be my teacher. That year would also mark my debut conducting the Festival Orchestra. This was very special because my piano soloist was . . . Walter Susskind! He played the Ravel G Major Concerto. I cannot describe the feelings that overwhelmed me throughout the rehearsals and public performance.

In September, the "great adventure" started. My relationship with Saint Louis Symphony would situate me by Mighty Mississippi for twenty-seven years—the first eight years alongside Susskind who could not have been more generous. When the orchestra began recording for Vox, he unbelievably permitted me to conduct the first albums. These comprised the complete works for orchestra by Gershwin, with my good friend Jeffrey Siegel as piano soloist. Susskind said that it was important to him that these first releases sell very well and put Saint Louis back on the recording map.

As a conductor, he excelled, quite naturally, in the music of his homeland. Listening to him rehearse and conduct Smetana's *Má vlast* was an object lesson in how to meaningfully convey a composer's intentions. Susskind needed to say little to get his message across, as his technique was always clear. This served him extremely well in the most underrated of conducting roles, the accompanist.

He was a favorite collaborator with Heifetz, Rubenstein and so many of that generation. As Susskind explained to me, "You have to become two different people. One is the conductor, leading the orchestra, and the other is the listener, standing aside a little and tuning in to the soloist's every musical thought." To this day, I have the utmost respect for those few who comprehend how to truly collaborate with a soloist. Susskind again: "No one should ever say how well you followed. That would mean you were behind."

I was never sure why Susskind left Saint Louis after less than a decade as music director. He had raised the ensemble up from the musical ashes after the highly controversial tenure of the Brazilian Eleazar de Carvalho. Under Susskind, the musicians were recording, touring and broadcasting. But Susskind grew restless. The board and concertgoers wanted a change. So he departed and I stayed on for two more years, but it was not the same and so I packed up as well.

Susskind proceeded to the position of artistic adviser for the Cincinnati Symphony, but his health was failing. After a brief stint, he moved west to Berkeley, where he died at the age of sixty-six. I was conducting in Israel at the time. The phone rang and when I heard the news, I was incapable of holding back the flood of tears. My other father was gone.

Mr. Susskind would have disliked a sad ending to his story. So I will recount another of the numerous tales that can be told.

The pianist Anton Kuerti was a good friend of Susskind from his Toronto days, and so it was only natural that they appear together in Saint Louis. After a performance, a dinner was held at the home of a man who boasted of his collection of private—in other words, pirated—recordings. He claimed to have all of the concerts from the Aspen Festival archives, where Kuerti also performed.

The three of us were appalled, but Susskind maintained his cool. With a wink to Tony and me, he inquired, "So you have the tapes of the festival in 1966?"

"Most certainly."

"Do you think you could let us hear the Chopin Piano Quartet Number Two from that season?"

Our host disappeared into the library, while we three formulated a totally outlandish comeuppance.

Upon returning, the collector was flustered, as he could not locate that performance. We did not let up.

Tony explained, "But in '66 we did the F Major, not the C Minor. That came the next year."

My turn: "I thought that the idea was to do the four of them chronologically?" Turning back to our host, I asked if he could find any of the Chopin recordings from that time.

Again, the man returned from the library totally flustered and Susskind hit him with the coup de grâce. He walked over to the piano and started improvising the tunes and rhythms from four completely nonexistent pieces!

"You remember that scherzo where Chopin combines both the polonaise and mazurka?" And so forth and so on.

This continued for about fifteen minutes. Best of all? We never confessed the prank to our host. I would bet that he spent the better part of the next two weeks hunting down those recordings.

I have never felt comfortable referring to my teachers and mentors by their first names, but I will break that rule this once. Every time I think of Walter, it is with that boyish twinkle, that gleam in his eyes that lit up the room every time he entered. Those little sparkles have never gone out of my mind.

8

The Juilliard

I've never let my schooling interfere with my education.

—MARK TWAIN

If Aspen seemed a laid back, familial type of music school, Juilliard was an entirely different universe. Pianists hung out with other pianists, violinists with their own kind, and so forth. There were only four conducting students in my first year, so we latched on to anybody we could.

The president of the school was the composer Peter Mennin. Although he was a fine administrator and visionary educator, I was sorry to have missed the opportunity to learn from his predecessor, William Schuman, the composer who had left to assume the directorship of Lincoln Center. During Schuman's tenure at Juilliard, a solid base of both musical and academic study was implemented which survived into Mennin's regime. The curriculum was rather broadly defined. To graduate, you had to meet the New York State Regents' criteria. So the school offered certain "traditional" subjects, albeit with a twist. The course "Song Text and Opera Libretto," for example, could satisfy the English component of the requirement for a college degree.

The most important of the non-performance classes was called "Literature and Materials of Music" and completion of a level of L and M was required for all students each year. It was an advanced form of that old standby, "Harmony and Theory." Conductors and composers had an even more difficult version of this course. My freshman L and M teacher was Hall Overton, a composer who had made a name for himself in the third-stream jazz movement, and who was constantly forgetting to flick the ashes from the cigarette that forever dangled from his lips. Smoking in classrooms was an accepted part of the culture then, yet I often wondered about the man's dry cleaning bills. He was not a bad teacher, his attitude cool and hip.

My freshman year was naturally devoted to learning the ropes. I seemed to be doing well with conducting and playing viola in one of the orchestras. By the second semester, I was forming chamber groups and presenting such works as the Stravinsky *Octet for Winds* and the Ibert *Divertissement*. There was even a performance of the Third Brandenburg Concerto with a very young Pinchas Zukerman as one of the three violinists. In retrospect, it is astonishing to think just how many of my peers at Juilliard would go on to have international careers—Itzhak Perlman, Emanuel Ax, Joseph Kalichstein, Jeffrey Siegel and countless performers, who are still active on the world's stages. In recent years I have suggested that we have a reunion of the classes of the '60s and assemble an orchestra for a fund raiser. But who would conduct? Levine, Conlon, Davies, Nelson, to name a few options. Maybe the gathering will materialize someday and we could invite a pupil from the preparatory division who played for me when he was eleven years old: Yo-Yo Ma.

In my second and third years, I lived in an apartment on 115th Street and Broadway, a half-dozen blocks south of Juilliard's pre–Lincoln Center home. Initially I shared it with a violist, Peter Sokole, who has since served in the Concertgebouw Orchestra for more than three decades. Peter was a bit active socially and he had a lot of visitors, so I frequently stayed in my room. During the next year in the apartment, my old pal and bass player from LA High, Ken Friedman, was my roommate. Ken was more like me, quiet and shy. He went on to become principal bassist of the Vancouver Symphony. My closest friend was Jeff Siegel, who has remained a constant confidant to this day. We went to movies, concerts and restaurants almost daily. In no time, we learned the trick of getting acquainted with the ushers at the various concert venues, and we rarely had to pay to get in.

In 1966, Vladimir Horowitz came out of retirement. When the concert was announced, organizers had already determined when the tickets would go on sale, and limited them to four per customer. The only hope of getting one was to stand in line overnight outside Carnegie Hall. I know that if everybody who claimed to be there actually was, about fifty thousand people would have surrounded the hall. I did get in that line, and when Mrs. Horowitz came around with coffee and doughnuts about two in the morning, I said, "I don't drink coffee, but could I have an extra doughnut instead?" She laughed and said, "Of course." I would never again see this woman smile.

The afternoon recital was easily the most anticipated event of my concert-going life to that point. Horowitz walked onto the stage almost a half hour late, but no one cared. He was present, and something remarkable was about to happen. There was a great, collective intake of breath when he missed some notes in the first phrase of the Toccata, Adagio and Fugue by Bach. After that, everything was pure musical magic. All those recordings I had listened to, the praise other musicians bestowed, nothing could come close to the live performance. Attending that concert was a reminder of how live performance remains more satisfying than the recorded equivalent.

Many years later, one of my record producers, Joanna Nickrenz, asked me if I had been at the once-in-a-lifetime recital. I said yes, and that I could relive the whole experience by listening to the commercial recording of the concert. She asked, "Did you really think the recording was of the actual concert?"

I said, "Of course. You can tell just because he missed those notes in the Bach."

She then produced a tape and asked me to listen to it. I was shocked! It was certainly not the same as my cherished recording. All manner of musical errors were in evidence. I asked what had happened.

Joanna explained how most of the material was recorded multiple times and that they had to leave in the opening because the entire audience heard the wrong notes. But while we all sat there in Carnegie, we were too enthralled to notice the others. That is why recordings can be so misleading. Even if they are unedited versions of the most sublime performances, nothing can replace the relationship of the artist with the audience. I have heard recordings of some of my own concerts that I thought were wonderful at the time; then, on rehearing, I notice poorly judged tempi, overindulgent ritardandos and a slew of wrong notes.

As important as Juilliard was, perhaps it was more revealing to observe the active concert life in New York. Jean Morel used to advise us to learn from the things that go wrong, because if you try to imitate what is good, you are merely a copy. There was a lot of good going on, though. We could routinely hear Bernstein, Szell, Ormandy, the underrated Martinon with the Chicago Symphony, and practically every artist that passed through the city. I still hadn't developed a taste for opera and it remained the weakest link in my musical chain.

The next two L and M teachers I had were Roger Sessions and Luciano Berio. Sessions was notoriously strict and students were forever trying to catch him in mistakes, especially when he would assign us to harmonize chorales.

"Mr. Sessions, the fourth note in the second bar of the alto clef should be a C-sharp."

He would erase the offending note.

"No, the alto clef."

He would erase the offending note.

"That's the fourth note, not bar."

He would erase the offending note.

"C-sharp."

And on it went.

Berio reminded me a little of actor Peter Sellers in his Inspector Clouseau role. The great Italian composer was the only person I had ever seen trip over a piano.

Not that this mattered. I was doing a lot of work conducting, playing piano for ballet rehearsals, as well as leading contemporary music concerts at school. My attendance in classes was spotty. The sessions with Morel seemed to be the one thing that I really cared about.

In 1966, I was invited to be assistant conductor of the New York Youth Symphony. I made my Carnegie Hall debut leading William Schuman's *New England Triptych*. Because I went to innumerable concerts at the Hall in my freshman year, the place did not seem so huge, at least from the audience. However, with that first step through the doors and onto the stage, I felt overwhelmed by the sense that the auditorium had at least quadrupled in size.

Schuman was there, and we began a friendship that lasted until his death. That made me regret even more that he had not headed up Juilliard during my student days. Perhaps his presence would have encouraged me to show up for more classes.

In my final year, my L and M teacher was Vincent Persichetti, another well-known composer who changed my attitude about classwork. This man made me curious about everything. He was rigorous but enthusiastic, and had a way of making the most boring contrapuntal exercises come to life. Persichetti also led us on great journeys of discovery. At the end of some classes, he would glance at his watch and nonchalantly make a remark along the lines of, "Well, we're out of time. By the way, do any of you know five piano concertos that start with the piano alone? See you Wednesday." We would rush to the library en masse. Of course, his lesson was not about getting five correct answers. It was about how composers handled the opening of works in piano concerto form. Persichetti succeeded in teaching without your realizing you learned something. I hated missing any of his classes.

In 1967, I was promoted to music director of the Youth Symphony and gradually Carnegie Hall started to seem its normal size. This is when my brother moved to New York to study, and I thought it would be a nice idea to perform the Beethoven Triple Concerto with him, Jeff Siegel and violinist Theodore Arm. Our mother arrived about two weeks prior to the performance to coach us in the work. She was demanding, as usual, but obviously we were achieving good results. Then about three days before the concert she said, "Let me see how you are going to bow."

We assumed she was kidding. We were professionals, adults, but it was no joke. So the four of us exited to a hallway, then returned to make a truly appalling entrance. She had us work on this over and over until she deemed us presentable. When we asked her why we needed to perfect this, she had an astutely perceptive answer.

"Because the audience judges you before you play one note."

A line I have never forgotten. Even though I still find my own entrances a bit awkward, I have come to realize that appearance does indeed count. But some artists go to extremes, and may be remembered for how they look rather than how they perform.

In my senior year, the specter of the great Juilliard challenge loomed. This was the dreaded L and M final exam. After four years of comprehensive study, final evaluation was based not only on how well you played, but on how much you learned in those classes. That test was legendary around the building on Claremont Avenue. Fail the exam and you did not graduate.

Tales were told of how we would be placed in a room alone and given a score to analyze. We would then be shepherded to another room in which more scores would be open on the piano, some quite obscure, which had to be identified. The example most often cited was the Second Symphony of Khachaturian. I was sure that if I didn't recognize the score in question, that would be my answer, even if it were an early Haydn symphony. On the blackboard would be words and phrases that we had to identify and translate. And these words may or may not have had any relevance to music. One tale claimed that a student defined *al dente* as a musical phrase played by a flutist who positions the instrument directly on the teeth.

I was scared to death. I had been a poor student at best and there was no way you could cram for this exam or fake it. I arrived and was handed the last four pages of the first movement of the Berg Violin Concerto to analyze. I felt sure to be assigned to the fifth ring of the musical inferno. I jotted down things that looked analytical and hoped I could explain a little something about the piece.

Upon walking into the room, I saw sitting around a table Persichetti, Sessions and Jacob Druckman. The sixth ring of hell now looked good.

There were the scores on the piano, the words on the board and the sweat on my palms. As I started in with my dissertation on the Berg, Mr. Persichetti stopped me and said, "Look, we all know you are a fine musician and we only have one question for you. Why weren't you in class more often?"

I explained that the school had assigned me so much conducting and piano playing activity that it was impossible to get to very many classes. The committee thanked me and sent me home.

Stories about that era at Juilliard could fill ten books. For me it was a period of musical intensity. However, during that time, I experienced so much isolation from the world outside the conservatory doors that I never even noticed the chaos that rocked my neighborhood as I walked to school up Broadway. Columbia University was just one block from my apartment, and although the area seemed more crowded with people than usual, I had no idea that hundreds of students had occupied several of the university's largest buildings to protest racial discrimination and Columbia's support of the Vietnam War.

These historic events lasted a week and ended in violent confrontations with riot police. But I remained oblivious because this external upheaval coincided with a period of intense personal struggle. Portions of my long-term memory had faded; I could recall even less about my childhood. I suspected I was having heart problems and my physician stated the trouble did not appear to be physical. I paid twice-a-week visits to a therapist, but still I grew further and further away from my past.

9

Jean Morel

The difference between ballet and opera is that when the dancers go to the top, they have to come down.

—JEAN MOREL

He sat at a small desk on the third floor of the Juilliard School, a burnt-out piece of cigar dangling from his lips. His accent was strong and his manner gruff. There were times when you wanted to quit, but Jean Morel forced you to stick with it, even if he was the reason for your discomfort.

There were many who felt the man should have, rightly, had a much more grand career, perhaps on a par with Pierre Monteux. Certainly he had command of the vast majority of French repertoire. But he was equally at home in all of the classics as well as in various contemporary styles.

Like so many others, Morel fled France during the war and wound up in South America. While in Buenos Aires, he married an American woman, who wound up running off with a visiting Texan.

This desertion scarred Morel forever, turning him sour against the country that he would soon call home. When he arrived in the States, he immediately secured a job conducting at the New York City Center Opera. Later, he would move on to the Met.

When the Juilliard School offered him a teaching position in 1949, the conducting landscape in the United States changed permanently.

On my first day as one of four terrified pupils, Morel seemed feisty, as if he was on the verge of proving how little we all knew. Five days a week, we would meet in his studio, always adhering to the same regimen, beginning with solfège exercises. I think I drove him nuts at my inability to master more than a few syllables, quickly invoking whatever sounds I could think of. With perfect pitch, I could sing the right notes, just with the wrong words.

"Slatkeen, what is zis fa-la-la?" was a mantra chanted pretty much at each lesson.

After that came dictation. In music, this means that the teacher plays the piano and the students write down the notes without peeking over the pianist's shoulder at the sheet music. Morel played, and our job was to take down the four-part exercises in the four different clefs we had so studiously learned for our entrance exam. Fortunately, I had studied theory as a youngster and could usually figure out the voice leading.

In the class of four that year, my peers included the Finnish bear, Leif Segerstam, Catherine Comet and John McCauley. We became friends, mostly to comfort each other after Morel's outbursts.

And he could be brutal.

Following the exercises, it was time to get around to actual conducting. The studio had two pianos. Three of us would play from the score, choosing among the instrumental parts, then the fourth student would conduct. Morel sat at his desk and commented often, typically with nothing but negatives.

On my first day, we started with a Haydn symphony. During the slow introduction, my left and right arms more or less mirrored each other in gesture. Morel looked up at me and quipped, "You could have left 'alf of you at home."

When a member of the class was having a rough time with a particular piece, he remarked, "Do not conduct. Go sell shoes. This country needs good shoe salesmen." Echoes of Modest Altschuler.

And if he really got upset, Morel would slam his hands on the desk and launch into a vitriolic tirade. It was a bit scary; however, growing up in a mostly Russian-trained musical household, I was accustomed to the behavior. But over the years, a few of my cohorts quit because they could not endure it any more.

On Tuesdays and Thursdays, we had the chance to work with the reading orchestra. Those young players were already bitter, not only because they did not make the top orchestra in school, but also because they had no desire to play in any orchestra in the first place. The competitive teenagers viewed their destiny as soloists. And Morel would be just as tough on the instrumentalists as on the conductors. "Why aren't you following what they are beating?" he would yell. "How can they conduct when you are playing like a wounded animal?" "You should spend more time practicing on your instrument and not on your girlfriend."

Like any great teacher, Morel was most severe with those he thought had genuine talent. There is much to be said for pushing hard. Today, there is often less criticism and more hand-holding. This kid-glove approach rarely produces the same kind of results as old-fashioned discipline.

Morel's attitude carried over to the Juilliard Orchestra, where we observed him on the podium.

His conducting technique was beyond reproach, as was his keen ear. One day, he stopped during a passage in Dukas' *La Péri.* "Monsieur third horn, your mute is not the same size as the others in your section." Since the bell of the horn faces away from the podium, the man could only glean this from hearing the sound. My fellow conductors and I were ready to give up and become shoe salesmen then and there. Morel also possessed the ability to solfège at the speed of light, perpetually delighted to show off his skills by singing the do-re-mi's of Chopin's *Fantasie-impromptu,* quite an impressive display by anyone.

His acid tongue inevitably got him in trouble everywhere. When leading the New York Philharmonic, he and the timpanist, Saul Goodman, had an angry verbal exchange. It got so heated that Goodman literally chased Morel back into the dressing room at Carnegie Hall, brandishing his mallets and threatening to murder the conductor. Morel had accused Goodman of purposefully ruining a concert. At Juilliard, the percussion studios were located behind the rehearsal room, but to access them, you needed to walk through the larger space. Every day, at exactly eleven forty-five, the large doors directly behind the conductor would open. The short Goodman would enter and say, in the thickest of New York accents, "Hi, Jean," pronouncing it as if addressing a girl, and in an angry tone. Morel would simply shrug and reply, "Oh, Goodman."

Morel had a penchant for correcting the percussionists. In his youth, he too was a percussionist, and he played the world premiere of Stravinsky's *L'histoire du soldat.* He also claimed to have attended the first performance of *Le sacre du printemps.* That is conceivable, but he would have been only ten years old. When we would ask him the truth about what happened at that infamous event, he would say he did not remember as he fell asleep amidst the din of the rioting underway inside the theater.

The Juilliard orchestra had its share of troublemakers, and every so often they thought they could put something over on Morel. They tried, and always failed. One violinist was constantly making remarks to his stand partner. When he got caught, and this was frequently, Morel would glower and say, "Ginsberg, you are a saboteur. You will be in the New York Philharmonic." Sure enough, a few years after graduation, Marc Ginsberg became that orchestra's principal second violinist.

During my final year at school, I conducted the orchestra in a performance of *An American in Paris*. I knew the concert went well and that Morel could say nothing bad about it. So I rushed up to the studio, where he was sitting at that desk, flecks of the cigar dribbling down his chin. He did not look up. There was a silence of about a minute before he grumbled, "Eet was not bad." That was the highest compliment he ever paid me and I was grateful for it.

He did have a gentle side. Once a month, Morel would take the conducting class to lunch at a restaurant right in the middle of Harlem on 125th Street. It was called Frank's. During each visit, he would place the identical order, a Dubonnet cocktail and fillet of sole. He regaled us with tales of the Paris opera, run-ins with renowned composers, and the history of obscure French composers. No insults allowed.

When Juilliard moved to Midtown, Morel appeared unable to adjust to the new accommodations. One afternoon, he got trapped in a stairwell and was forced to spend the night there, waiting for the school to reopen the next morning in order to be freed. The Juilliard Hilton just did not suit him; his health and his mental state began to deteriorate. The school relieved him of his duties and he would spend his remaining years alone in his apartment.

I had convinced Walter Susskind to let Morel guest conduct a subscription concert in Saint Louis. When the date neared, storms were covering the Midwest and the pilot of the plane carrying Morel, Susskind and the orchestra's artistic administrator, Jim Cain, said that the flight might have to be diverted to Tulsa. Morel, who had said nothing on the trip, quietly muttered, "I do not want to go to Tulsa."

Richard Holmes, the legendary timpanist for the SLSO and a conducting student of Morel's, met them at the airport. Rick had arranged for a private nurse to care for Morel during this stay. Susskind allowed me introduce him to the orchestra. It would be nice to report that the experience went well, but Morel was a mere shadow of his former conducting self. The sharp ears were present, and his technique was clearly a joy to watch, but there was none of the fire and temperament that defined his work at Juilliard. Once in a while, something special would come through. It may not have meant a lot to the orchestra, but personally I was transported back to those glorious days at school.

The final performance over, Rick and I took Morel to the airport. In those days, security permitted us to accompany him onto the plane. As we strapped him in, Morel grabbed Rick's coat sleeve. Both of us could see him crying. In a frail and weakened state, he said, "After all these years, I never realized that I had any friends. Merci."

Rick continued to pay Morel's medical bills, until Juilliard realized how embarrassing it would be if the public got word that he was not being covered under the school's health and pension plan. Jean Morel died in 1975.

Everyone who played under his baton has a different story to tell. But each of these musicians all agree on one thing: they can recall everything about the pieces of music Morel led. Most who became members of major orchestras still hear his voice when a different conductor tries to make a correction. Whatever the repertoire, Morel brought a thorough understanding of idiom and style to each rehearsal and performance. Every piece played under his direction lingered in the memory.

And Jean Morel's legacy continues through many of today's most notable American maestros. James Levine, John Nelson, Dennis Russell Davies, James Conlon, Jorge Mester and countless other conductors. All were recipients of the best possible tutelage from one of the only people who could actually teach this strange art.

How can one sum up these incredible four years at Juilliard? The short Frenchman in the blue rehearsal coat, with little crumbs of cigar caught between his lips and waiting to pounce at any moment, said it best:

"Eet was not bad."

10

What the Composer Tells Us

So much of what we do is ephemeral and quickly forgotten, even by ourselves, so it's gratifying to have something you have done linger in people's memories.

—JOHN WILLIAMS

During one memorable rehearsal at Juilliard, we had a rare opportunity to watch a composer and conductor interact. The piece was the Third Symphony by Roy Harris and the conductor was my teacher, Jean Morel. The composer was seated midway back in the auditorium. There is a section in the piece where Harris had made a cut years earlier. The excised portion had always been omitted in performance, but the publisher continued to distribute parts with the offending section. Morel, somewhat of a literalist, chose to perform the missing pages.

When Harris heard the start of this section, he sprang up from his seat and cried, "No, no! I got rid of this part years ago. Please put the cut in."

Morel responded, "Monsieur Harris, this is not like a last will and testament. You cannot change what they have sent to us. We are playing what you wrote."

This discussion continued for a few minutes, and the composer conceded he was not winning the debate. Thus, the original version of the symphony would be played. Morel was smiling.

Situations are not always so confrontational. Such problems are handily avoided if the conductor and composer are in contact with each other prior to the rehearsals. When the score arrives, and if it triggers questions, it is always best to be in communication so issues are resolved well in advance.

Perhaps there was no conductor who collaborated with more composers than Serge Koussevitzky. In fact, Koussevitzky made it possible for the American composer to be accepted into mainstream orchestral life. His advocacy of Schuman, Copland, Bernstein and so many others would inspire and instruct other conductors desiring a full agenda of new music on their plates.

Koussevitzky's achievement is all the more remarkable when you consider the rumor that the maestro was actually unable to properly read a symphonic score. To learn pieces, he had two pianists come to his home where he would stand in front of them and conduct as they played. My own suspicion is that he detected single instrumental lines, but like any number of conductors, had difficulty assembling multiple lines in his head. This was not the ideal solution, but he got extraordinary results.

Relationships between composer and conductor did not develop until the late nineteenth century. Prior to that time, performer and author were one in the same. We don't have much documentation as to how, for example, Beethoven conducted music other than his own. Certainly there are cases where a great composer turned over the interpretive chores to someone else.

In spite of the attention paid in recent decades to "historically informed" or "authentic" performance practice, nobody still has any idea of how Mendelssohn played Bach. It seems as if these musicological concerns have applied to recreating how a composer might have "authentically" heard his music during his lifetime, not how others viewed the material through succeeding generations. Gustav Mahler made extensive edits to the complete Beethoven symphonies, and, on paper, the information is readily available (see chapter 29). Yet we have scant indication as to how Mahler actually conducted these Beethoven works.

Listening to recordings can be equally frustrating. Wilhelm Furtwängler, revered as a Brucknerian, frequently presented this composer to the public, and we have the audio documentation to which we can refer. But what are we to infer from Furtwängler's diverse takes on the Eighth Symphony, which are available in different versions and in wildly varying tempi? Not only do we come away confused about the conductor's thoughts, we still have barely any sense of how Bruckner might have performed this work.

The dilemma continued though the twentieth and into the twenty-first century. Composers also seem to find interpreting their own works extremely challenging. Each composition naturally reflects something about its creator at the time and place the piece was written. In retrospect, it is impossible to replicate precisely what you thought and felt at some earlier moment in life. Recordings by the master composer-conductors including Bernstein and Boulez show that their thoughts evolved and transformed as the years progressed. In some cases, the later recordings are faster, and in some, slower. Bernstein committed his First Symphony to disc three times and Boulez recorded *Le marteau sans maître* twice. Not only are the timings altered, the overall feel of the performances is varied substantially as well.

I observed Aaron Copland conduct many times, and I was struck by how tempo seemed his lowest priority when leading his own material. The composer came to conducting later in life, and he enjoyed it immensely. Copland said that he enjoyed conducting because he would get paid for just waving his arms around. His demeanor with the orchestra was rather curmudgeonly, perhaps because the performance occurring onstage was not the same one that was in his head. "Perky, perky!" was his way of urging musicians to go faster. Like innumerable composers, Copland's technique was limited, but seeing such a legend on the podium compensated for most of the weaknesses.

Stravinsky certainly qualified as another legend, but unlike Copland, he rarely championed other living composers, preferring Tchaikovsky to his contemporaries. As a conductor, his posture and movements were quite angular and stiff. Like Copland, his own tempi were slower than we expected. One night, I was privileged to attend a Lincoln Center event where the composer directed the New York premieres of a couple of recent pieces. The giant little man emerged from the wings to a thunderous ovation. Alas, the pieces were not well received and the audience response at the conclusion was tepid. I think the composer would have preferred catcalls and booing to apathy. It was disheartening to see the master for the last time in these circumstances.

A few composers today are good podium minders. Ollie Knussen and John Adams come to mind, but almost inevitably, the organization's music director or management asks them to program other music in addition to works of their own. Maybe that idea succeeds when the works planned are also by living composers, or others who influenced the composer's music. But often it smacks only of a marketing idea, as if the administrators lacked sufficient confidence in the ability of the composer's music to sell tickets. The composer as conductor is about the closest we get to the old days when people flocked to hear Paganini, Liszt or Rachmaninov play their latest compositions.

There must have been tremendous excitement when the giants of the past both wrote and performed their compositions. Learning about the genesis of how these works came about is fascinating, but for our purposes we need to know about the process today.

Let's start with how a new piece of music for orchestra is brought to life.

History has mostly moved beyond the times when kings and courts had resident composers. The Thomaskirche put Bach on a salary; Haydn enjoyed a long association with the Esterhazys. But today's composer relies almost exclusively on commissions, on royalties for past performances, rental and sales of music, and occasionally revenue from recording. Often an orchestra has a fund set aside for new music, and sometimes it will solicit benefactors for a particular project. The cost of a composition depends on its length and on the stature of its composer, running from $500 to $2,500 per minute. Contractual agreements typically include the premiere, exclusive performing rights for perhaps a year and first recording rights.

If the music director plans to conduct a new piece, he or she usually has a say in selecting the composer. Sometimes, a composition will result from a competition, wherein the top prize is a professional symphonic premiere. In these circumstances, the music director may or may not have participated on the jury that picks the winner. Every so often, conductors must face this situation, and they might not be in sync with either the triumphant artist or his or her musical style. If you agreed to play the piece, the only course of action is to pretend that it is the greatest composition ever written since the B Minor Mass. Deep inside, tacitly, you know that you will never perform it again.

In a more likely scenario, the conductor has actually been the driving force behind the commission. And sometimes you have to raise the money yourself. There are always citizens who enjoy the new, and love having their names attached to the creation of a work of art. In Washington, I was particularly fortunate to have the support of John and June Hechinger, who were active sponsors of practically all of the contemporary music I premiered. This made my job easier, as all I had to do was visit these wonderful people, tell them what I was thinking and ask them to fund a particular project.

Another way of securing a world premiere is to uncover existing works that have not yet been performed. This is easier than you would think. Many composers have had commissioned works withdrawn for varying reasons. This can occur when the performer is not satisfied with the work, or the composer has a change of heart about his or her own composition. A slightly different situation occurred with the pianist Lang Lang, who had commissioned a concerto from Jennifer Higdon. After the work was complete, Lang Lang decided that it was just not for him, and it took two years before another pianist performed the work.

Another example of a displaced premiere occurred in 2010. In 2000, the composer Lewis Spratlan won a Pulitzer Prize for his 1978 opera *Life Is a Dream*. This award was given only for the second act, which was given a concert performance. When the work was written, the opera company for which it was intended went bankrupt and could not mount the piece. It was not until 2010, more than thirty years later, that the opera was finally presented.

The final composition by the Argentinean great Alberto Ginastera was *Popul Vuh*, based on the Mayan book of creation. The Philadelphia Orchestra commissioned this piece, and Eugene Ormandy was supposed to premiere it. Ginastera died in 1983, reportedly leaving one movement incomplete. The conductor was also ailing and passed away two years later. Incoming music director Riccardo Muti had no interest in the piece, so it was forgotten. The pianist Barbara Nissman called the work to my attention, as I had learned many of the composer's pieces and loved his music. When I laid eyes on the score, I deduced that the composer actually had completed the work. The world premiere took place in 1989 in Saint Louis and I performed it with the originating orchestra, Philadelphia, in 2008.

The quantity of never-before-played, extant compositions is huge, but finding them requires research and diligence. Sometimes the effort is not worth it, as the music may not be of the quality one hopes. Just presenting these curiosities for the sake of novelty might seem fine at the time, but it can backfire.

In 1981, a symphony by Mozart surfaced after lingering in Germany for a few hundred years. It was in F major and was assigned the Köchel number 19a. Allegedly the wunderkind penned this at the age of nine. The world premiere was given by me and the Mostly Mozart Festival Orchestra at the White House. President Reagan attended, and I remember telling the audience that the symphony is only for small string orchestra, two horns and two oboes. "This does not reflect the recent cuts in the arts budget," I said, eliciting some gasps. The work was charming yet not particularly memorable.

The esteemed music critic for the New York Times, Harold Schonberg, wrote on July 8, "The little F-Major Symphony has no great individuality. A 9-year old is not going to write music of searing emotional intensity. For the most part, the symphony goes along in predictable patterns. But it is elegant and well proportioned, it has a lovely, singing slow movement with some very individual accompaniment figures, it moves with confidence, and it surely is as good as almost anything written in its period."

Ten years later, scholars discovered that the whole thing was a hoax, with no evidence that the work had been written by Mozart.

Naturally, different composers produce their work at their own individual pace. An organization tends to offer a commission about a year and a half before the tentative date of the actual premiere. All parties agree to fees, the length of the work, and the specific forces involved. Upon receiving this information, the conductor will commence building a program into which the new piece will fit. Most of the time, but hardly always, it is slated to appear at the opening of the concert. Some musicians argue that this arrangement is unfair to the composer, as audience members can calculate roughly how long the piece lasts, then arrive just in time for the concerto. However, if the commissioned piece reaches twenty minutes in length or longer, the rules change. It is possible to start with an overture of some kind, do the new work and save the big symphony or concerto for the conclusion.

Once in a while, a new work is of sufficient breadth and substance to warrant last place, after intermission, but to pull this off takes a very confident management and conductor. Obviously, if the work is a full evening's length, no shuffling is necessary, but for the most part, orchestral institutions have stuck with a short opening work, followed by a concerto and ending with a symphony. One reason may be due to the paucity of composers writing huge symphonies. The cost of a forty-five-minute piece is also a factor. A new concerto usually clocks in at twenty-five minutes or so, and unless the soloist is extremely high profile, the piece is scheduled before the intermission.

All commissions start out with the best of intentions. If the conductor knows the composer, so much the better. There will at least be the knowledge of what is coming, from a stylistic point of view. Unless the writer has a major epiphany, the new opus will carry on either in the general corpus of the composer, or be reminiscent of the most recently completed work. In Saint Louis, we were fortunate to have four composers in residence. Joseph Schwantner, Donald Erb, Joan Tower and Claude Baker, each of whom stayed with the orchestra for three years. We had performed their music prior to the actual residency, so the players were already familiar with the various musical idioms. Performing their new works therefore presented few difficulties.

Knowing the style of a new work is equally important for guest conducting appearances. For my own debuts with major orchestras, many programs have included pieces with which the ensemble has had no experience. The orchestra needs to be given a sense of direction, especially if the composer is one not previously encountered. Belief in the piece itself is as crucial as thorough knowledge of the score. Very few things are worse than a half-hearted commitment to the task at hand. It happens once in a while, but the conductor must be persuasive or else he or she risks loss of the players' respect.

On occasion, I have consulted with the composer to discuss various aspects of the piece. One amusing moment occurred with Steve Reich. He was writing a piece for Saint Louis. It called for double string orchestra—two divided sections resembling a large-scale octet—winds and percussion. About three months before the premiere, I asked Reich when the score would be available. He said he was finished with half of it and would send it to me. I could never have imagined how literal his words would prove to be. What arrived in the mail was just the lower half of the score, the part for the second string orchestra! The remainder came about a month later.

Contracts contain specific language concerning the date when the work is due. Some composers are efficient and finish well before the deadline. Others are notoriously late; their music might arrive only days before the first rehearsal. A conductor's ability to assimilate a score also varies. For some, it is a long methodical process. Others can get the gist early on and focus on details as the time approaches for performance. Limits also fluctuate as to the number of pieces an individual can learn in a season. Familiarity with the compositional style is helpful.

When the score arrives, the first thing I do is look at the instrumentation list, which normally appears right after the title page. I need to find out if we may need any unusual instruments, or if the composer has exceeded the contractual number of players allowed. Synthesizers and computer-driven devices usually fall into the purview of the percussionists or the keyboard player. The performers must be given their parts well in advance in order to cope with new and evolving technologies. Sometimes special instruments must be rented.

We all differ in our ways of learning a piece of music. My own method is divided into four parts. First, I take a cursory glance at the entire piece, trying to get a feel for the sound, structure and shape of the work. Many conductors go to the piano and attempt to play what they see on the page. I admire those who can do this, but think it occasionally prevents you from being able to mentally hear the orchestral color. My own preference is to imagine the sound that I see on the page, without any instrumental assistance.

The second phase of new music score study involves a return to the beginning. How do the instruments interconnect? What passages look particularly difficult, either for the orchestra as a whole or for the solo parts? Are there concerns as far as dynamics go? Will some instruments overpower others, and was this intentional on the part of the composer? Do we know how softly a crescendo begins and how loud it gets at the end? Are there notes that are not playable on the specified instrument? Who plays which part in a string divisi passage? This list goes on and on.

But the most critical question is probably, "How much rehearsal time will it take?"

Supposedly, Arnold Schoenberg had fifty sessions for the premiere of *Pierrot lunaire*. And this piece is scored for only seven instrumentalists and one vocalist! Today we are governed by rules and regulations. Rehearsals can only last a specified amount of time, and with orchestras, there tends to be a routine division of labor each week. New music fits into the weekly schedule the same as familiar music. If we are lucky, and plan in advance, it is possible to begin rehearsing a new work the week before the performance, but you must make sure that you have the same musicians present both weeks.

It does not matter if a piece is new or old. The same care and attention have to go into every bar. There is often the criticism that the newer music gets short shrift in the overall rehearsal scheme. In fact, it is the standard repertoire that receives less attention. There have been numerous times when I have devoted most of the rehearsal to the latest creation, leaving the traditional works for shorter touch-ups. Sometimes this resulted in an extraordinary performance, as the instrumentalists were on the edge of their seats, waiting to see what I would do that had not been rehearsed.

No one can know what constitutes "enough rehearsal time." For some, there is never enough. Regardless of the repertoire, orchestra members should be made to feel confident that they know the work, and that nothing will interrupt the flow of its performance. This means that all concerned understand the ethic and emotional content of a piece, as well as the notes. As always, I try not to speak too much or too long at rehearsal, preparing as much as possible in advance so that I can anticipate the problem areas. If time permits, I might ask the composer to say a few words to the orchestra at the start, but generally, I prefer to let the music do the talking.

So far, the study process has been primarily horizontal, examining the piece as it progresses, start to finish, and then trying to gauge what is needed to put it together. Now comes the third step, the vertical. Instead of seeing the work as a whole, individual lines are analyzed. The colors are viewed in isolation as opposed to blended into the entire musical fabric. The process can be a grueling ordeal if the piece is dense. You separate each voice in your head, figuring out how the sonorities were created. This phase, too, is the best time to really get the work into your body.

Sometimes it is helpful to be alone and conduct through some passages. The physical—motion, movements—must supplement the mental. Just as with a standard repertoire work, you must constantly remind yourself to envision how the players will see your gestures. Then comes the matter of tempo.

A few composers notate tempos in their scores with such precision that you must be a mathematician to decipher the glyphs. A metronome, or device that produces regular ticks settable in beats per minute, is sometime used to assist the conductor in finding the correct tempo. Ever since it was invented, however, there has been controversy as to its real value. The pianist John Browning once told me that his good friend Samuel Barber was reluctant to put in metronome indications, as he felt that *moderato* and *vivace* told the performers everything they needed to know. But his publisher, G. Schirmer, insisted and so, against his desires, they are in the music.

No conductor carries a metronome to the podium for a performance, but some do keep one around for rehearsals. Even that can be a problem, as your internal clock changes naturally, making a tempo seem right one day and wrong the next. And who can really discern the difference between the speed of a quarter note at 112 or 114 beats per minute? Still, the markings are there and they give us a rough idea of what the composer intended. How can we be accurate during the concert?

Here is a little trick that can help you sense these rates without a metronome. Every musician has certain tempi in their memory that remain pretty much inflexible. For me, *The Stars and Stripes Forever* always goes at 120 beats per minute. "Sempre libera" at 84, *Boléro* at 72. It may seem silly, but once in a while it is possible to just remember these works when those indications come up in other pieces of music. After a while, tempo becomes ingrained in the body's physical memory and these references are no longer needed. The last thing you want is the sound of one piece to be in your head while another work is being played in front of you.

With this phase of study completed, you are ready to communicate to the composer specific problems that you might have discovered. Perhaps you perceive a wrong note, a misplaced dynamic or a passage that needs more clarity in the orchestration. E-mail or telephone contact is an option, or you may prefer to wait until the composer arrives for the orchestra's first rehearsal.

Finally the time has come to go through the piece, just the way you did when it first crossed your desk. Start at the beginning and imagine that the performance is underway. I do not actually physically conduct, but just sit and try to hear it. Pacing is crucial. Mentally, you can only approximate how the some contemporary work will sound when played. The increasing use of electronics also affects our ability to intuit the sonority.

Some composers will make a recording of their piece with computer instruments and send it along in advance. This can be useful but also dangerous. Hearing an electronic representation can provide an idea of the speed, overall shape, and approximate timbre of the work, but it falls short of replicating the actual sound of the orchestra. My best advice to a novice is to learn the work thoroughly before listening to any recording. I find that most of these aural aids wind up seeming a bit faster than is practical for live performance. No composer has ever erred on the slow side.

With preparation complete, it is time to start rehearsing with the orchestra.

How does the conductor know how much rehearsal is needed? The entire program must be taken into consideration. The more complex the new work, the less time there will be to rehearse the other pieces. Even with a short new composition, the technical demands for both conductor and orchestra could mean that the remaining works on the docket will not receive so much attention. My advice is to get a feeling for how much time the new work will need, and program accordingly around that piece.

You commission a new work, create a full concert around it, and hope that you have guessed correctly. To have a command of the general language that the composer employs is helpful. This will give you an idea of how the work might progress. Always be sure you schedule the new music at the first rehearsal.

If you are giving the new work its premiere performance, the composer will likely be present from the start. Once in a while, he or she is unable to attend, in which case the conductor must keep absolutely accurate tabs on what does not seem to work. It can be a tempo, a passage that is not playable by a particular instrument, balance issues and similar details. The ideal situation allots enough time to go through the piece from beginning to end. If the notation is not complicated, a run-through might be possible, but sometimes the compositional technique is unusual, requiring the conductor to explain what the various notational symbols mean. In compositions that employ traditional notation, it is quite possible to play through the piece. A lot of rough patches are inevitable, but the composer will come away with his or her curiosity and expectations satisfied.

At this particular rehearsal, I don't anticipate much interaction. It is simply an opportunity for all the musicians to get a rough idea of how the piece goes. The pianist and composer Marc Neikrug tells the story of the initial rehearsal of his flute concerto. The conductor was Lorin Maazel, and after the rehearsal, Marc wanted to offer some corrections.

Maestro Maazel spoke to him from the podium, saying, "Now is not the time."

The next day, amazingly, everything fell into place quickly. Maazel looked out into the hall and addressed the composer, "Now you may speak."

There was nothing Marc could say.

Rarely does rehearsing proceed this smoothly. In my experience, there will always be things to fix. Mr. Maazel is correct in trusting his players to sort out much on their own. Most of the time, I ask composers to jot down every thought, perhaps indicating things in the score that they were not happy with. As we go through the written list, I make notations in my copy of the score, marking the places where changes and corrections are mandatory. Sometimes I will actually list those on a piece of paper, bring it to the next rehearsal and read the list aloud to the orchestra.

For me, these methods have worked most effectively in rehearsal with John Corigliano. One of the reasons our partnership has succeeded over the years has to do with John's excellent ear.

On one occasion in Stockholm, I was premiering a new symphony by a Swedish composer. His music resembled a surprising mix of weak Shostakovich and even weaker Walton. At one point I had a question about a note in the timpani.

"Should that be a D or a D-flat?" I inquired of the man.

The voice in the hall screamed, "I don't know! I don't really know!"

I was convinced that he was on the verge of leaping to his death from the balcony.

Yes, there are composers who mark many things in the score but can't pick out these details when listening. John knows exactly what he wants, and it's often more efficient to have him address the orchestra directly. I invite him up to the podium, he rattles off the things he would like to be different, and every so often I chime in or conduct just the questionable passage. The players respect his hearing abilities as well as his craftsmanship. Plus they know that I trust him. He can get picky, but with an eye to the end he wishes to achieve.

Changes are always necessary, whether the piece is hot off the press or has been around for a while. No two performances can or should be alike. That rule applies to every style of music in the concert hall. If composers of our time reflect on some of their earlier work and make alterations or adjustments, then isn't it within reason for conductors to make changes too? Most often, the composers will respect the conductor's experience and go along with whatever amendments might be suggested.

Not all composers enjoy bounding up to the stage at rehearsal. They might come to the edge of the proscenium, or simply remain at the seat they have chosen for listening purposes. The lone disadvantage to the farther location comes when members of the orchestra have questions. The distance from the brass section to the audience can make verbal communication difficult, and with the composer present, everyone has a chance to get the new piece right. It amuses me when I have invited the author of the work to share the podium, yet orchestral musicians direct their questions to me. Similarly, perhaps because they believe that only the conductor should speak from the podium, a composer will convey recommendations to me rather than address the players involved.

A lot of what I have described in this section assumes that conductors are given at least four rehearsals per concert. Sometimes there are more, and sometimes less, but one constant is the dress rehearsal. My preferred working method is to give notes to the orchestra before the play-through. We might even perform these passages out of context. The run-though follows and the composer gives further critiques. It is always appreciated when the composer thanks the orchestra for all of its hard work.

As thorough as the rehearsals may have been, there are other problems that might arise regarding the performance. For starters, the conductor must know precisely where the composer will be seated during the concert. Many embarrassing moments for me have resulted when, at the end of the work I have made a sweeping gesture to the audience, fully expecting the composer to rise and perhaps join us onstage. Instead, I have pivoted around, surprised to see that person emerging from the wings.

Every composer loves to take a bow, but many do not give thought to appearance on stage. Just as the performers have a dress code, it is important that anyone coming on stage be appropriately dressed and groomed for the occasion. It is equally important to know if the composer is expected on the stage or will simply bow from a position in the audience.

Once I premiered a piece that we all knew would receive a tepid reaction from the crowd. I asked where the composer planned to sit and was told not to worry. He would be offstage and I should come and get him.

"But what if there is not enough applause to justify a return?" I inquired.

"Not to worry."

Worry was not on my mind when the work concluded. I stepped off the podium and the 8:20 *Flying Zephyr* went whizzing by, overtaking my place and bowing deeply to the five or six people who were still clapping.

It is impossible to get into the minds of those who create music. There is something about the abstract nature of sound that does not readily lend itself to verbal explanation. Even with the composer present, we can never truly fathom the turmoil or ease underpinning a composition. Although most conductors are not composers, the concept of fashioning something out of nothing is unparalleled in giving the conductor insights into the creative process. For that reason, I highly recommend that every budding maestro try their hand at writing music. More than likely, however, these compositions will never be heard, much less receive a second performance.

As for composers, getting that second hearing is possibly more important than the premiere. Hopefully, the conductor will have enough faith in the author to program the work in subsequent appearances with other orchestras. One benefit is that audiences are then introduced to important new repertory by guest conductors as well as their own music directors. I have always encouraged visitors to program music that is not so familiar to the local audience. My initial live exposure to the majority of works from the English canon came via Sir John Barbirolli, many French pieces through Charles Munch, and Bruckner from Leinsdorf.

Working closely with the composer is still the optimal method for getting to the truth in a given composition. You must have the courage to fight for those composers in whom you believe. Inevitably some people will question your choices, but that faith is the foundation of your musical credibility. And at the very least, you have realized the intention of the composer, no small feat.

11

Second Banana

Between the wish and the thing, life lies waiting.

—PROVERB

There is probably no harder role in music than that of the staff conductor. You have to know every piece of music in any given season, and if you are career driven (and what conductor isn't), you hope that someone cancels.

For a notable few this is exactly what happened. The case of Leonard Bernstein is well documented, as are the legendary starts of Arturo Toscanini and Michael Tilson Thomas, but it is not just a matter of being in the right place at the right time. A great deal of effort goes into this seemingly thankless task.

Let's start with the basics. How do you get the staff conductor job?

In Europe, there are very few apprenticeships of this kind with symphony orchestras. History shows us that most conductors of earlier eras worked in opera houses as répétiteurs, coaches or rehearsal pianists. They rarely got to conduct. If an opportunity presented itself, there was usually a performance with no rehearsal. For many, the opera was a dead end. For others, it was the starting point of an uncertain future.

Quite often, some authority will say something like this: "You need to have a background in the opera house to be a conductor of substance." I don't think this applies anymore. If you look at the majority of conductors during the last half of the twentieth century, you will find that most came to opera later rather than earlier. The names read like the history of orchestral life in the latter half of the twentieth century: Leonard Bernstein, Seiji Ozawa, Simon Rattle, Pierre Boulez, Daniel Barenboim, Zubin Mehta, Eugene Ormandy and even James Levine. Staff conductors, of course, must learn and digest the repertoire, just as they need to have a broad knowledge of orchestral, chamber and vocal literature, but they no longer have to serve their apprenticeships in the pit.

There may be another reason why some conductors have not opted to avail themselves of opportunities in the theater; they began to feel that the vast canvas of orchestral repertoire was sufficient in order to satisfy their own musical taste. Orchestral scores in the twentieth century were becoming more and more numerous and complex than their counterparts in ballet and opera. The basic technique required for *Peter Grimes* by Britten, written in 1944, is not much different than the tools needed for *Tosca*. On the other hand, conducting the Third Symphony of Lutosławski demands an entirely new set of skills with regard to beats and gestures. John Adams' *Nixon in China,* written just five years after the Lutosławski, is technically grounded in the nineteenth century.

Still, the opera house can provide a good beginning for some individuals. In the United States, it is more difficult to take this route because there are not so many full-time opera companies. On the other hand, orchestral life continues to flourish, sort of, with a number of assistantships up for grabs every year. Most orchestras have established some process by which they select staff conductors. Typically an audition is usually required. In other instances, the music director will handpick the assistant, and the orchestra will need to trust that decision. This can backfire on the boss if the person chosen turns out to be weak, but it can also boost the integrity and esteem of the music director if the second-in-command is strong.

Once you become an assistant, you must try to make the most of the opportunity. All of a sudden, your life is no longer your own. You will pass endless hours of study and preparation for works that you will only get a chance to watch others rehearse and perform, but that alone can be tremendously exciting for the fledgling conductor. A top orchestra's season may include as many as three hundred pieces of music, and the assistant must digest all of these in just a few months. He or she may not realize it at the time, but all of this knowledge will serve well as a foundation for the future, as will the observation of the diverse personalities on the podium.

The opportunity to observe various conducting styles is invaluable. Whether the conductor is a seasoned professional or just embarking on a career, he or she has a great deal to offer. Actually, I tend to believe that you can learn more from the conductors who do not do so well. Perhaps this is because the greats cannot be imitated, and trying to emulate them only results in a copycat approach instead of one you can call your own. However, by observing the weaker directors carefully, it is possible to avoid making their mistakes. These might occur in matters of technique or basic approach. Do the conductors talk too much without results? Are they clear or vague in the beat? Do they seem to elicit the respect of the orchestra, and if they do not, what is going wrong?

Keep watching and listening.

When might an assistant first be called upon to conduct? Possibly for a regularly scheduled rehearsal, a young person's concert, or a last-minute substitution for an indisposed conductor.

But let's back up a bit. I think the most difficult moment a conductor faces is the initial encounter with a professional ensemble. You may have spent years working with community, youth or academic orchestras. Now it's a whole new ball game, with new sets of rules in play.

It is important to keep in mind your past symphonic experiences. Your stick and rehearsal techniques have developed around what best suited the ensembles previously directed. If you have spent the majority of your time conducting amateur ensembles, you have not had an opportunity to concentrate on issues of interpretation, sonority or subtle balance. Rather, you have dealt with matters of ensemble, intonation and just steering the group through those fundamental elements without too many traffic accidents. Yes, you still teach all of the above, but you are not conducting students anymore. You have to be prepared as never before. Every nuance of the score needs to be reflected in your beat and your body language. Your demeanor in front of the orchestra must be more direct and to the point. Professional orchestras hate time wasters.

The role of the assistant conductor has changed in much the same ways as the orchestra. There is more variety in the repertoire; seasons are longer, union regulations more complex. The number of musical styles that must be mastered continues to grow. Some newcomers balk at doing pops concerts and even children's programs. The full range of genres is part of the assistant's experience and can all be put to use later, even kids' fare. Developing skills in every area is crucial for the apprentice. Conducting scores from Broadway, motion pictures and jazz is now a requirement for the assistant. Not everyone likes all music, but as a young conductor, you must embrace all styles and genres in order to learn. Perhaps you can discover a corner of the repertoire that you never knew existed.

I always request prospective assistant conductors to submit programs for young people's concerts. And I also ask them to ad lib some of the speech they would deliver at such a presentation. The art of verbal communication with the audience has become de rigueur for the assistant conductor. The more comfortable you can be addressing the audience, the greater your likelihood of success.

Be creative, I advise prospective assistants. Come up with concepts that are fresh and manage to convey educational value. Remember that almost two generations of audiences have grown up in the visual media age. Create an atmosphere of imagination, where the music takes the listener on a journey with no visual aids. Give some historical background and provide a context for every piece you present to young people. Ensure that everyone can relate to the sounds they are hearing. Remember, you are molding the audience that will listen to you twenty years from now.

Perhaps the assistant will be given a full subscription program to conduct. It is important to consider very carefully what music will be performed. At this opportunity, you need to convince the orchestra, audience, management and the press of your worth. Utilize your strengths. The concerto and its soloist will probably be assigned. Unless you are extremely uncomfortable with the repertoire, go along with this selection.

Then, choose a substantial second-half work, but don't go overboard. Choose a piece that you have previously performed, taking advantage of the fact that you are already familiar with the musical content. This is not the time to take a stab at Brahms' Third. Next, find a program opener that will grab the audience's attention and make the crowd eager to stay for the second half. If possible, select something by a living composer and a piece the orchestra has never played. Spend a lot of time in the music library, perusing scores from the orchestra's repertoire.

The orchestra will already know you from the young people's concerts you have led. They are not looking for anything different in the way of conducting technique. What is different is that you finally have more time to get your musical ideas across. Later on, I will discuss in more detail the actual rehearsal process, but for the moment, let me say just a few things about the relationship between the assistant and the orchestra.

Most orchestras will not call you "Maestro." Since they got to know you by your first name, they will probably continue using it for most of your early career. For the almost ten years I spent in the secondary role in Saint Louis, I was always called "Lennie" or "Leonard." When the reverse occurs and you single out one musician at rehearsal, much will depend on how close you have become to that player. If you know them well, the first name is fine. Otherwise use Mr., Ms. or Mrs. You can also address them by the instrument and position they hold. "Third trumpet, a bit louder please." Do not assume that they are all your good friends. Keeping a professional demeanor on stage is a critical part of the assistant's job.

Not only is it important to know what to say, it is equally important to know how to say it. Since you have observed other conductors, you probably noticed that the best of them wait until the orchestra is quiet before uttering a word. Everyone in the orchestra needs to hear what you are saying. Do not yell, but give your directions in a firm, direct way. Imagine that you are always talking to the back stand of the second violins. This will apply when you are a seasoned veteran as well.

It is perfectly fine to stay on stage during the breaks, getting advice from the musicians. Many will be eager to help you. Do not take it personally if there is some criticism of what you are doing. Listen, nod in agreement and analyze it later. Your only goal is to make great music.

Most of the audience attending your first subscription concert will not have seen you conduct. To them you are just another conductor, albeit one who spends the whole season with the orchestra. These patrons really want you to succeed, as you are part of the community. The same applies to the orchestra, which will continue working with you for the duration of your contract.

Speaking of your contract, my recommendation is to try and secure a two-year agreement for the initial phase with the orchestra and then continue on a year-to-year basis. As you will likely not have yet secured a manager, the details of this document will be negotiated between you and management, perhaps with the assistance of a lawyer.

How long should one remain an assistant?

My usual rule of thumb is four or five years maximum. In Saint Louis, I was given several titles in order to keep me around: Assistant, Associate, Resident,

Associate Principal and Principal Guest Conductor. All this in just ten years! The danger of staying too long in this role is that you can become typecast as a professional assistant, and it might be difficult to secure a major music directorship in the future. Eventually you must leave the protective womb of your first position.

There is tremendous satisfaction in doing every aspect of this job well. You will have learned a lot of repertoire, found out the best ways to work with other musicians, discovered how complicated it is to run the orchestral machinery and developed meaningful community relationships.

Congratulations! You are now a professional conductor!

PART
TWO

It may be hard for an egg to turn into a bird: it would be a jolly sight harder for it to learn to fly while remaining an egg. We are like eggs at present. And you cannot go on indefinitely being just an ordinary, decent egg. We must be hatched or go bad.

—C. S. LEWIS

12

A Career Begins

It is not as difficult as I thought it was, but it is harder than it is.

—EUGENE ORMANDY

You cannot know how much of a hand fate plays in the decision-making process. Toward the end of 1967, I was faced with a number of options and had no idea which road I would follow.

First, there was the possibility of remaining at Juilliard. I had completed my bachelor's degree and certainly the prospect of continuing studies with Morel was most appealing. I was already conducting frequently around New York, and Julliard had asked me to do some teaching as well. These things provided enough security that I thought maintaining the status quo did not seem like such a bad idea.

Second was an experience that would ultimately leave a very bad taste in my mouth. At that time, the New York Philharmonic hired its assistant conductors through the Dimitri Mitropoulos International Competition. Claudio Abbado was among those who had won. One day I got a call inviting me to meet with some of the organizers of the contest. Assuming they wished to encourage me to enter, I went to Lincoln Center to see this group. It was not as I had anticipated. Yes, I was asked to consider entering the competition, but there was a significant string attached.

Almost all the winners of the past years had been from other countries. There had not been an American in quite a while, and the group thought it was time for this to happen. A few had watched me conduct and thought I would be perfect for the job. That was when I realized something was not right. They informed me that if I entered, I would be assured of winning and would become an assistant conductor to Leonard Bernstein.

Aside from the entrance exams into Aspen and Juilliard, I had never been or wanted to have any part of a competition. I have held true to that through this day, at least at the professional level. But the discovery that this one would be rigged was something I simply was not prepared for. What made it more shocking was that I knew some members of the panel and could not believe they would participate in such a scheme. I did not answer them that day, and I also never applied. No one ever sought to discuss it further.

The third option was to accept the invitation to go to Saint Louis and be Mr. Susskind's assistant. I did not know if I was ready and felt that my only source of meaningful advice would come from that of my teacher, Jean Morel. It was amazing how thoughtful the man could be. I knew he wished for me to stay and continue my studies. Yet he also said that the best way to be a conductor was to conduct. He felt that entering the professional ranks would be the logical step. I would go to the city where my father had spent his youth, and as the man said, "What goes around, comes around."

A sizable obstacle stood in the way. The country was mired in Vietnam and the Conscription Act was still in place. If I left school, I was eligible for the draft and might have to trade in the baton for a bayonet. Well, not really. It had been determined that if I went into the service, I would join NORAD, based in Colorado Springs, and work as an arranger. This was a military organization which had an outstanding band. I was forthcoming about this from the start with the symphony's management and they understood the risk in hiring me. It was possible that I might need to leave in a couple of months. Nonetheless, I chose Saint Louis and would have to let the draft cards fall where they may.

I arrived in September 1968 and recognized some familiar faces. The artistic administrator of the Aspen Festival, James Cain, was hired for the similar position in Saint Louis. Of course, Mr. Susskind was there, and a few Juilliard alumni had become members of the orchestra during that season. Also in Saint Louis were older musicians who had played with my father, including Isadore Grossman, my dad's primary violin teacher in the '20s.

My compensation was the handsome salary of eight thousand dollars for the year and I found an inexpensive apartment where I wound up sleeping on the couch most of the time. This was the second year in the orchestra's newly refurbished home, a former movie palace renamed Powell Hall. It had, and still does have, splendid acoustics: warm, reverberant and well suited to a luxurious sound. Still, Susskind had a lot of work to do. His predecessor, Eleazar de Carvalho, was not so interested in the sound of the orchestra, and also, controversy marred his five-year tenure. The orchestra required a strong leader and Susskind fit the bill.

Sure enough, six weeks after getting settled, Uncle Sam announced that he wanted me. From the outset of my new life in the Archway City, I had continued regular visits to a therapist. Anxiety attacks and recollection of less and less of my past were now commonplace. I had considered using this to excuse me from the draft. Medical deferment seemed like a better option than 4F.

I went downtown for the examination that would determine whether I was qualified for military service. In the morning, they administered a written test; one section dealt with spatial relationships and another with identifying machines and tools. Not exactly my strengths; I was pretty sure I had done poorly. Then, in the afternoon, came the notorious physical exam. Generally, I had been a healthy specimen, but on that day, anxiety and fear overwhelmed me. My blood pressure, which was and continues to be textbook perfect, shot through the roof. They took me to a room where various military types kept popping in to check if I was all right. Finally the chief medical officer told me to try to calm down and get my clothes. Uncle Sam did not want me after all.

In that first season, I was scheduled to lead eighty-three children's concerts, a series of ten Sunday afternoon programs, some touring performances and a subscription concert. My initial program was part of the "Sunday Festival of Music" concerts, this one featuring Viennese selections. I was conducting each piece for the first time, and I felt a bit scared. Saint Louis had two newspapers in those days and the notices were somewhat mixed. More significantly, the reaction of the orchestra was also mixed.

My first full-length symphony program took place in Kennett, Missouri, a small town in the south of the state. The concert featured Tchaikovsky's Fourth and we had just one rehearsal. I opted to conduct from memory but on that night, fraught with anxiety, I could not remember how the piece even began. The first hornist, Roland Pandolfi, saw my plight, waved his arms and mouthed, "Over here." I gave the downbeat and the horns got me through the initial plunge.

My first children's concert was in Canton, Missouri, near Mark Twain's birthplace. This program included Dukas' *The Sorcerer's Apprentice* and was notable for two things. First, my lack of poise in speaking to audiences. I really had no experience and knew that my verbal communication skills were not convincing. Second was learning that orchestral musicians sometimes show their humanity in amusing ways. At one moment in the piece, the music is fast and furious. It then dies down for a bit. There follows a slow transitional section where the contrabassoon plays a low F-sharp, all alone. All musicians know this spot and on that occasion, the contra player did not come in. In the following bar, instead of the silence prescribed by the composer, the young people were treated to the vocal stylings of Brad Buckley, uttering "Shit!" It is tough to appear unflustered in such an instance and the orchestra and its young assistant just made it worse, trying not to laugh. I guess we managed to finish together, but who knows the impact we had on the children. Perhaps Mark Twain would have approved.

Next came my first subscription concert, which had been slated for early October. A long history of labor disputes had plagued the orchestra, but for Susskind's first season, negotiations would progress until his opening concerts had transpired. After a few weeks, talks collapsed and my concerts wound up as the first ones canceled. Naturally, I was disappointed but I got paid, and as it turned out, something personally important came out of the layoff.

To keep busy, I did some teaching in the public schools and began talking to civic groups. Gradually I became more confident about my ability to relate to other people. In the center of the city, the majority of nightlife used to be concentrated around Gaslight Square, but the late '60s had reduced the area to a set of run-down and decrepit buildings. One of those housed a small radio station that billed itself as "Radio Free St. Louis." It was run by a group of slightly aging hippies, most of whom lived on the premises. Whoever got up first in the morning would turn on the transmitter. There was no NPR at the time and stations like these were usually referred to as alternative, or underground, radio with little or no format.

One day, while the strike was still on, I was asked to come down and do an interview. The staff seemed surprised by my familiarity with so many different genres of music. At the end of the program I was offered my own show. I agreed, and so every Thursday for three years, from two until six in the afternoon, *The Slatkin Project* aired on KDNA, 102.5 on your FM dial. I selected an eclectic mix of any music I could think of. Using the station's library and my own record collection, the program drew a lot of listeners. It was also possible to connect up to six phone lines and have call-in conversations with residents all over the city. I learned what they liked and disliked about the symphony. Best of all, sitting alone in the studio, I could hone my speaking skills and discover how to communicate to a large number of people at one time.

Ultimately, the station fell victim to the expanding airwaves and, as the '70s arrived, alternative radio gave way to other forms of listening experiences. It didn't help that KDNA was busted a couple of times for drugs and violating all sorts of building and FCC codes. But I loved every minute of my three years there. Much of what I would do in programming for the orchestra could be traced to comments people made over the airwaves. The previously limited scope of a conductor's activities had changed for many.

When the orchestra returned to work, a lot of effort was put into restoring the public's confidence in the ensemble. My role as a more active public figure became clear even in those early days as an assistant. The orchestra and management were very supportive of some of the new ideas we were creating. Concerts combining our players with rock and folk artists, local groups and jazz ensembles were concepts that had not been previously tried. We presented the first live performance of *Jesus Christ Superstar*; however, our top priority was still a focus on the mainstream symphonic repertoire.

In the summer, the orchestra moved across the river to the campus of Southern Illinois University to play a series of concerts at the Mississippi River Festival. The festival was under the auspices of the school, but the symphony organized all the programming, including the pop acts that occupied the early part of the week. Jim Cain had minimal knowledge in this field, so he left it up to me to recommend which rock-and-rollers he should book. In doing so I got to meet Janis Joplin; Yes; Jim Croce; Emerson, Lake and Palmer; Joni Mitchell; plus others who were hot and whose records I was spinning on the radio.

Saint Louis did not have a youth orchestra and I vowed to rectify this deficiency. With the symphony's support, we founded the Saint Louis Symphony

Youth Orchestra in 1969. Because one of the criteria for students' acceptance to the group was participating in their school's music program, at least three institutions established such a program just to send their talented students to audition. More than six hundred young musicians auditioned that first year, and we took 125.

During the first rehearsal, as everyone got settled into their new environment in Powell Hall, I was reminded of my own happy times playing in similar youth orchestras in Los Angeles. The first notes we sounded were of the Stokowski transcription of the Passacaglia and Fugue in C Minor by Bach. Maybe the ensemble was not so good, intonation poor, technique negligible, but to me it felt heavenly.

By this time, my mother had relocated to Chicago where she began teaching; she also took over the cello classes of János Starker at Indiana University. I would take the forty-five-minute plane flight to visit her and to hear the Chicago Symphony on a regular basis. Developing professional relationships with the likes of Solti, Giulini and Leinsdorf was invaluable.

Also during this period, several smaller but good orchestras offered me music directorships. I said no, waiting it out for some position that felt better suited to me. So I stayed in Saint Louis where I was learning a great deal and conducting a lot. I had met and worked with outstanding soloists such as Michael Rabin, Géza Anda, John Browning and Jean-Pierre Rampal. Guest conducting was filling up my calendar year.

I married for the first time: a woman named Beth Gootee. Neither of us was ready for this commitment and it barely lasted a year and a half. We lived in the South County of Saint Louis, real suburbia, and I still did not earn that much. But life was comfortable enough and I was just glad to be working.

A phone call in 1974 changed everything.

13

A Life in the Year

Every time is the first time.

—SHURA CHERKASSKY

On November 14, 1943, slightly less than a year before I was born, a conductor named Leonard jumped in at the last minute, replacing an ailing conductor. That afternoon, history was made. Substituting for an indisposed Bruno Walter, Leonard Bernstein made his debut with the New York Philharmonic, and it hit the front page of the *New York Times* the next day.

Three decades later, in 1974, the Phil saw another Leonard make an unscheduled debut.

It was on Sunday afternoon when I got a phone call from the orchestra's executive director, Nick Webster. Riccardo Muti, scheduled for his second American appearance with the orchestra, was not on the plane that arrived from Italy. No one could locate him and it is unclear to this day why he failed to materialize. Illness was cited, but the fact remained that the expected guest simply was not in New York.

In any event, there was no Muti and there was no assistant conductor to fill in. With little time to find a replacement of stature, the management of the orchestra decided to take a chance on a young American once again. Up until then, I had performed with several orchestras in the States and a few in Europe, but none of these was on the Philharmonic's level of expertise. This was the moment that every conductor dreams of.

I asked what was on the original program. Prokofiev's Symphony No. 5, already a repertoire piece for me, was the major orchestral offering. Byron Janis was the piano soloist in the Beethoven Third Concerto. We had never worked together, but I had such respect for his musicianship and artistry, and I assumed that he would be a pleasure to accompany. I couldn't change this particular piece on the program anyway. The opening piece was the *Waverley Overture*, Op. 1, by Berlioz. I told Nick that none of these would be a problem.

That night I saw the Berlioz for the first time. Fortunately, I owned a copy, but had never opened its covers. The overture is a lesser piece and I suspected this would be the only time I would perform it.

My next step was to call my mentor, Walter Susskind. He was overjoyed at the news, and if he had not been conducting in Saint Louis that week, would have flown in for the occasion. His only advice? "Take a deep breath before you give the first downbeat."

Plane reservations were made, the hotel booked and bags packed. Monday I arrived and readied myself for the rehearsal. At this point, I knew that my plan of action, after saying good morning, was to play straight through the Prokofiev and not say a word. Let me get to know them and vice versa. I did not have enough time to get apprehensive and so, when Tuesday morning rolled around and the hour approached, I felt prepared.

But it was not all smooth sailing.

The Philharmonic had a reputation for notorious treatment of conductors. As a student, I had witnessed my share of less than respectable behavior toward the person on the podium at Philharmonic Hall, as the venue was called then. I also knew many of the players in the orchestra, some of whom attended Juilliard with me. Gerard Schwarz was the first trumpet, Marc Ginsberg the principal second violin, and a majority of the first chairs taught at the school. Logically, I anticipated no difficulties.

During the play through, a few odd things occurred. When I went back and started to actually rehearse, a clarinetist stopped me and said, "At this place I play on the A clarinet. Usually it is done on the B-flat instrument, and I know that your score is in C. What notes do I have?"

I told him the proper sequence and inquired as to why he was doing it on the A clarinet. He said he preferred the darker sonority, but if I wanted it on the other instrument, he would accommodate me.

In the second movement of the symphony, a passage for three trumpets has repeated eighth notes going in somewhat chromatic lines. I stopped and remarked that the second trumpet had a wrong note, which I had noticed when we had read through the work. The player explained that he had been playing that note in this orchestra for thirty years. I apologized and informed him that he had played it incorrectly all that time.

Then, when we reached the Finale, I paused and told the viola section that the beginning of the Allegro was not together. The principal of the section contradicted me, "It is together." I repeated that it was not. He then said it would be fine at the concert. In response, I stated that I would feel better if it was together now.

The conductor's dressing room is on the third floor. After the rehearsal, I went there and sat down to ponder what I might have done wrong to provoke these awkward moments. Orin O'Brien, a bassist in the orchestra, and the first woman to join the Philharmonic roster, came up and said, "You did a great job!" I asked her what all those uncomfortable interruptions were about. She responded that the Philharmonic routinely did these little tests on conductors on their first outing. This seemed peculiar to me, as seasoned professionals know immediately whether the conductor is any good. Orin felt that perhaps the time had come for the group to stop these sophomoric pranks. She assured me that going forward, I would see no more shenanigans, and indeed, the remaining rehearsals went smoothly.

Byron Janis was already experiencing some of the symptoms of a debilitating disease that would ultimately curtail his playing career. Still, it was a pleasure working with him, and there were some moments when the old spark reignited. As far as the *Waverley Overture* was concerned, the less said the better. Maybe it is a piece best left in the hands of the person I replaced.

There were four performances. I wish that memory served me well, because I really can't recall how everything went. The orchestra was gracious and played superbly. Audiences were enthusiastic. Reviews were mostly positive. Donal Henahan of the *New York Times* wrote, "He conducted Mr. Muti's original program with a professional aplomb and made a considerable splash at times with Prokofiev's Symphony No. 5." The headline in the *New York Post* read, "Philharmonic is saved by Slatkin, a Supersub." The *Post*'s Robert Kimball penned, "Despite—or because of—the difficult circumstances, the orchestra responded with conviction, involvement and a spirit that are not always features of the Philharmonic concerts." I was immediately re-engaged, the most important affirmation of all.

After the second concert in the series of four, Byron fell ill. Jerome Lowenthal, who came in at the last minute and with no rehearsal, replaced him. We met just prior to the performance and ran through a couple of crucial spots in the Beethoven. All went well, despite a lingering sense of disappointment that Janis was incapable of doing the whole series.

My debut with the Phil may not have garnered the same media attention as Bernstein's, but there was no question that this pivotal set of appearances would alter my conducting life dramatically. And it happened quicker than anyone could have predicted.

Two months later, I was summoned to Chicago, this time to fill in for Daniel Barenboim. The health of his wife, the cellist Jacqueline du Pré, was deteriorating rapidly from MS, and Daniel wanted to be by her side in London. He had canceled a number of dates, and one coincided with some free space in my calendar.

I had in fact led the CSO in 1971, in a children's concert as well as in a light program held in the parking lot of a shopping mall. These substitution performances would mark my subscription concert debut in the Windy City.

During this period, Barenboim and the orchestra were engaged in recording a cycle of the Bruckner symphonies. When I inquired about the program, I was told to avoid the scheduled music and assemble my own ideas for this appearance. This was fine. Although I keep a large repertoire in my head, Bruckner was not among the composers I really knew well. I admired the music, but it simply did not speak to me.

Given pretty much free rein, I selected a menu that would consist primarily of pieces unfamiliar to the orchestra. With no soloist, I had a chance to really put a different kind of spin on the offerings than was the norm for Chicago. The program was as follows:

Purcell/Slatkin   *Chacony*

Vaughan Williams   Symphony No. 6

Intermission

Piston   Symphony No. 2

Ravel   *La valse*

With the exception of the Ravel, each work was receiving its CSO premiere. I had never presented the VW in public, but a season earlier, Walter Susskind had scheduled it in Saint Louis. During the dress rehearsal, he summoned me to his podium and said he wanted to go out in the hall so he could listen to the opening. Thirty-five minutes later, I had led the whole work straight through. When I asked Susskind why, he answered that he wanted to confirm that I was doing my job and prepared at any instant to jump in.

Boy, did that advice pay off!

Rehearsals and concerts went beautifully. At that time, Chicago had four newspapers. I hit the quadrifecta, as the critics were unanimously positive. Again, as in New York, I was invited to come back, and have been a regular visitor with both orchestras since.

In Chicago, on the afternoon of my opening night, where was I? In a movie theater, watching *Blazing Saddles*, which had opened the previous day. For me, emptying the music out of my head for a while worked like a charm to control any nervousness.

Very shortly after this, in April 1974, another maestro fell ill. This time it was Sir Adrian Boult and the orchestra was the Royal Philharmonic in London. I had management representation in the United Kingdom, but had yet to conduct in the capital. Arrangements were swiftly made for me to step in.

Not so fast.

It seemed that governmental powers were not pleased with the selection of an American for this engagement. The European Union was in the early stages of growth, and some officials preferred that either a conductor from Britain, or at least an EU member, should serve as Boult's temporary replacement. They also cited my lack of experience with major symphonic ensembles.

I called John Edwards, the orchestra manager in Chicago, as my agents believed they were powerless in this situation. Just when it appeared that my London debut would be put on hold, a pair of letters were sent on my behalf, one by Sir Georg Solti and the other by Sir Michael Tippett. Both musicians were revered by the British and their opinions carried a lot of weight. Solti argued that if I was sufficiently good to lead the New York Philharmonic and Chicago Symphony that season, I was certainly capable of standing in front of the RPO. In addition, he noted that the only method for obtaining the kind of experience they desired was to conduct engagements such as this. Sir Michael wrote in praise of my commitment to British music.

The government office reversed the decision and reinstated me. The program was a bit unusual. For one of the scheduled works, the composer, Sir Lennox Berkeley, would conduct his own Third Symphony. The opener on this all-English program was Walton's *Portsmouth Point*, and the concerto was the one for violin by Frederick Delius. I had a couple of weeks to learn it.

Sir Adrian had planned Vaughan Williams' *Job* as the concert's second half. I was totally unfamiliar with this work at the time, and managed to substitute the same composer's Sixth Symphony, still ringing fresh from the Chicago appearances.

Rehearsals took place in Watford, about thirty-five miles outside of London. The soloist in the Delius was Wanda Wilkomirska. She had a strange habit of walking around while playing, and at one point I glanced up from the score to see her standing next to the timpanist, oblivious and in her own world, far away. Fortunately, this behavior only occurred at the rehearsal.

For the concert, Royal Festival Hall was full, and the audience remained silent during the incredible last movement of the symphony. There was no applause for almost half a minute at the conclusion as the final chord died away. The press was enthusiastic. Perhaps one reason is that they had rarely heard a foreign-born conductor present English music.

Over the years, I substituted for several conductors who became indisposed: Giulini, Bernstein, Steinberg, Tennstedt, Eschenbach, Leinsdorf, Levine, to name but a few. During one season in Pittsburgh, I replaced three conductors. For the last of these, the orchestra had put a sign on the dressing room that read, "Leonard Slatkin. Principal Substitute Conductor."

Sometimes I wonder what would have happened to the course of my career if all three conductors had been able to fulfill their engagements back in 1974. Possibly nothing would have changed and my work would have progressed anyway. You never know when the call will come, so it's crucial to live by the Boy Scout motto, "Be prepared."

14

John Edwards and David Hyslop

We serve an art—a great art—and we must hope and pray that we are worthy of it.

—JOHN EDWARDS

Their appearances could not have been more different. One was short, pudgy and balding; the other tall, lean and, well, two out of three ain't bad. The men had a lot in common: first and foremost was their love of the orchestra.

John was born in Saint Louis in 1912, and although extremely passionate about music, he would go on to earn a master's degree in English literature from Harvard in 1934. He returned to Saint Louis that year to work as a music critic for the city's now defunct second newspaper, the *Globe-Democrat*. During those years he also served part-time with the orchestra, mostly assisting in public relations.

Following that, John accepted a job as assistant manager of the National Symphony in Washington before promptly being rehired as manager with Saint Louis in 1939. After just a short time with the SLSO, he once again relocated to become business manager of the Los Angeles Philharmonic and the Hollywood Bowl, a position he maintained for just three seasons.

Other moves took John to Pittsburgh, Baltimore, back to the NSO and once again to Pittsburgh, where from 1955 he held the title of general manager for twelve years. Clearly the accumulated experience would pay off.

Still, his biggest mark would be made during the next step. In 1967, John became general manager of the Chicago Symphony. He was the force behind the hiring of Sir Georg Solti, and the pair would bring that orchestra to international prominence by both recording and touring throughout the United States, Europe and Japan.

Because of his phenomenal knowledge of music and his savvy business skills, John earned the nickname "dean of American symphony orchestra managers." He received numerous honors and became the number-one advocate of the American Symphony Orchestra League.

Perhaps his Saint Louis background was what triggered his interest in a young conductor just beginning in that city. John had invited me up to Illinois to attend concerts by the Chicago Symphony. He also gave me my first conducting opportunity there in 1970 with the Civic Orchestra, the training arm of the CSO. After that concert with them, John provided his counsel and told me that if I ever needed to discuss anything, I should run it by him first.

He was my beacon, always steering me on the right path. John put me in touch with Mariedi Anders, who would become my first agent. Whenever offered a guest date, I automatically called John to help decide if I should accept or decline. At that point in my career, I did not understand why I should decline any opportunities, but at times John would flatly say that I wasn't ready or that I just should not pursue that job.

In 1976, I was offered the music directorship of the New Orleans Philharmonic. This followed a week of concerts with the orchestra, but I really did not think it was the right fit for me. I called John and described the position, adding, "I assume that this is to be declined."

"No, Leonard. I certainly know about the offer and you are going to take it."

"Why?"

"You will find out later."

That was that. I truly did not know what thoughts underlay John's advice. But after a two-year stint, it hit me that my mentor was absolutely correct. The orchestra itself played well, but was mired in problems. The hall wasn't conducive to a really pleasant sound. The organization went through four executive directors in that short span. I had to wade through the tedious audition process. Decisions, which I had only observed from the sidelines in Saint Louis, were now in my hands.

John obviously wanted me to discover if I had the stuff it takes to be a music director. I made a lot of mistakes, but each one was a learning experience. Indeed, running an orchestra was completely different than merely conducting.

Less than two years later, I was conducting a series of concerts in Buffalo. During the course of that one week, offers came in from three other orchestras, each including a music directorship. Those cities were Minneapolis, Cincinnati and Saint Louis. I had been working regularly in the Twin Cities at that point, Saint Louis had been home for almost ten years, and I had appeared in Cincinnati several times. Again, I called John.

Each of those orchestras was approximately equal, musically, and the population of the cities was similar. I anticipated that John would lean toward the locale where I was less well known. But his decision flew in the face of convention, and he told me that I was to return to Saint Louis.

Very few conductors had gone back to the place where their professional lives had begun. This time John explained why the choice was correct. "Now you know that you are equipped to run a full-time major symphony. What you need is the best management team behind you."

The other two organizations had wonderful leadership, but John knew that someone special was coming to Saint Louis.

His name was David Hyslop.

Born in Upstate New York, Dave's background differed considerably from John's. His career path was less varied and his outside interests were in jazz and sports, but his passionate love of classical music somehow led him to the orchestral world.

Like John, David spent some of his early career in Minneapolis, as assistant managing director. He quickly moved, in 1972, to the Oregon Symphony Orchestra as its general manager. We met there a handful of times. While guest conducting an all-state orchestra in Portland, Dave came to see me with an invitation to do a set of concerts with the Oregon Symphony. That led to a job offer. Of course, I consulted John and had to politely turn the position down. David would later call this one of his great disappointments, but it was personally one of my best decisions.

In a very short time, he had helped build a solid foundation in Oregon which attracted notice throughout the orchestral field. David was now the go-to person for any major job opening. In 1978, he accepted the executive director position in Saint Louis, and quickly came to me with his second proposal.

By then, we had grown better acquainted and found we had much in common. This paid off through our similar thoughts as to how to best function as a team. Joan Bricetti was hired as artistic administrator, and we now formed a trio of very strong-willed people, working to shift the orchestra in new directions.

One of my first assignments from Dave was to write a list of my perceived strengths and weaknesses. It was a basic corporate technique with new employees, but rarely used in the arts. I learned a good deal about myself through that exercise, especially when I stopped fantasizing and dealt with reality. I had presumed that conductors do not have weaknesses.

We put together long-range plans, a set of goals and objectives to follow regardless of outside influences. Each time we achieved an important goal, we established a new one. There were times that the three of us fought tooth and nail, but we held such respect for each other that we would manage to reach an agreement. This period was remarkable, and to this day, I never take but a small part of the credit for what we accomplished; it was the product of all of us striving toward a common end.

Dave became much more than my boss. We were good friends. Sometimes, that friendship helped shape important decisions.

We had a concertmaster vacancy and narrowed it down to two finalists. Both were wonderful candidates and each had played with the orchestra for a couple of weeks. Still, the audition committee could not make a final recommendation for the position. They handed the dilemma over to me. I kept wavering, too.

Dave suggested that we go to a basketball game to take our minds off arguably the biggest decision a music director will ever make. The concertmaster has a critical role to play in both developing and maintaining an orchestra.

There we sat, at the now defunct arena, at a not terribly good game with the Spirits of Saint Louis. There was no talk of music, only commentary on the game, the occasional dirty joke and snacking on something that passed as food.

Midway through the third quarter, I turned to him and said, "Dave, I know which one it will be."

He smiled, knowing full well that taking my mind off it would be the perfect way to get me to make a decision.

The two of us would frequent jazz clubs, comedy clubs, movies and sporting events. Everyone knew that no decision would be made without the two of us in total agreement. I continued to consult John for the big decisions, but David was becoming the person to whom I would grow closest.

He organized our first overseas tours, as well as made sure that our orchestra paid an annual visit to Carnegie Hall. In 1984, when *Time* magazine declared that the Saint Louis Symphony was the second-best orchestra in the country, Dave wondered why we did not top the list. Number one, according to the magazine, was Chicago. The first person to call us with congratulations of course was John Edwards.

But Utopia has a deadline.

I was in Minneapolis that same year when the phone rang to notify me that John had died at the age of seventy-two. A lot of us suspected something amiss when the man would nod off at either a concert or even a dinner. The cause of death was a stroke. The news hit me hard, but by this time, I had David to lean on. We organized a pension fund concert in John's name.

A couple years later, Joan Bricetti would also suffer a stroke, fortunately not fatal. She needed to leave her position and that meant that the three-person team would be torn apart. We tried several replacements but never replicated that group. It was a tough period for Dave as well. Certain factions of the board did not agree with the directions we were taking.

In a deli in New York, while on tour in 1990, Dave informed me that he was accepting the presidency of the Minnesota Orchestra. This may have been the hardest career decision of his life. I was stunned, though my reaction was tempered with understanding. His successor, Bruce Coppock, did a superb job, but I was sensing that perhaps it was getting to be the time when I should leave Saint Louis.

Dave and I have remained close to this day. I call him "Kid," and he signs off as "Zoot," after the legendary sax player Zoot Sims. There are very few occasions when we do not toast John's memory. I could not have asked for two better mentors, professionally and personally.

15

Keeping It All Together

When you are not practicing, remember, someone somewhere is practicing, and when you meet him he will win.

—CHARLES "ED" MACAULEY

When the house lights dim and the concertmaster makes an entrance, followed by the conductor, what comes next is the culmination of a process that is at the heart of music-making: rehearsal.

A concert with a professional orchestra will require roughly eight to ten hours of rehearsal time, assuming it is for a normal program with at least one standard work. In the summer, single rehearsal concerts are common. Pops concerts rarely take more than two sessions. Sergiu Celibidache, the eccentric Romanian conductor, would frequently ask for as many as fifteen rehearsals, and would instruct the musicians not to bring their instruments to the first three.

There is a legendary story of Sir Thomas Beecham, who was about to begin rehearsing the Second Symphony of Brahms with the New York Philharmonic (although the ensemble's name changes depending on who is telling the tale).

"Gentlemen. You know this piece and I know it. Let's just read it at the performance this evening."

The second clarinetist said, "Maestro, I have never played this work before."

"You will love it," responded Beecham.

What happens when almost one hundred musicians assemble on a Tuesday morning, with the intention of having a two-hour program ready by Thursday night?

Naturally, different conductors have different personalities and working methods. Some like to talk a lot. Others keep many of their thoughts to themselves. Each orchestra responds distinctively to each conductor. There is one certainty: every instrumentalist makes up his or her mind as to the relative merits of the conductor within the first few minutes of rehearsing.

My own rehearsal methodology has changed a great deal over the years. When I was starting out as assistant in Saint Louis, I very rarely had more than one rehearsal for any program. Whether it was children's concerts, family programs, outdoor events or concerts on tour, time was scarce. Observing how my colleagues handled time management issues was always informative.

Rehearsals fall into what are known as services. For American orchestras, a service is customarily defined as a period of two to two and a half hours. Under the Tuesday-to-Thursday scenario, the initial rehearsal is a single two-and-a-half-hour session. Wednesday counts as a double service day, with the afternoon rehearsal being the shorter of the two. The concert is preceded by a dress rehearsal. There are naturally exceptions: choral works, operas, and tours; but for the most part, the four-rehearsal format is the norm.

This may seem strange, but one of the decisions you must make is whether you will stand or sit at the rehearsals. Usually a stool is provided, but I used to heed the advice of Erich Leinsdorf. He claimed that if the conductor sits at rehearsal, it is an invitation for the players to relax a bit more than he thought they should. For most of my career, I usually stood.

Stagehands are your best friends. When you arrive on the platform, they will ensure that the podium is positioned precisely where you would like. Another important detail is choosing the optimal height of the music stand. This placement will be marked and some orchestras even keep a record of the position where each conductor prefers the stand. There are few things worse than having to reach low down to turn a page or banging your hand on the edge because it is too high.

You must even think about where you will put the scores you are not conducting. One orchestra has a little table set out for this purpose. Some conductor stands have a built-in shelf below. If you are working on a pops concert, there might be ten or twenty works on the program. It is best to double-check that you have organized the scores in the correct rehearsal order. Also, it's a good rule of thumb to bring scores for the entire concert to the first half of a rehearsal in case a player has a question about a piece that will be rehearsed later.

The librarians of an orchestra are critically important, both before and during the rehearsal process. If there are questions about editions, or cuts, they are the people who make sure any deviations are marked in every part. Sometimes you do not bring your own scores for each piece, and the librarians will show you what copies they have on hand. For a standard work there might be one score covered in markings by previous conductors plus another copy that is clean. My initial outing with the Tchaikovsky First Piano Concerto in Washington DC had an amusing moment. Having performed this a number of times, I felt that using any old score would do. The one that was handed me contained almost no markings at all, except a gigantic blue crayon indication on the first page which read, "HORNS!!!!"

You might also be asked if you prefer to have a baton waiting on the stand or if you will carry your own. In some situations you may be asked if you want an extra one out there, in case yours accidentally breaks or you fling it into the audience. In Detroit, there is a hole in the upper right corner of the stand where one of my predecessors, Paul Paray, had kept the baton when he was not using it.

There are usually three or four rehearsals for a subscription program. For me, the first day, no matter how well acquainted I am with the orchestra, is devoted primarily to reading through a large portion of the program, regardless of how familiar or unfamiliar the music might be to the players. I will likely start with a piece that they know so there is little more required than learning the potential problem areas, information I file away for the next day.

Jean Morel would tell us, "Conduct from what you receive." This meant that you use the rehearsal not only to convey your thoughts and concepts, but also to take in what the collective has to say. My debut with the Philadelphia Orchestra contained the Second Symphony by Rachmaninov. This was a "house piece" for musicians during Ormandy's tenure. They played it with the same regularity as other orchestras performed, say, Beethoven's Seventh.

A few of my tempi were a little faster. Rubatos had different inflections. Dynamics, perhaps, contrasted a bit more. The read-through was basically Ormandy's Rachmaninov. I listened carefully that day, and made mental notes as to where I might tell the Philadelphians something novel.

If a program features a work that is unfamiliar to the orchestra, not just a premiere or first local performance, that piece is normally scheduled for the second part of the rehearsal. This is the time when you most likely will speak to the orchestra about specifics. Some scores cannot be read through without comments. There are matters of beat patterns, instructions to comprehend before anybody can play; perhaps unusual techniques of sound production, places that must be done slowly the first time, and so on. No matter what, you always want to provide as much sense of the whole as possible.

I have a philosophy that works this way. Come into each rehearsal with a "game plan." Know what goals you want to accomplish at each session. If you succeed, stop. If not, make adjustments and come to the next rehearsal with a more practical approach. There are numerous examples of conductors getting angry as the clock approaches the end of the rehearsal period; the personnel manager pops out from the wings, looking like an executioner with a pocket watch, ready to chop off your head if you dare go one second into overtime.

You should look at the clock, but these days, maybe two or three devices visibly remind everybody of what time it is. One orchestra even has a digital readout that counts down! You and your ensemble might be just two bars away from the final chord of that Schubert Symphony but you are not allowed to finish it.

In Chicago, when I was conducting *Salome*, an opera that lasts an hour and forty minutes, we had come to the first sitzprobe, where the singers join the orchestra for the first time, minus sets or costumes. It is just a reading with everyone. I had rehearsed the orchestra alone several times and remarked that it would be nice if once the singers arrived, we would play the opera straight through, no stopping. And that would suffice as the whole rehearsal.

As it turned out, the orchestra had a clause in its contract stating that no rehearsal could exceed an hour and a half, then must be followed by a thirty-minute break. I asked the chairman of the orchestra committee for an exception; if we could tack on the extra ten minutes, then everyone could go home early. He said that members had fought hard for this clause due to other conductors abusing the contract, and that we could not have the extra time. So we started, and at the designated hour, when the deadline arrived, I announced intermission. A half hour passed, the orchestra returned, we picked up right where we had left off and finished the remaining ten minutes of the opera. The orchestra had to stay twenty minutes more than was really necessary. As Morel often said, "The musician's union is often for the musicians, but against the music."

One guest conductor in Washington was leading a rehearsal of the Verdi Requiem with the chorus, soloists and orchestra. The clock was running out, but he was running on. The personnel manager walked out and halted the proceedings, mid–"Libera Me." The conductor was furious and launched into a tirade about the rules, in particular those of American orchestras. The reason he wanted to finish the piece was so that he could eliminate the rehearsal the next morning. That might have worked if he had explained his intention at the outset.

The truly critical element of that first rehearsal is getting a sense of how the orchestra does each piece. If you decide that actual rehearsing is necessary at the initial meeting, plan in advance which movements or portions of a given piece you want to work on. Because the string section makes up the majority of the players, most of your remarks are directed toward them, but don't let that rehearsal turn into a discussion exclusively devoted to bowings. Although a professional group is accustomed to it, the winds and percussion section get a bit annoyed with this process after a while. Sometimes I will ask for a strings-only rehearsal to sort out these matters before the other sections arrive.

Another time-saving device is to ask the librarians to mark the string bowings into the parts and send them out in advance. Most conductors do not have the luxury of owning complete sets, and so they have to use whatever parts are available. A top-tier orchestra will, in fact, have two sets, one for the music director's exclusive use which cannot be changed, and another set for the guests.

How does the orchestra know about the requirements that the conductors would prefer? Are there any particular seating preferences, wind doublings or markings that need to be put into the parts? How does the conductor know what is normal for each orchestra?

Staffs have developed questionnaires, and for the past fifteen years or so have sent them to conductors about four months prior to an appearance. These cover matters such as the size of the string section each piece calls for, the length of each rehearsal, the editions of music on hand and the order of the pieces slated for each rehearsal.

I have found one aspect of this last item troubling. Generally, the conductor is asked to rehearse in descending order of resources needed for each program. For example, let's say that a program consists of Brahms' Second Symphony, the Bruch First Violin Concerto and Haydn's Symphony No. 68. Clearly the

Haydn requires far more rehearsal as the piece is not played often, but since it uses the smallest orchestra, its slot will always fall at the end of the day when the musicians are getting tired. Some organizations are more flexible than others about this process, but each musician is paid their full salary, regardless of when they are required to be on stage. The only consideration that matters should be what's best for the music.

Just as you must know what you want to accomplish in a rehearsal, it is equally important, in my mind, not to utter redundant or superfluous remarks. Some conductors literally write in their scores what they are going to say and when to say it. Orchestra members are justifiably upset when the conductor stops and says something, even though the ensemble has executed exactly what the conductor asked for.

When you do stop, address the specific subject that you wish done differently, whether the length of note, fixing a passage that was not together or correcting intonation. Never repeat a passage without reason, even if you need to pull a reason out of thin air. You can always resort to explaining you were not happy with the way you conducted it the first time, and can the orchestra do it again? The musicians like it when the conductor admits a fault; just don't try it too often.

After the preliminary encounter, it is time to evaluate how it went. What didn't work and which passages do you think can be left alone? How much time will you need to spend on each piece the next day? Where could your beat patterns and gestures have been clearer?

If there is a new piece, or if the composer is present and will offer comments, you need to go through the score prior to rehearsal and figure out where adjustments need to be made. I cannot emphasize strongly enough the extreme importance of time management. Know your goals and how much time you have available.

With its pair of rehearsals, Wednesday is when you get down to the nitty-gritty. Details must to be sorted out, balances well defined and interpretations refined. If players have questions, you must be prepared to answer every one of them. Someone might notice that they have a note that seems at odds with another section. A slur might be missing. Matters of long notes versus short ones commonly crop up. Achieve as much as possible, because the next day will go by faster than you can imagine.

Assuming that there is a soloist on the program, it is imperative that you meet with that person and attempt to understand what they are thinking and feeling. Your dual purpose is to accommodate and simultaneously collaborate. Most instrumentalists have a solid idea of how they want to interpret the concerto. They will have performed it many more times than you. If you disagree with the approach, well, the likelihood that you are going to change the soloist's mind is slim. Accept their approach and make it seem as if you had exactly the same thoughts all along.

A dress rehearsal is, of course, not that, literally—at least not for the instrumentalists. But it is an opportunity to go straight through the program. I almost always ask to do this rehearsal in the order of the concert. The reasoning is simple. It gives the musicians, especially the strings, a better idea of the stamina required for the duration of the concert. Stage setup changes, a piano move, percussion redeployment and so on are done in the concert context. And even if you have led the program countless times, you can conceptualize the physical and, potentially, the emotional demands of the evening performance. I do warn the players that if needed, they should take it somewhat easy and save their energy for the concert. Inevitably, this idea lasts for about two minutes, as I throw myself into the run-through, and the result resembles a performance more than rehearsal.

After you have finished each piece, review the spots that you thought did not go well or that could use a bit more tidying. Now if you are doing, say, a Strauss tone poem, how can you remember what went wrong twenty-five minutes prior to the end of the piece? My way is to simply turn over the edge of the page where the transgression took place. Once you go back, it is easy to remember what needs fixing. The problem is that sometimes the dog-ears do not stay put and the page reverts to its original state. Some conductors use little scraps of paper or Post-it notes as bookmarks that they drop in mid-piece.

In theory, the dress rehearsal should not surpass the length of the concert, but seldom is this the reality. Sometimes we will ask the musicians if there are places they would like to do again. However, the last thing that a conductor should want is to end the rehearsal mired in minutiae. Conclude on a positive note. Thank everyone for their hard work, telling them how much you look forward to the concert.

A few other items worth mentioning may not seem relevant to the music, but still they affect how the rehearsals transpire.

When I started in Saint Louis, the concertmaster, Max Rabinowitz, and the principal cellist, John Sant'Ambrogio, took me to lunch. They were generally complimentary, but after a few weeks of observation, they had a few suggestions. The first was to use a stronger deodorant. This was coupled with changing shirts at the intermission, as I used to perspire profusely. I know, it's disgusting, but the physical nature of conducting does not always produce the most attractive sights or aromas.

The reverse is also noteworthy. Heavy colognes and perfumes wafting across the strings create a distraction. A small number of people may be allergic. You must find the right balance of fragrance if needed. Try to avoid any scented product when working with singers.

Conductors should wear a long-sleeved shirt. If you are outdoors, and the weather is hot, short sleeves are fine but only if they are secure at the ends and not flapping around. You get the picture. I once got in big trouble for the way I suggested that female members of an orchestra should be held to the same standard as the men when it came to onstage attire. The males traditionally have to conform to a single style, whether tails or tuxedo. The women tend to have more leeway in choice of garments. This means that some dresses or blouses will have bare arms and others half or fully covered. Audiences see us before a single note is heard, so the visual homogeneity matters.

Don't come to rehearsal disheveled. Photos of past generations depict the conductor and orchestra in jacket and tie. Stiff formality is not necessary, but beachwear isn't appropriate, even at the Hollywood Bowl. Sloppy appearances can lead to sloppy performances, not that being well groomed guarantees a great concert, but it doesn't hurt.

In the evening, you will no doubt arrive at the hall extra early. Some conductors habitually will cut it close. In a few instances, the maestro literally gets out of the car fully dressed, and walks through the stage door, then immediately to the concert platform. In young adulthood, a lot of musicians do not pay careful attention to their appearance. There are plenty of exceptions, of course. Matters of taste dictate how you wish to look, but this concert marks the first time the public will view you as a conductor. A little coaching in attire and stage deportment is in order.

These days, there is a tendency toward a more individualistic image. However, orchestras don't appreciate deviations in personal style until you have established your credentials. As a rule, men should dress in a manner similar to that of the gentlemen of the orchestra. Attire is one item in your budget where you should splurge on quality and make sure your formal outfit properly fits. Get a good tailor to make alterations, especially to the shoulder area. Demonstrate for him your widest beat pattern so the clothes are adjusted. The tails or tux should remain straight no matter how much acrobatic skill you might be showing off. Own good-looking and sensible shoes. You will work on your feet for a couple of hours. Plus, the concertgoers seated in the front row will have a close-up of your feet for most of the night, so no scuffs, please.

Dress for women is slightly more complicated. Just as you should conduct in a manner that suits you, so should you don what best complements your style. Some female conductors choose black tuxedos, the same as their male counterparts. Some have formal gowns made. An attractive and pragmatic alternative for other women is a well-tailored pants suit. Whatever you choose, do not let it distract from your music-making. The last thing you want people talking about is what you wore rather than what you conducted. Although a few soloists have pulled it off, visual distractions tend to obscure the musical results.

You might not have contemplated it during rehearsals, but you need to accustom yourself with the walk to the podium. It is the audience's first sight of the conductor. A few venues have difficult entrances. Topping the list is the Concertgebouw in Amsterdam. You must descend what seems like one hundred stairs to reach the podium. A set of double doors is opened and you start at the top, gazing at the sea of audience members not only in front of you, but directly alongside the stairs as you make your way. The trick is not to look down but get used to the distance of each step. I am not sure if the hall has insurance to cover a botched entry.

In some venues, the entrance might be on the side opposite the first violins. Vienna's majestic Musikverein has conductors coming in stage left. This causes some awkward moments if the guest is not used to entering from this side. You need to either climb over the podium or walk around it to shake hands with the concertmaster. When there is a pianist, you acknowledge the soloist, shake the leader's hand, and then exit in the other direction. Danny Kaye used to do a ten-minute comedy routine about the conductor getting lost within the orchestra en route to the podium.

The rehearsal process is not so dissimilar to a practice of a sports team. The manager works out the plays and drills the players over and over. When it comes to the game, he tries to stay on plan, but circumstances usually mean adapting. The conductor does the same, and if everyone knows his and her parts and how they fit in, it is easy to adjust to any deviation from the practice session.

There was a time when I hated to rehearse. I thought that all that was necessary was to be physically clear, and then the need for words would be minimal. With the passage of time, and with more experience under my belt, rehearsing became just as important as the concerts. Getting ideas and interpretation across to the orchestra in whatever means possible meant going deeper into the musical meaning of a work, although it always seemed there was never sufficient time to get it perfect.

Then again, there is always this philosophy:

Practice makes perfect.

No one is perfect.

Why practice?

16

Playing for Keeps

Some of us will do our jobs well and some will not, but we will be judged by only one thing. The result.

—VINCE LOMBARDI

Running an orchestra is not that different from being the CEO of a medium-sized corporation. You are the superior to whom the majority of the staff reports, but you must still answer to others. Your decision-making determines the direction the organization will take. Your job is to shape the company within the established parameters. It is easier for the board to dismiss you than it may have been for them to hire you.

This last aspect does not apply when it comes to employing the musicians of the orchestra. That process is long, and it involves a complicated set of rules that vary from ensemble to ensemble. In earlier times, the conductor simply hired those musicians he wanted and fired those he did not want. No explanation required. Today, the procedures are more complex and, for the most part, more fair.

When a vacancy occurs, orchestras in the United States place an advertisement in the Musicians' Union newspaper. The ad outlines which positions are available and the minimum salary per year. Each organization has its own way of handling the auditions. Here is a rough idea of the process.

The personnel manager's office receives applications. Only basic information is requested, but this usually includes references, a brief curriculum vitae and whether the applicant holds US citizenship. Problems obviously can arise if the musician wins the audition but is denied the job due to immigration restrictions.

The first round of auditions is done two ways, either live or by recording. If the opening is for a principal or titled position, up to four hundred candidates might apply. You can imagine how time consuming this would be if every applicant appeared in person, so increasingly orchestras are using recordings to sort out who qualifies for the next round. It also saves a lot of money for individuals who might otherwise travel thousands of miles to play for only five minutes. In some cases, people with an outstanding musical background might automatically place into the later rounds of the process. Once in a while this can backfire, as an extremely talented individual, fresh out of conservatory, may be passed over simply for lack of experience.

The music director typically does not participate at this early stage in the selection phase. An orchestra committee, weighted with more players from the section that has the vacancy, listens to all of the auditions. The performance level can fluctuate wildly and the stress of the audition can take its toll on even the most seasoned performer. It is up to the committee to consider these factors in reaching a decision.

You might be asking, "How does the committee know if the recording is legitimately rendered by the applicant?" It doesn't, although I do not know of many instances where auditionees have submitted recordings of other in-strumentalists. The tape or CD is also tricky to judge, as the quality of sound can vary tremendously. In the opening round, the committee is looking for technical ability, not sonic excellence. You cannot know about that until you hear the musician live. Whether live or recorded, the whole of the first phase can take quite a while.

Before we leave this initial step, one other subject regarding the process needs some clarification.

Over almost the entire course of my conducting career, one matter having to do with the audition procedure has annoyed me. I understood it when I began in the profession, but as we get deeper into the twenty-first century, its relevance seems questionable. I am referring to the blind audition.

Many readers may be unfamiliar with what I am talking about. Let me fill you in.

As I said, in the past, the conductor hired whomever he wanted. Whole or-chestras were formed simply by a selection process governed by one individual.

As time went on, the members of the orchestra became part of the audition procedure. Usually they offered advice, yet the conductor hired his choice. Gradually, more attention was paid to the wishes of the ensemble. So a balance was reached. Most of the time, the right people were hired, based solely on musical ability.

Then the '70s arrived and things changed.

An African American timpanist, Elayne Jones, sued the San Francisco Symphony, when she was in her first season. After this initial year, she was notified that her contract would not be renewed. Elayne charged that the reason she did not get tenure was due to racial discrimination.

Ultimately, the suit was dropped, but the effects were immediate. From that point on, live auditions were held behind a screen usually placed in front of the candidate onstage. Anonymity became the watchword. Carpets were put on the floor so no one could hear what kind of shoes were being worn. No spoken words were allowed, either from the candidate or the audition committee. Numbers were assigned to those playing, no names ever announced. The auditions were almost literally blind. Orwell's 1984 had arrived in the music world a decade early.

To this day, this process has remained unchanged in most every major American orchestra.

The musician vying for the job never sees his or her judges who might later be sitting next to them onstage. The impersonal nature of playing into a screen seems like the antithesis of what will be expected of the instrumentalist if he or she gets the job. Thus the audition procedure is, at best, an artificial method of selecting the right musician. Some players do not audition well, but are more than qualified to join a professional orchestra. Just because they may not perform proficiently behind a screen does not indicate that they will fail to excel within the orchestral ranks.

Let's return to the actual process.

It is becoming more and more frequent for members of an orchestra to audition for a promotion; that is, assistant clarinet to principal, second violin to first and so forth. The artistic reason is clear but this career move involves a salary increase as well. Customarily these musicians automatically enter at the later rounds of the audition. Of course, if a current member of the orchestra lands the job, it creates another vacancy, another set of auditions.

The music director, in consultation with the musicians, chooses the audition repertoire. There is a fairly standardized list of pieces for each instrument that orchestras tend to use. Strauss' *Don Juan* will always be on a violin repertoire list. You would not dare overlook *Afternoon of a Faun* for a flute audition. The applicants know in advance what music will be requested, with the exception of ensembles that have a sight-reading component. This skill is in greater demand these days, as several orchestral programs during a given season must be prepared in a single rehearsal; often the sheet music doesn't even show up until the day you have to play it. But the committee's judgment is fundamentally based on the prepared music. The applicant is also required to play a concerto. Usually this work is specified but sometimes the choice is left up to the performer. I prefer the latter inasmuch as it represents what the instrumentalist believes are his or her strengths.

During an audition, the candidate might play some orchestral excerpts with the section, or a string player may be asked to participate in a quartet with three of the current members of the string section. This technique is quite useful and helps the orchestra evaluate the capabilities of the candidates to lead, follow, blend as a group and play with the appropriate stylistic characteristics. And obviously, these things can only be tested in orchestras that agree to remove the screen at some point in the proceedings.

The time has come for the decision. Each candidate has played for about twenty minutes. A variety of works have been heard. What happens next? Again, each orchestra has different rules for the actual selection. Usually a vote is taken. Sometimes the committee and the music director will agree on just one player, but it is possible to have two or three if it seems they are equally qualified. The personnel manager tallies the votes and announces the results to the committee. Let's say there are nine orchestra members and the music director. You would think that if a majority votes for the same candidate, that person wins automatically. Not necessarily. Even if nine people vote for the same musician and one against, discussion can change the outcome. The votes are secret but in this situation, there are two courses of action. Either the dissenter can speak up to explain why he or she voted that way, or can remain silent and pretend that the lone vote came from someone else. But ultimately, it is usually the music director who has the final say about who is hired.

I usually ask the principals what they thought and why. I also voice my opinion. This can take a lot of time. Most musicians want to pick the right person. It is possible that they wish to see a coworker advance, even if a seemingly more qualified person comes from the outside. Music performance is not objective. As director, you must know what you are looking for and be able to verbalize it. You must not be insensitive to the feelings of the orchestra, but you must have a clear vision of what you want.

In most orchestras, the music director can override the committee, but when the vote overwhelmingly favors a particular applicant, there is probably a good musical reason. Only when the vote is close do you need to exercise your authority. Remind the orchestra that hiring is ultimately your decision and because no consensus was reached, you need to make sure the players fully support your conclusion. Another possibility in a close vote would mean asking a handful of candidates to play again. This can go a long way toward eliminating or reinforcing doubts. All the reservations can be addressed and another vote will be taken. Eventually a winner will emerge, but sometimes questions linger. In this case, some organizations opt to wait and hold a whole new set of auditions at a later date. You get to go through all of this again. Ultimately, you must pick the person based on his/her artistic integrity. There can be no compromise.

Similar to the hiring of a professor at a university, a trial period precedes the granting of tenure. This period of time completes the evaluation, and if questions remain, the player is relieved of the position. I like to think that we have reached the point where the process provides a definite winner, but on some occasions I have had to consider refusing tenure to a new player. The best action is to first have a few talks with the musician to determine the cause of the problems. This usually results in improvement and the individuals taking their place as full members of the orchestral body.

Naturally there are stories galore, true and apocryphal, about what goes on at an audition. In Saint Louis one year, we had vacancies for both violin and cello. Back then, we used to set up one day for listening to musicians exclusively from our own area. Very rarely did this produce much interest, but those who applied needed to be heard. For these auditions, we had arranged for violinists in the morning and cellists in the afternoon. A gentleman who showed up for the first audition did not do very well, and we assumed that was the last we would see of him. But lo and behold, in the afternoon, there he was again, playing equally poorly on the cello. He did not get either position.

The same union rule applied when I was music director of the Grant Park Festival in Chicago. The auditions were held in a room at city hall. An elderly man entered, announcing that he was present for the viola audition. We noticed that he was not carrying an instrument or case.

"Oh, am I supposed to play?'

We sent him back to the warm-up room and he returned, viola in hand, but minus his bow.

"I'm sorry. I'll go get it."

A few minutes later he returned. We asked what he would like to start with.

"The first movement of the Bach G Major Suite, but I forgot to bring the music. I'll go get it."

"Never mind," we said. "Just play a few bars from memory."

He managed a total of four. Needless to say, the gentleman did not join us that summer.

My favorite story has to be the audition that occurred in my last year as a student in Aspen. At the beginning of each summer, all the students had to be placed in one of the several orchestras. This meant about four days of non-stop auditions. We always limited them to around ten minutes, asking individuals to start with music of their own choosing.

A cellist entered the room and told us that he would play a piece that he wrote. We had never had that happen before. The work was one where there were lots of leaps, scratches and unpleasant sounds, very '60s.

After two minutes of this, Walter Susskind asked the young man how his sight-reading was.

"Show me the piece that I cannot sight-read!" boasted the confident cellist.

We conferred and came up with the second movement of Tchaikovsky's Sixth Symphony. It is in 5/4 time, and although not really that difficult, it can reveal a lot about a player's rhythm and sound.

The cellist stared at the music for a minute and said, "That's the piece!"

We had no idea that this was a setup. The cellist and school administrators had arranged the prank in advance. A good laugh was had by all.

Now that we know the process for hiring, perhaps we need to learn something about the flip side, dismissal.

There is only one way to get into an orchestra. You have to win an audition. Granted, there are rare exceptions, for instance when a player is promoted or the music director assigns a position. By contrast, the number of ways a player exits the ensemble are numerous. The majority come about through the musician's retirement or relocation to another orchestra.

In America, you can play in an orchestra for as long as you want. You can even retire and continue to work for the orchestra. There is little incentive to leave it. Most musicians do not wish to admit they no longer possess the requisite skills that got them the job in the first place. And, surprisingly, most music directors are reluctant to underscore those deficiencies. It does come down to a matter of opinion, after all.

Just as in the past, when instrumentalists could be hired directly by the conductor, they could be fired just as easily. No reasons were needed, just a "You're outta here" from the music director. All that has changed, and much for the better. The mechanism for dismissal is long and cumbersome, so most music directors prefer to avoid the headaches. Again, the rules vary from orchestra to orchestra, but tend go something along the following lines.

There are essentially three reasons to contemplate releasing an orchestra member: insubordination, insobriety and musical incompetence. The first does not occur very often, the second is difficult to prove, so the third is the reason most frequently cited.

As with hiring, each orchestra has its own set of parameters for this procedure.

The conductor has an initial meeting with the player under consideration for dismissal and says, "Here are some problems I have been noticing. I hope you will take steps to resolve them." There is a follow-up meeting a few months later. If the circumstances have improved, everything returns to normal. If not, the conductor states that the conditions for employment in the orchestra have not been met and therefore the player's contract will not be renewed. At this point, at least one other member of the orchestra will be present and the witness must take very accurate notes.

The player's recourse is to go to the union and fight the non-renewal. Sometimes the individual accepts his or her fate, accompanied by some sort of severance agreement negotiated with the management. If this does not occur, a formal meeting convenes between a committee of orchestra musicians and people from management. In Washington, fifteen players voted on the relative merits of the dismissal. I was the only representative from the administration. When there are significantly more musicians than management, more than likely this works in favor of the player. Sometimes, it is painfully obvious that the player must go.

At this point, assuming that no decision can be reached, an arbitrator becomes necessary, somebody whom both sides agree upon. This person comes from a list provided by the union. Arbitrators can use whatever means they want to determine the fate of the player. Sometimes testimony alone is all it takes. Sometimes the musician is asked to play. Every word from the sessions is evaluated. Eventually a verdict is rendered. If the arbitrator sides with management, the player can be dismissed with no compensation. This rarely happens. Instead, a kind of plea bargain is negotiated. After all, there was probably a time when that musician contributed a great deal to the orchestra. The past service deserves compensation. If the decision comes down in favor of the instrumentalist, he or she is reinstated.

This process can take two years or longer. No wonder most music directors are reluctant to go through it. One misspoken word and the musician returns to the orchestra anyway. This may seem harsh but, in fact, the music director has the upper hand in the long run. If the decision favors the player, the conductor can restart the whole process. Most musicians do not want to endure the stress a second time. The music director must be completely convinced that the action is in the best interests of the orchestra. It cannot be personal. There is no tougher decision that you will ever face in your role as a leader.

It works quite differently with the staff. The music director certainly must have input in regard to the hiring and firing of the executive director and artistic administrator, but nearly every other employee is not in his or her province. If there are real conflicts, they are brought to the attention of either the executive director or the board itself. Needless to say, the conductor has no influence on who serves above him or her.

It is easy to understand why some music directors delegate these responsibilities, but to me, it is part of the job. In a profession that aspires to the noblest of
heights, some decisions can seem insensitive and callous. Those actions are a
facet of the artistic imperative. Change is inevitable. We can only hope that conductors can perceive the same faults in themselves as those perceived in others.

There are no amusing stories about dismissal.

17

Running the Ship

Never tell people how *to do things. Tell them* what *to do, and they will surprise you with their ingenuity.*

—GEORGE S. PATTON

When attending an orchestral concert, you assume that no matter who is conducting, the person on the podium serves in the identical capacity as did the one who stood there the previous week. However, one obvious difference would be the number of weeks that the individual performs with the ensemble.

Conducting in the concert is but a small fraction of the music director's job. Generally, the principal conductor is also responsible for most of what happens in day-to-day orchestral life. He or she is the boss. At least, that is what the public thinks. After all, people rarely hear the names of the administrators, members of board of directors or numerous employees that comprise a symphonic organization. I have always felt that the duty of the music director is to take the credit when things go well, and take the blame when they do not.

It might help to back up just a little in music history. Orchestras at the beginning of the twentieth century were customarily run by boards. This elite membership, along with the music director, determined what the arts community needed from their local orchestra. In some instances they also chose the programs. Seasons were not very long and the players lacked the financial security they currently enjoy. As late as the 1950s, the majority of major orchestras did not perform much beyond twenty-four to thirty-six weeks per year. And the music directors were present for most of the concerts. The term *jet set* had not come into use.

The conductor was expected to reside in the orchestra's home city, although some exceptions were inevitable. Toscanini, Reiner, Szell made their orchestra's city their home. They became a fixture of the city's cultural life. In fact, they virtually dominated and shaped the artistic vision of their environment.

As seasons lengthened, the concert calendar mandated a larger number of guest conductors. Too many weeks led by one person was deemed unhealthy for the orchestra and audience. As a result, the control wielded by the music director began to erode. Increasingly, decisions were left in the hands of executives, and a new position, artistic administrator, came into being. In a sense, this resembled the European role of the intendant, although the conductor still had most of the control over the programming.

Present-day conductors have differing definitions about what their job actually is. Some choose to regularly participate in the community; others just finish their concerts and leave town. However, music directors seem to share certain universal responsibilities, whether they like it or not. Because the United States does not have an active and strong system of government support for the arts, this enormous obligation falls to the individual cultural organizations. As head of an orchestra, in conjunction with the executive director and board president, you form a troika, more powerful than having one boss alone. In depressed economies, you must convince reluctant donors to contribute even more money by emphasizing the value of your product to the community.

To accomplish this, the ideal presentation must demonstrate how the orchestra relates to today's audience. With attendance down, audience age rising and repertoire often stale, it is no wonder, with the abundance of entertainment alternatives, some people opt to stay away from symphonic events. The conductor remains the figurehead of musical society in a given community and the most visible means of showing leadership comes in one form: programming, programming, programming.

The heart of the orchestral season lies in the music played. To that end, the programs themselves reveal a great deal about the music director. Since there is generally only one full-time professional orchestra based in a region, the music director must plan a musical agenda that, while reflecting his or her personal musical tastes, also addresses the needs of the larger community and provides the broadest possible experience for the audience. Almost every kind of music will be performed in a single season. The music director must engage in as many of these styles as is reasonable. It makes sense to go with your strengths for most of the season. Whether he or she admits it or not, it is simply not possible for any one musician to feel comfortable with the infinite variety of musical thought.

When planning a season, the music director must look and see what the orchestra has and has not performed in previous years. It is helpful to draw up a three-year plan of works you wish to present. In the early stages of putting together a season, it is not necessary to factor in the desires of guest conductors.

It has been said that an orchestra is like a museum. That, of course, is insulting to both institutions, but to some degree, the statement is valid. Most of the public expects their ensemble to play a varied collection of works. And like a great museum, it should have its areas of specialization. We live by the works that have survived the test of time. We are also judged against other institutions in this way, so concertgoers expect a balanced season of works representing the various periods of music history.

Portions of that history are a little difficult to define, as the manner of performance style for earlier periods comes into question when executed by the contemporary orchestra. How the conductor chooses to perform baroque pieces, for example, is truly an individual matter. Along with these works, the season must include a representation of new pieces. This can take the form of music not previously performed by the orchestra, or compositions by living composers created just for these concerts. In addition to preserving aural history, we must help to expand it.

I believe that the orchestras which find a balance between the old and new are the organizations with the best chances of survival in an increasingly competitive market. It becomes imperative for the music director to find those areas where his or her orchestra can be unique. There can be fabulous performances of the finest works in the literature, but the orchestra must be known not only by how it plays, but also by what it plays. As a student, I looked forward to the Cleveland's Schumann, Chicago's Strauss, Boston's Ravel and Philadelphia's Tchaikovsky. Those orchestras played these and countless other composers with a distinctive sound and style that, perhaps, is missing these days. Professional performances tend to be uniformly excellent, with an accent on uniform.

The music director puts on paper what he or she would like to do on the programs. Now comes the selection of the guest artists, both conductors and soloists. Often these performers may have limited dates available, so you have to approach them early in the planning stages. This can cause compromises in your own programming, as some artists only have a handful of works prepared per season. What if you want to schedule the "Great" C Major Symphony by Schubert for yourself and simultaneously guest conductor X is insisting on performing the piece? The decision will depend on how much you want to do the Schubert, as opposed to how much you want to have this particular conductor in that season. Remember, you can always program the work for yourself in future years.

A pretty good rule of thumb is to hire guest conductors who are especially strong in repertoire where you are weak. This is not such an easy pill to swallow, as most of us think we do everything equally well. There are several works in the Austro-Germanic canon that I don't feel close to. I always try to find conductors to fill in these gaps. This means getting to know the conducting work of others. It also is where a solid artistic administrator can be most helpful.

In balancing a season, the choice of new, lesser-played or contemporary music becomes challenging. Most guests will submit their party pieces. It is quite rare, even today, to find conductors who offer much from the twelve-tone school, even though that system is more than one hundred years old. They know it will be difficult for the public, and management discourages guests from this kind of programming. The younger conductors, who should be on a quest for adventurous forays with an eye on capturing positive critical notices, are concentrating on the standard works, or those pieces they know the orchestra and audience will find palatable. So the tough sells usually land on the music director's plate.

It is nearly impossible for a conductor to observe colleagues in action. They are rarely conducting in the same city at the same time, unless one has opera performances. To assess the quality of their work, the music director should have absolute confidence in a right-hand person. Remember, the public will not realize that someone besides the music director might have selected the guest.

Much the same goes for soloists. Marketing departments will tell you which ones are proven box office draws. Your own taste can tell you something else. An orchestra is not in the business of making money, but it is also not trying to sink the ship financially. A balance must be achieved between established artists and young, or not-so-well-known, soloists that you believe in. If a proven violinist is available and you are not in sympathy with that person's musical approach, attempt to assign him or her to a guest conductor.

Repertoire discussions will also come into the mix. Usually, soloists don't offer a lot of concertos in a given season. Generally you choose a work from the list presented by the artist that best fits into the season. Another way to select the soloist is to choose a work you would like to do, and then locate the appropriate musician to play it. This method can work effectively to introduce a young or unknown talent. There will be people that you will want to have visit on a regular basis, so try to establish relationships with several artists so they can become familiar to your public, even if they are not so well known to other orchestras or audiences.

Members of the orchestra need to be given consideration. Each ensemble normally employs several musicians capable of outstanding performances as soloists. Certainly the concertmaster and other principal string players fall into this category as do most of the principal winds. It is always wonderful for morale if a player from the middle of the violin section can stand in front of his or her colleagues and show off. One outlet for handling this is to devote a whole program to soloists from the orchestra. This can result in very creative programs, including works for multiple soloists and orchestra.

Now you have all the pieces planned. You have constructed a balanced season. How do you know it will work? You don't! At best it is a knowledge-able guess as to how ticket sales will go despite your belief in the artistic merit. When I was in Saint Louis, David Hyslop and I developed a method to deal with the guesstimates. We would examine each program and assign it a number from zero to two. Two represented a guaranteed sellout and zero meant lots of subscriber turn-backs and no-shows. A good example of a two would be a Mozart concerto followed by Beethoven's Ninth. A zero is the ever-popular all-Stockhausen evening. If in the course of a twenty-four-week subscription season, we came up with a total of twenty-four points, we would forecast a successful year.

This system required us to be ruthless on the programs and ourselves. If a concert featured a well-known soloist, but also had a new piece, we might rate it a one. A conservative program with no soloist might get half a point. In all this, remaining faithful to our artistic integrity was key. Yes, we would adopt some changes, but it mostly worked. We knew which programs would reach a large audience. But we knew we had to take chances, too.

Because Saint Louis was then on the periphery of the national musical consciousness, we had to develop a long-range plan that would score points on the broader musical map. At the same time our primary concern was our local audience and subscribers. If we could not succeed at home, there was hardly any sense in also losing money on the road. We basically kept our programming in line with the mainstream, not overemphasizing the innovative aspects of our plan, nevertheless advertising a solid season with great artists and strong programs. Once in a while we presented a rarity. For the most part these could be woven in with traditional fare. We were also aiming for a national audience; to bring nothing but the standard repertoire to New York, Boston or Chicago was asking for a critical pounding. We had become known for our programming of American and Slavic music, two areas of repertoire not so much explored during the reign in the United States of primarily Austro-Germanic maestros.

Saint Louis did hear its share of exotic works, but a lot of these were in preparation for tour appearances. They did not draw so well at home, but on the road in major venues, they packed the houses for single performances. In one case, we were cited as being the finest orchestral event of a season. It was during these trips that we presented works such as William Bolcom's *Songs of Innocence and Experience,* and the American premiere of Nicholas Maw's *Odyssey* as well as Peter Maxwell Davies' *Worldes Blis.* New York concertgoers heard the local premieres of works by Terry Riley, Steve Reich, Elliott Carter, John Williams, Alberto Ginastera and many others. Defining the orchestra's role when playing in New York, where we focused on unusual repertoire, was quite different from our home persona where we concentrated on the standard orchestra canon for most of the season.

Perhaps equally important as performing these works was our belief in the pieces themselves. The orchestra gave as much, if not more, to these unusual projects. We became a major force on the East Coast. Much the same is still true today, as the current music director, David Robertson, has also been developing an audience base for his own concepts of programming on the road.

In Washington, it was pretty much like starting my career over. I followed the seventeen-year reign of Mstislav Rostropovich. His credentials as a cellist were beyond legendary and eclectic. But as a music director, he pretty much stuck to the Russian repertoire, with the exception of a few ventures into new music. Although he may not have displayed the same extraordinary talent conducting as playing the cello, his musicianship was never in question. In any event, I inherited a somewhat undisciplined orchestra. As he told the musicians on a farewell cruise given for him up the Potomac, "I love each and every one of you like a child. There are some of you I should have sent away from home, but I could not. I will leave that to Mr. Slatkin."

Thanks a lot, Slava!

The first order of business was to establish a working relationship with an orchestra I had not guest conducted very often. After announcing my departure from Saint Louis, a call came from the then chairman of the Kennedy Center, James Wolfensohn, asking me to come to Washington. A concert was hastily arranged to see if the orchestra and I would make an ideal match. On paper it looked good but the performance was average. At intermission, Jim said that he had a guest that he wanted me to meet, and he proceeded to bring President Clinton and family to my dressing room! The president asked, "So you are going to be part of the Washington family?" It was impossible to turn him down and I now found myself in the nation's capital.

The situation was not easy going and the first problem I encountered involved the Kennedy Center Concert Hall. This rectangular building has been described as the crate in which the Washington Monument obelisk was packed. Acoustics in the main hall were dry and the members of the orchestra could not hear one another clearly. It was certainly a far cry from the warm sound I had experienced all those years in Saint Louis.

However, there was a bit of luck on my side. After twenty-five years, most of the theaters in the Kennedy Center did not meet the latest codes for either disabled access or fire safety. The concert hall would be the first renovated, and we were given the chance to work with acousticians and architects in an effort to solve some of the problems. Our budget was limited, but the suggestion was made to eliminate almost 250 seats and place choral seating behind the orchestra. There were battles about the color of the seats and of the hall itself. But in the end, it wound up a considerable improvement over its predecessor.

At one of the re-dedication concerts, I asked President Clinton to conduct *The Stars and Stripes Forever*. He requested a conducting lesson at the White House. It was obvious that the man knew the piece and what to do, asking me, "How do I conduct the ritardando before the big brass entrance?" At the performance we lost power to the microphone, and so without amplification I could tell the audience how good our new acoustics were. Then I said, "Ladies and gentlemen, I've grown quite weary of conducting this piece, so I would like to introduce our new assistant conductor, President William Clinton." Clinton would later joke, on several occasions, that this was the first time he got one hundred people to follow what he wanted them to do.

The music director is charged with the responsibility of determining what the overall nature of an orchestra's sonic profile will be. There was no doubt that the Kennedy Center was the exact opposite of Powell Hall. The two differed so thoroughly that a comparison simply was not possible. After several seasons of experiments with setups, risers and almost everything else that affected sound and balance, I concluded it was of critical importance to have the cellos and basses face the audience instead of playing straight across the stage. This triggered turmoil within the orchestra. I pleaded for them to be patient, to try this configuration for a few months, listen from locations in the hall and then decide. Eventually I won, but dissatisfaction lingered among some of the musicians. My successor, Christoph Eschenbach, kept my solution but shifted the double basses to the rear of the stage wall, something I wanted but the bass section had overruled. Ah, the advantage of being the new kid on the block.

American music formed a sizable part of my tenure, to nobody's surprise. After all, this was the *National* Symphony of the United States. The instrumentalists probably would have preferred focusing on the standard fare. They had tired of the vast amount of Russian material and now they were going to get their fill of Copland instead of Tchaikovsky. I tried to chart a balanced course, leaning toward my strengths during the first few seasons. Our initial recording, the Corigliano First Symphony, won a couple of Grammy Awards and promptly put us on the national map. We toured a good deal, memorably across the United States as participants in a program called "American Residencies." This gave us a chance to visit different sections of the country and evaluate the state of music at each stop. It was evident that our education system was failing, especially in the arts. I tried to work with the White House and Mrs. Clinton in developing a public service campaign to raise arts awareness.

Over time, I met many high-achieving people who had not pursued musical careers, but cited their childhood training in music as a key to success. Names such as Alan Greenspan, Sam Donaldson, Colin Powell, Donna Shalala, Condoleezza Rice, Andrea Mitchell, Paula Zahn and many others all had the benefit of learning an instrument early in life. We came up with a plan to create television ads where a famous figure would dress as a child, posed with the instrument he or she had played, and a young person would dress as the adult's professional counterpart. The whole visual element would convey a powerful message through seeing celebrities and role models promote music education. Everyone loved the idea, except a leading education group in the area which declined to work on raising money for the ad. Perhaps someone will follow through with it in the future. Although education is typically the purview of others, it is vitally important that the music director participate. Whether conducting, speaking or simply lending a name as an advocate, engaging in your community's education programs is critical in this day and age.

In my first season, the *Washington Post* ran an article referring to cutbacks in Fairfax County, at the time the wealthiest region in the States due to the dot-com industry, military contracting and financial services. The board of supervisors was holding a meeting to discuss the upcoming budget. One item on its agenda proposed to eliminate the fourth-grade string music program as well as field trips to cultural institutions downtown. I decided to attend one of these sessions, even though I was a resident of Maryland and not Virginia.

When I arrived, the meeting was well under way. Each person had four minutes to make his or her case for a favorite cause. Some seemed justified and a few were partisan and frivolous. When I stood at the rostrum, I could not help but notice that the general makeup of the board fell roughly in my age group. So I threw away my prepared notes and told them this story.

"All my life, I was a product of the public school system in Los Angeles. There was always music education. At my high school, we had three choruses, two bands and an orchestra. Rehearsals were always at normal school hours, not before or after the basic curriculum.

"When I was in fourth grade, a woman named Mrs. Otto would come to school twice a week. We would sing, learn how to play some instruments and make up games based on musical principles. In many ways she was the most influential person in my earliest days.

"When I return to Los Angeles to perform, every so often someone comes backstage. They say, 'You probably won't remember me, but we were in elementary school together. Do you remember Mrs. Otto? I didn't go into music, but she made music come alive for me.'

"Perhaps some of you had a Mrs. Otto when you were young. If so, please think about that person and what he or she meant to you. And please do not deprive your fourth graders from having their very own Mrs. Otto. Thank you."

The board members discussed this briefly, adding stories of their own musical education. That night the board reinstated the funding. I felt a sense of accomplishment. The next year, the program was slashed.

The American music director must deal with similar circumstances within the symphonic organization. Several facets of fund-raising come with the job, duties that many conductors truly do not enjoy. I have always believed that if it is my orchestra, I need to do as much as possible in the community, just to gain credibility for the orchestra and myself. Others feel that maintaining a distance, acting like an aloof kind of old-school maestro, is more effective. For me, a closer connection to the neighborhoods where I lived resulted from being seen shopping at the market, taking out the trash, going to the ball games and dining at various nearby restaurants.

The NSO was structured in a way that was radically different from its constituents. My orchestra had its own board, but the Kennedy Center also had one. Jim Wolfensohn felt that the KC group must have some say in NSO life, especially as deficits crept up. He found a way to merge the two boards while keeping them independent. The Kennedy Center board would incur a percentage of the deficit, and in turn, would utilize the National Symphony as needed. Jim departed about six months after I arrived, as he had accepted the position as head of the World Bank. The person who brought me in to change things would only be there on my side for half a year.

The new administration had a different idea. I don't think they were at all thrilled with the integration of the two boards, as it must have been tricky to divvy up who gets what. As such, I never went on a fund-raising call, as any prospective NSO benefactors could potentially be in the gun sights of the KC. An organization hires people based on their strengths, and to take away one of mine seemed a waste.

Somehow we managed. A couple of tours were canceled due to lack of funds, but we traveled twice to Europe and Asia as well as Carnegie Hall. I think that audiences enjoyed our performances, especially on the West Coast, but we failed to really capture the imagination of the public.

We strived to be the "Great American Orchestra," spreading the gospel according to Aaron Copland. Every opening program had a representative work by a native composer. Festivals were developed, big stars brought in and dignitaries from all over the world would listen to us in the somewhat cavernous Kennedy Center.

One project, and perhaps the initiative of which I was most proud, was the National Conducting Institute. For nine years, aspiring maestros came to DC for three weeks, spending their time learning about how a major orchestra was run, from public relations and marketing to development. They observed me work with the orchestra for a week, and then came their turn. With immediate feedback from the musicians, each conductor received a crash course into the workings of this complex profession. By the time the three-week session ended, they had a complete picture of what lay ahead.

During the almost decade of the institute's existence, I learned that there are no hard-and-fast rules. What worked for one conductor did not necessarily apply to another. If a student struggled to clearly convey a passage to the orchestra, I might take the baton out of the leader's hand and see if that solved the problem. One young charge had an annoying habit of calling the musicians "you guys" in rehearsal. I went offstage, grabbed a ceramic coffee cup, and for each instance he uttered this phase, dropped a quarter noisily into the container. After a dollar and a half had accumulated, he asked what was going on. I replied that the amount in the cup would be what he owed us after the rehearsal. The Pavlovian effect worked and the conductor did not have to mortgage his house.

Virtually every student who attended the institute found employment in the music profession. I will follow their development with interest. This was also the time when I probably got the closest to the members of the orchestra. After each of my rehearsals we would gather in a room and discuss what worked and what did not. I outlined my plans for the next day and was open to any criticism held by either the musicians or the conductors. Of course, I could also give as good as I got.

At the turn of the century, I was undergoing a major shift in my personal life. Life on the road is one easy excuse, as is midlife crisis. I found myself searching for companionship away from home. Perhaps I was trying to avoid responsibility or attempting to remind myself that I could feel younger. Consequently, I engaged in activities that should not have happened, and perhaps would not have if I had realized the impact of my actions on my family, friends and orchestra. As a result, everything suffered—relationships, rehearsals and concerts.

Whether this was a direct reason for the abrupt non-renewal of my contract I will probably never know. It was on a Friday when I got a call from my agent, Doug Sheldon, saying that the NSO wanted to extend my current agreement by one year, after which time I would leave the orchestra. They wanted an answer by Tuesday, barely any time for negotiation. The reasons cited were board dissatisfaction with my programming and orchestra dissatisfaction with my rehearsals. I had been notified once, several months before, about the orchestra complaint, but this was the first I heard about any problem with the board.

With the help of some friends at the Kennedy Center, I got the extension increased to two years, allowing my son to finish middle school at an educational facility where he had been for almost his entire life. I tried to fathom this mess, especially after discovering that the majority of the players who wanted me out were people whom I had hired. The musicians took sides and for several weeks the situation was chaos. I blew up at a board meeting and started grousing to almost everyone.

There was no question in my mind that for about two years I had not done a good job, so they had justification for letting me go. On the other hand, by the time the pink slip arrived, things were again going well. We had done spectacular and well-prepared performances of operatic work, as well as complex contemporary pieces. It did not matter. Too much, too late.

The following season, my second to last, we faced a severe budget crunch. I had two big projects planned: the world premiere of Chris Rouse's Requiem (which meant bringing in a chorus) and a concert version of Strauss' *Salome*. Then they offered me a choice: pick one over the other. The Requiem, obviously, would not draw much of a crowd, and already aware that this would be near the end of my tenure, I opted for the Strauss. It was one of the saddest decisions I would ever have to make as music director. If the NSO applied the same fund-raising principles as other orchestras follow, I would have been out there hustling bucks to cover both projects. The rules said I could not do so, but at least I had the satisfaction of a superb performance of the opera.

The final year of performances in DC was outstanding. I cheated, however. All of the big-name soloists performed with me, leaving the smaller-budget artists to conductors who were under consideration as potential candidates for my job. I had nothing to do with the hiring of these musicians or their programs, and that was fine with me.

The orchestra made a presentation to me after one of the concerts. It was sweet but accompanied by a slight distance. I was still not Slava. And yet the NSO had become a better ensemble, and also had begun to reclaim some national attention. Trips to New York introduced unusual repertoire, but nothing seemed to catch on locally the way that the Rostropovich concerts had.

At my last performances, Yo-Yo Ma was soloist in one of my favorite works, Bloch's *Schelomo*. I had asked him also to perform a composition of mine for two cellos called *Dialogues*. The second soloist was Sol Gabetta. My closing selection was *Pines of Rome*. No real speeches, and I was glad. Farewell programs can be rough. Lorin Maazel told me that for his finale in Cleveland he had chosen the Verdi Requiem. "Never have the words *libera me* had so much meaning as on that night!"

In 2005, the longtime music director of the Nashville Symphony, Kenneth Schermerhorn, died. This loss coincided with a pivotal moment in the history of the orchestra, as they were getting ready to open a new hall. Kenneth had been instrumental in securing the funds for the project. With no set musical leadership, the organization needed someone to shepherd the ensemble into new territory.

I became musical adviser to the orchestra, a position I held for three years. I did not have an interest in becoming Ken's successor. But this new situation actually suited me well, as I could conduct a few weeks a season in Music City and mostly steer clear of the responsibilities of music director. Because it was an exciting time for the community, and the orchestra itself was quite good, I threw myself into the job.

In the span of my brief tenure, we opened the hall, dedicated an organ, hosted the League of American Orchestras and recorded several albums for Naxos. One of those, a disc of music by Joan Tower, went on to win a couple of Grammys, the first such awards for the Nashville Symphony. After a search, they selected Giancarlo Guerrero to fill the still-vacant music director position.

During my final season in DC, I had a guest conducting date in Detroit, an orchestra I had not led for over thirty years. I was not aware that they were looking for a music director. That week, with Prokofiev, John Williams and Walton on the program, I had a wonderful time. Apparently the feeling was mutual since, in the space of five days, we agreed that a true relationship could develop.

Most of the board had been attending a retreat up on Mackinac Island, but word soon filtered northward that something special was happening in Detroit. Gradually members returned home and receptions and dinners were hastily arranged. By the end of the week, all sides felt we needed at least one more set of concerts together prior to making a commitment.

About a month later I found myself at the orchestra's summer home, Meadowbrook, located about fifteen miles north of the city. At one time this was a major festival; however, the economy had reduced it to less than a month's work. The original intent was to create a middle-of-the-country Tanglewood, but the plan never materialized. Still, this bucolic setting has charms that make for a pleasant evening of picnicking and listening.

Initially, I had been invited to lead a single program, but knowing that the orchestra generally played two or more of these alfresco concerts during a given week, I wondered why I was not conducting the whole package. It turned out that the Sunday program starred the Von Trapp Family Singers, four grandchildren of the *Sound of Music* heroine. Since I had no hesitation doing a pops-style concert, we agreed that I would add this second concert to the Beethoven scheduled for the previous night.

All went well, and maybe superior to the downtown concerts a month earlier. The chemistry was definitely there. We sealed the deal, although my start was delayed by an ongoing series of contract negotiations between the management and orchestra. I did not want to get caught or used as a bargaining chip. The issues needed to be settled before I would sign.

Now I had returned to the middle of the country, albeit the extra cold part. The orchestra had been without artistic leadership for five seasons, but sounded excellent. It performed in one of the great halls of the world, a bit smaller than most and full of rich sonorities. Just what I wanted.

But Detroit was also filled with huge economic holes, and this preceded October 2008, when the stock markets tanked. Some journalists wrote that following my less-than-successful tenure in Washington, I really needed to turn around an organization. However, all I thought about was that Detroit would be the ideal place to make music, and would perhaps allow me one more opportunity to make a contribution as a music director.

A music director must have a solid staff to rely on. In Saint Louis it was there. In DC it fluctuated. Detroit had every ingredient for artistic and managerial success, but digging out of the fiscal morass was formidable. In a very short time, I immersed myself in the community, worked in schools, gave lectures, went to the auto shows and figured out how to make a Michigan U-turn. The orchestra players learned my manner of working quickly and I learned how hard I could lean on them.

There were already some outstanding educational activities taking place under the umbrella of the DSO, including the Civic Ensembles. On Saturday morning, five hundred young people came to Orchestra Hall, where they were divided into five orchestras. In addition, they received individual lessons and in many instances instruments as well. It resembled a kind of El Sistema. I immersed myself in this world, working with the youth groups in rehearsal and performance.

Immediately behind the hall is another educational facility, the Detroit School for the Arts. It is a magnet school and another five hundred students are taught subjects as varied as filmmaking and saxophone. Again, I tried to get as involved as possible. In addition, I threw myself into various activities at other schools, middle, high or college levels. In a city struggling to climb out of social and economic difficulties, these educational institutions were oases. At one point I met with the supervisor of schools. He told me, somewhat proudly, that 30 percent of the Detroit public schools had music education. My response was that this meant 70 percent did not. A dialogue began as to how the DSO might provide leadership by implementing programs that could bring the arts to these schools.

In many ways, Detroit was closer in philosophy to what I had been accustomed to in Saint Louis than in Washington. The distance from the East Coast made me feel a bit more isolated, but the city is a few hours by car from Chicago, Cleveland, Toronto and Pittsburgh. I had an orchestra that was respected by the industry if not free of the problems plaguing the business.

Most of my experience with ensembles abroad had been spent as a guest. Whether in England, Germany, France or Spain, I was content to conduct these orchestras on a part-time basis. Over the years, I had conducted all the major British orchestras, spending regular periods with the LSO, LPO, Philharmonia, RPO and BBC.

It was probably just a question of time before a British group would ask me to serve as its principal conductor. In the meantime, a few offers had emerged from other European orchestras. I wanted to wait for a London posting. In 1999, the invitation came from the BBC. Sir Andrew Davis had been leading the orchestra for nine years and was stepping down. I had worked with the BBCSO on several occasions in the past, mostly with contemporary music and on tour. It seemed like the perfect job. Every performance would be broadcast, there would be an emphasis on English music, and I would be able to tour often with my own ensemble.

It did not work out quite as I expected. Several in the orchestra opposed my candidacy, but I did not know this at the time. I was convinced that we could accomplish mutually beneficial, musical goals. The problem was figuring out whose goals they were.

As with most government orchestras, the BBC operates according to a hierarchy and chain of command that dictates policy for the season. The principal conductor has little or no control of programs, even his own. I gamely went along with the presentation of obscure composers whose musical style did not fit comfortably into my convictions.

Rehearsals and some performances took place in the studios at Maida Vale. Their concert hall is the Barbican, on the other side of town. Similar to most London orchestras, the BBC is only permitted to rehearse there on the day of a performance. To me, this makes it almost impossible to develop a sense of sonic profile. And the constantly varied repertoire, although commendable, also works against cultivating an orchestra's individual sound.

More disheartening was the organization's attitude that because every performance was being heard on the radio, the number of people in attendance was less important. On some evenings we played to perhaps four or five hundred people, despite ticket prices that were among the lowest in the world.

It was only with the summer Proms that we attracted the kind of enthusiastic crowds I had hoped for. Everyone loves performing for this audience. They are quiet when needed, and vociferous in their approval. Having the opportunity to play a half-dozen times in the Albert Hall was a dream. But even there, the directive to play new music could conflict with proper preparation of some of the programs. Also, the orchestra only got into the hall on the day of a concert, as the place is booked solid with presentations by groups from across the globe.

The hope I had for touring disappeared, as the BBC was making financial cutbacks. A proposed American tour featuring all-British music was scrapped, including a proposed Carnegie Hall presentation of Britten's *War Requiem*. In lieu of this trip, we taped two programs for television that revolved around Korngold and Rózsa. They were fun to do and seemed to be well received, but did not air outside of England. The project did give me the opportunity to spend a week in Hollywood, location filming and running around from studio to studio.

A wonderful anecdote came to light when I stopped in at Warner Brothers. The archivist of the library showed me scores and parts that my mother used in her role as first cellist. Then he told me this story.

It seems that fellow Austrian émigrés, the composers Erich Wolfgang Korngold and Max Steiner, were not the best of friends. One afternoon they happened upon each other.

Steiner asked, "Erich, how come my music is getting better and better and yours is getting worse and worse?"

Korngold replied, "It is simple, Max. I am stealing from you and you are stealing from me."

I really hope this story is true.

During my second year in the post, the BBC asked me to step down, but agreed that I should continue for two more seasons, bringing the total to four. It was clear that this idea had been in the administration's mind from the start, and it was probably for the better. The chemistry simply wasn't particularly strong between the orchestra and me. Nonetheless, we shared some fine performances. And I was there when it mattered most.

18

Leonard Bernstein

The joy of music should never be interrupted by a commercial.

—LEONARD BERNSTEIN

Just as people remember where they were when Man first walked on the moon, when JFK was assassinated or when they had their first kiss, I will never forget the first time I saw Leonard Bernstein.

He was presenting a television program, standing on an enlarged version of the first page of Beethoven's Fifth Symphony. Musicians were placed next to where their instruments appeared in the score. It was November 1953 and I was nine years old.

Until that time, the only Americans I ever saw conducting were Alfred Wallenstein, music director of the Los Angeles Philharmonic, who did not make a big impression on me, and various conductors in the motion picture industry. The podium seemed the province of long-haired, older European men with exotic accents. Yes, there had been a handful of Americans on the scene. However, most had either been born abroad or were the offspring of immigrant parents. Bernstein was our nation's first homebred maestro.

His accomplishment remains an inspiration to all conductors in the United States, and it is not possible to forget that Bernstein paved the way for Americans being accepted on the podium. My generation grew up with his televised Young People's Concerts. As aspiring musicians, we bought his recordings, read his books and listened to his lectures.

When I was a student at the Juilliard School, Bernstein was still the music director of the New York Philharmonic. One Friday at lunchtime, someone from the administration office came down to the cafeteria and announced that he had a couple of tickets to that afternoon's performance downtown. (Juilliard had not yet moved to Lincoln Center.) Students rushed to get those seats and I was lucky enough to win the race. I had no idea what was on the program and didn't care. It turned out to be a Haydn symphony—No. 87—and Mahler's *Das Lied von der Erde*, a work I did not care for at the time.

It didn't matter. Watching the master was always a joy to me. Some cynics inevitably carped about his podium gyrations, but all you have to do is watch any video to witness a clarity of beat and, more importantly, a genuine musical meaning conveyed by every gesture.

During those years, I tried and failed to get backstage to meet Bernstein. Even an attempt to bribe an usher didn't work.

While I was music director in Saint Louis, the orchestra and I recorded a few albums of his music. This was a formidable task. After all, we had the composer himself conducting his own works in what were assumed to be definitive performances. Initially I was reluctant to take on these pieces for disc, but EMI could not get Bernstein due to his exclusive contract to conduct for Columbia, and later, Deutsche Grammophon.

But we had a little piece of history on our side. In 1945, Bernstein made his initial recording with a major American orchestra. It was his First Symphony, "Jeremiah," and the orchestra was Saint Louis.

Everyone believed that the two of us had been acquainted for a long time. This was not the case and not for lack of trying. In 1984, Bernstein was on tour with the Vienna Philharmonic. I was in Chicago at the time and, of course, needed to attend at least one of the concerts. A post-concert dinner had been arranged and I was invited. Finally I would meet my American idol.

It was not to be. At the close of the concert, while shaking hands with pretty much all the members of the orchestra, Bernstein stumbled off the podium, fell and landed on his chest. Medical personnel hurried him offstage immediately, and he was rushed to the hospital. We would later learn that he fell onto the medallion he habitually wore in performance, one with the likeness of Dimitri Mitropoulos. Bernstein sustained some bruising and our meeting was thwarted again.

Other attempts to get together, both before and after this, were doomed as well.

Two years later, we would finally meet fact to face. It was at Tanglewood in the summer of 1986. I was scheduled to lead the Boston Symphony on a Friday evening concert and Bernstein was conducting the student orchestra on Saturday. Knowing that he would be in Lenox that weekend, I felt confident that by programming one of his works, he would show up. The piece I chose was the early ballet *Facsimile*.

I thought that the best course of action, rather than just wait until my concert, would be to attend one of his rehearsals. So I arrived at the Music Shed a half hour before the starting time. While I waited in the parking lot, I was cornered by the conductor, Maurice Abravanel, who was a lovely, gentle man. Then I saw Bernstein pull up in his convertible. I could not dismiss Abravanel mid-sentence, and it was already five minutes past the rehearsal's scheduled start.

Bernstein got out of his car and headed toward the stage. My then-wife, Linda, hurried over to him and said, "Maestro, there is someone you need to meet." I dashed over and introduced myself. He looked me in the eyes and exclaimed, "My God, finally," and proceeded to give me a gigantic hug.

Instead of entering the rehearsal, he and I chatted for about ten minutes while the orchestra warmed up. The first thing he asked me was why I did so much of his music. My reply was simply that I loved it.

"But *Facsimile*? No one plays this piece and it isn't even an anniversary year. No zeros or fives."

"Your music does not need a special occasion, like some composers." Then I added facetiously, "Like Elliott Carter."

Bernstein shot back, "No, you are wrong. Mr. Carter's music is played far too often."

Ouch!

My performance with the BSO was not very good. I exaggerated tempi and really did not have enough time to put together the unknown piece properly. For decades, musicians had repeated horror stories of Bernstein's public tirades against performers if the maestro did not like how they played his music. I braced myself for the assault that I anticipated at intermission.

"Well, it was not what I intended when I wrote it," he said.

My heart sank further.

This was followed by, "But I can see how you arrived at your conclusions." Then he proceeded to dissect my interpretation at such length that it delayed the start of the second half of the concert.

I sensed that after a long and distinguished career, he was beginning to realize that for his compositions to survive after he was gone, they would have to undergo interpretive changes similar to those frequently made by Bernstein himself when conducting the music of other composers.

We became friends but not close. I saw him a few more times, usually at Tanglewood. Once, we even taught a conducting class together joined by Seiji Ozawa, Lukas Foss and Gustav Meier. The proceedings were dominated not so much with our teaching as by Bernstein personally taking Foss to task for failing to achieve his potential.

The last time I heard from Bernstein was backstage at Avery Fisher Hall in 1989, minutes before I was to conduct his *Songfest* with the Philharmonic. The phone in the dressing room rang and when I picked it up, he conveyed how sorry he was that he could not be with us. It was obvious to me that his emphysema had worsened.

Less than a year later, he died.

But that is another story.

19

Alice and the Carter Affair

Be what you would seem to be—or, if you'd like it put more
simply—never imagine yourself not to be otherwise than what it
might appear to others that what you were or might have been was
not otherwise than what you had been would have appeared to
them to be otherwise.

—LEWIS CARROLL, *ALICE'S ADVENTURES IN WONDERLAND*

October 7, 1976. America was nearing the conclusion of the bicentennial celebration of its revolution. In Chicago, on that night, another revolution was born.

I had not planned on attending, but a couple of days earlier in the week, the executive director of the Chicago Symphony, John Edwards, called me and said that something extraordinary was taking place and that I should hop on a plane for the premiere of David Del Tredici's *Final Alice*. Because I was still based as an associate conductor of the Saint Louis Symphony, this was not so hard to arrange, as it was only a forty-five-minute flight.

Del Tredici was one of six composers who had received a commission that year to write a work for a round-robin project, wherein each composition would be played by the other five participating orchestras. John Cage wrote a piece for the Boston Symphony, Leslie Bassett for Philadelphia, Elliott Carter for New York, and so on. Of the six pieces, the Carter and Del Tredici seemed to attract the most interest.

Back then, David's music was completely unfamiliar to me. I had understood that he was a die-hard serialist who, like a number of composers, was moving away from that school and taking his music in a fresh direction. Over the past few years, the man had become obsessed with *Alice in Wonderland*, with *Final Alice* his biggest statement to date.

In the mid-'70s, most of the musical establishment looked upon premieres with little enthusiasm. To tolerate anything unfamiliar seemed more of an obligation than pleasure for the audience. For that memorable night in Chicago, János Starker was on hand to play the First Cello Concerto of Saint-Saëns during the first half of the program—hardly enough to fill more than twenty minutes.

Why such a brief work before intermission?

Because what came next was one of the most significant events to grace a concert hall in the second half of the twentieth century. Onstage, with Sir Georg Solti conducting, sat a Mahler-sized orchestra, plus sirens, a theremin and other assorted unusual instruments. In a semicircle around the conductor were two saxophones, a mandolin, banjo and accordion. And soprano Barbara Hendricks would jump into the national spotlight with a performance unlike any I had previously witnessed.

The revolutionary premise was simple: Could a composer write a work that sent us hurtling back in time harmonically yet at the same time seem contemporary? The answer was an overwhelming yes! Here were big tunes, fugues and virtuoso playing by everyone. The audience leapt to its feet and gave an ovation typically reserved for famous soloists after a concerto by Tchaikovsky. And people exiting the hall came out whistling, humming and actually singing the melodies of the preceding sixty-five minutes.

Overnight, the musical world changed.

Since the premiere, I have had the opportunity to perform the work several times. At those first performances, Sir Georg made a substantial cut in the work's middle section. One of the hallmarks of David's writing is his inability to stop. You ask for a ten-minute piece and you get a half-hour extravaganza. I found the omitted material remarkable in that it introduced sounds and ideas unexplored during the course of the piece. This section also included important, albeit difficult, music for the soprano to sing.

In Saint Louis and Minneapolis, we featured different singers on different nights. Ms. Hendricks did the pared-down version and Judith Kellock performed the entire work. The arrangement was a bit confusing for the orchestra, but once they saw which soprano came onstage, they knew what to do.

In London, we tried another tack completely. Phyllis Bryn-Julson dispatched the sung parts and Claire Bloom recited the narration. Splitting the role seemed like a good idea at the time, but in retrospect, it took something away from the sheer virtuosity of a single performer getting through the whole piece on her own.

Alice lay resting on my music shelf for quite a while thereafter, as if the world had passed her by. Then, for my final season in Washington, I decided to program major works by American composers I've championed throughout my career. I asked David, now that thirty years had passed, who sings it. His answer was a definite, "Hila Plitmann is who you want." I had not known of her but it turned out that she was the go-to vocalist for matters contemporary.

Although she had performed some works by David, *Final Alice* was not among them. She learned and memorized the piece in less than a month. The performances were extraordinary. Hila chose to completely immerse herself in the character and the realm she inhabited. We all wished that someone had made a video, and I hope that will not take another thirty years to accomplish.

Since that Chicago premiere, composers have been able to freely write what they wish, with academic formalism coexisting comfortably alongside minimalism, neo-romanticism and the gamut of musical *isms*. That one night in October was the catalyst that gave them permission and changed the contemporary musical landscape in America.

Although there had been works written before *Final Alice* that explored a new Romanticism, none of those pieces was as big and bold as what David had accomplished. Berio, Rochberg, Druckman, the minimalists and others sought new directions in their music, but it was *Alice* that stormed onto the scene in the biggest way. That night in Chicago created an atmosphere of change for almost every composer, musician and audience member of the time.

The second work in this round-robin project to receive a good deal of attention was by Elliott Carter and its premiere went to the New York Philharmonic during the tenure of Pierre Boulez. This happened in February 1977. Word of the work's technical challenges spread, although some considered this composer's earlier Concerto for Orchestra more difficult. The title of the new piece was *Symphony of Three Orchestras*.

To receive funding for the project, each of the six participating orchestras had to perform the other five works. By the mid 1980s, I had established a significant relationship with the Chicago Symphony. In fact, for a couple of years, almost all of its concerts were conducted by only four men: Georg Solti, Claudio Abbado, Erich Leinsdorf and me. An orchestra member wag dubbed us "the Gang of Four," after the political opposition faction in 1960s–70s China.

Each of us knew our roles. As music director, Sir Georg presided over repertoire choices. Abbado, the principal guest conductor, pretty much did what he liked. Leinsdorf and I picked up the slack with works the other two did not perform. For instance, during this period, I did all the Sibelius symphonies over seven consecutive seasons—not exactly a composer associated with the other three maestros. And, of course, I was called on to cover the majority of the American repertoire during the season.

For several years, John Edwards had asked me to do the Carter. I politely declined. It was clear that neither Solti nor Abbado was going to take it on. Leinsdorf had a particularly rough time with Carter's Piano Concerto and told me that he never again would conduct a piece by him. In 1984, after three failed attempts to persuade me, John finally won. His directive was blunt: either I do the piece or the CSO would lose about a quarter of a million dollars.

I had performed some Carter before, notably his First Symphony; a ballet score, *The Minotaur*; and his truly wonderful Variations for Orchestra. Only the last even remotely resembled the *Three Orchestras* work. But in the '70s, Carter had moved on to very complex structures that simply did not speak to me. Once in a while, I would try studying a piece or two, just to see if I could warm up to this style, but the writing did not appeal to my own aesthetic.

Whenever I opened the score to the symphony, I would close it right back up. The concept of the piece was highly imaginative. The orchestra is divided into three groups. After a brief introduction, each group plays its own short, four-movement symphony simultaneously, creating a degree of organized chaos. A short coda rounds it out. The piece is only seventeen minutes long, but Carter packs a lot into that short span.

Eventually I got the hang of it and felt moderately comfortable with the idiom. The music is inspired by a Hart Crane poem, "The Bridge." And that knowledge helped me relate to the emotion that Carter was attempting to express. But a lot of tough corners remained, metrically as well as texturally. I requested, and received, extra rehearsal time so I could work with each group separately, and I later put them together.

Then things got interesting.

At the dress rehearsal, Mr. Carter sat quietly in the hall. We played the piece through for him and when we were done, I asked if he had any comments or corrections for us. All he mentioned was one place where he wanted the cellos to be "more espressivo." That was it! We were far from perfect and whole passages went awry, yet the composer did not say a word about ensemble, intonation, tempi or anything else—just that one remark.

I was now pretty confident that what he wrote on the page was not what he heard. Most other composers I had worked with always wanted to ensure that we were approximating what was written. Mr. Carter seemed oblivious to this. Maybe he simply wanted to confirm that we were conveying the emotional content, but I was not convinced. Too many things had gone wrong and the composer should have noticed.

We went back and tried to fix as much as time allowed. The orchestra also wanted to repeat a few passages in the interest of getting them right. Twenty-five years later, the piece does not seem as daunting as it did in Orchestra Hall that week, but it is still a challenge.

Backstage, during the rehearsal's intermission, Carter and I discussed what would happen at that evening's performance. To demonstrate some of the work's guiding principles, I had prepared a set of cues (short musical examples from the piece) for the orchestra to play at the concert just prior to the full performance. The composer did not want me to say anything at all, telling me, "The music speaks for itself." I countered that the audience would likely hear the piece only this one time and should be informed as to how and what to listen for.

Carter then said that if I elected to speak, all I should do was read the Hart Crane poem. I explained that this was printed in the program book, so that action would be redundant. Clearly we had a conflict, and I was quite stubborn in those days, so I decided to proceed with my talk.

The concert began with Ravel's *Menuet antique*, a lovely piece that I thought would balance well with the Carter. After a setup change, the orchestra returned to the stage. I walked out and took the microphone. Whenever I conduct a piece that is particularly difficult to absorb, I traditionally open with some sort of lighthearted remark, then move to the serious business at hand. Perhaps with the Carter, this is where I made a crucial mistake.

"Ladies and gentlemen. You will notice that the next piece on the program is entitled *Symphony of Three Orchestras*, but I want to assure you that neither the Boston nor Philadelphia is here with us. It is just the Chicago Symphony!"

Cue laughter.

From his aisle seat in row 10, Elliott Carter stood and walked up the red carpet to the exit. Most people did not recognize him, thinking it was an elderly man leaving for some personal reason. But I could see him clearly, as could the orchestra. We went on with our demonstration of metric modulation and where each of the three orchestras was located physically on the stage.

When we finished performing the work, I could make out the offstage frantic gestures of the CSO artistic administrator, Martha Gilmer, as she motioned a signal to let me know not to ask Carter for a bow. I mouthed, "I know," to her and left the stage. We got three curtain calls for the piece that night.

When the first half ended, Martha reported that Carter had gone to the box office and in a rather huffy tone said, "I did not need to come to Chicago to be insulted." One of the stagehands quipped, "Where *did* he want to go for that?"

Intermission saw a flood of musicians coming to my dressing room. They thought that the talk was perfect and supported me, but the opposite point of view was expressed to me at dinner by John Edwards. He reprimanded me for not honoring the wish of a distinguished composer. I said that the audience deserved to know how to listen to this type of music. John was adamant, telling me that if I chose to speak at the next concert, Carter would not attend, but if I agreed to say nothing, he would.

All this took place on a Thursday. The next day, at nine in the morning, the phone rang. It was the music critic of the *Chicago Sun-Times*, Robert C. Marsh.

"I want to thank you. In all my years with the paper, I have never made the front page until now. Even when Solti was appointed."

When I hung up, I called down to the front desk to get a copy of what had been written. Sure enough, there it was!

"Noted composer walks out on CSO."

That angle had not even crossed my mind. The orchestra was furious and the article quoted some of the members. The feeling was not that we performers had insulted the Carter; rather, that the composer had turned his back on us.

The second performance was that afternoon. As is the case with Friday matinees in the States, the audience tends to be older and predominantly female. I had found from my other concerts over the years that this crowd was receptive when confronted with new music. But this time they expected the now-controversial speech and demonstration. I walked onto the stage, faced the orchestra and just played the work through. Acknowledging Carter, I left and that was it. One bow only. No further applause, quite a contrast to the night before. The piece had made no impact whatsoever.

Mr. Carter had to be elsewhere on the Saturday night when we had the final performance of the program. So I was able to reinstate the talk. Once again the reception exceeded merely polite. I knew it defied his wishes, and perhaps the day will come when this music is not so difficult to digest, but listeners need to be informed through more than program notes alone. Those conductors comfortable with on- and offstage presentations need to serve as the strongest advocates for all music. And if we do our jobs properly, the audience might just return to hear additional works by the same composer.

But the story has a coda too.

About a year later, I got a call from Nick Webster, executive director of the New York Philharmonic. He told me that Zubin Mehta needed shoulder surgery and had to cancel five weeks of performances. Would it be possible for me to fill any of the vacant slots?

I asked for the dates so I could check them against my own schedule. Nick was particularly interested in a specific week. When I asked him why that one, he replied, "We are supposed to play the Carter *Symphony of Three Orchestras*."

"Nick, do you know what happened in Chicago last year?"

"Yes, but Mr. Carter has asked for you."

"Why?"

"He thinks you do the piece very well."

Unfortunately, I was unavailable to fill in any of the weeks for the Phil, but I realized that I needed to repair some of my foolishness. So I phoned Mr. Carter and asked if I could have the premiere of his *Three Occasions*. He granted this and came to the concerts in New York when we played it with the Saint Louis Symphony. I apologized for my behavior in Chicago, but insisted that my talk had helped listeners appreciate his works. We chatted and Carter admitted that perhaps his demeanor was wrong headed. He had mellowed, too.

20

As the World Turned

When I die, just keep playing the records.

—JIMI HENDRIX

Authors have books, scientists have theories, and painters have the canvas. Even the composer has the printed music. But when it comes to performing artists, after a lifetime of devotion to the cause, they could only leave behind memories and memorabilia, such as program books. At least that is how it was until the early 1900s.

The twentieth century provided a new and innovative way of preserving the musicians' art in sound. The recording medium allowed the listening audience an opportunity to, at least, hear performers, whether singers, instrumentalists or conductors, practicing their craft. We owe a great deal to Thomas Edison. In 1877, when he uttered "Mary had a little lamb" into his tinfoil recording device, a new era had dawned.

Not long afterward musicians realized the potential of this invention. Enrico Caruso embraced it. Herbert von Karajan refined it. The "historically informed" crusaders would not be in the forefront without recording. Whole careers have been fashioned from it.

The history of the recorded art is readily available. Information not written about is the actual process of making an orchestral disc. As with most aspects of music, there are various ways to do it. I have recorded in America and Europe. Despite the differences, the process starts in the studio with one person, the producer.

Probably the first people in this profession had it easier. The extent of the job entailed checking for decent sound and letting the performers go their own way.

That first medium, the wax cylinder, was limited to one take, with no opportunity for editing. In addition, it only recorded about three minutes at one time.

Today, producers have twenty-four and forty-eight tracks to deal with. The miking techniques are complex and the soundboards look like panels on a 747. Most sessions, at the basic level, need at least one engineer, the person who will move around equipment and set levels. It is not uncommon now to see four or five people on the production team. But for me, in 1975, just two people sat in the booth and one hundred onstage.

The first recordings in nearly two decades by the Saint Louis Symphony were made for Vox, one of the earliest of the budget labels. The low cost of the discs also meant a sacrifice in actual recording time. In the days of the LP album, you tried to get all of the music on one disc, about forty-five to fifty minutes in two three-hour sessions. The Gershwin project, the first integral cycle of his complete orchestral works, would occupy three discs but would be done in six sessions, over just three days. I had a distinct advantage of having witnessed my parents record constantly throughout their careers. Especially helpful was watching my father conduct his Hollywood Bowl recordings.

To be a bit more secure about some not exactly standard repertoire—the Second Rhapsody, *Lullaby for Strings* and Gershwin's own Suite from *Porgy and Bess*—we scheduled two concerts so we could prepare the pieces. The other option was to just record them cold, but that really could not be done given the time constraints. The pianist in the four works featuring the keyboard was Jeffery Siegel. Rehearsals went fine, and the concerts were outdoors as this was our summer season. But Jeffrey developed a kidney stone and was in severe pain. Plus, the second concert was rained out!

The day before the sessions began, I was introduced to the dynamic production team of Marc Aubort and Joanna Nickrenz. Marc was the engineer with enough credentials to give him access to any recording facility in the world. Joanna, whom we nicknamed "Razor Ears," would produce. The pair had been working together for many years and we were lucky to have them.

We had to sort out the recording order. How could we get 150 minutes of music taped in 18 hours? That second number is misleading. The orchestra required a total of one hour in break time during each three-hour session. That meant that we were facing twelve hours while the machines were running. That sounds like a lot of time, but it really isn't. The music is surprisingly difficult, and the recorded art needs greater accuracy than a concert. In our favor was the quantity of solo piano passages in the pieces with Jeffrey. Because he was not operating on a union contract for this, he could drop them in after the sessions were over, but the union rules said he had to play them once with the orchestra onstage. I cannot fathom the logic in this.

We started with *An American in Paris*, the Gershwin piece we probably knew best. Marc had scouted out the Powell Hall acoustics and took a guess as to the best placement of the microphones. Nevertheless, it still took a good twenty minutes of balancing with the orchestra to feel secure. I stepped into the booth during a short break and listened to the playback to determine if it was the sound I wanted. Did it capture the atmosphere of the hall? Was it natural? Too much brass? Not enough woodwinds? Plus, we were recording in quadraphonic sound, a precursor of today's surround sound, so the rear channels needed adjustment for hall ambience.

Most musicians prefer a single, complete take of a piece, whether an overture or a movement of a symphony. It provides the producer with a framework and overview of how the artists want the piece to go. After that initial stab, the musicians take another break and head to the control room—the green room in Saint Louis—and listen to the playback. Because so few in the orchestra had made a recording in recent memory, the room was jam-packed with people chiming in about this or that. "Is my solo free enough?" "I can't hear myself." "The brass is too loud!"

Normally, as we would learn when we had a bit more time, the pattern wound up with an inevitable second take, but we had to immediately start putting the pieces together. Joanna was amazing! We began at the beginning of the work, and she would stop us about two bars after something that either was not correct the first time around, or did not go well on the second try. I used to think that I had good ears, but she topped everyone I have ever met, with the possible exception of Jean Morel.

Communication between the stage and recording booth is done in two ways. When the producer calls out, "Take forty-two," for example, a red light goes on to signal us to be quiet and start recording. Through a monitor located near the podium, the producer and engineer can talk to the entire group onstage. Of course, because those mikes are all over the place, they pick up all our chatter, too. Once in a while that can be embarrassing. There is also a telephone near the conductor's music stand. This is for circumstances when those in the booth are not sure if what they are about to say is confidential. The message could be about intonation, ensemble or simply wrong notes. After trying both ways, I asked that everything be out in the open for all to hear, and did not use the phone again.

When we had completed *An American in Paris*, Joanna asked if any orchestra members wanted to repeat particular passages. This was very smart, as she helped build confidence in all those onstage. To save a little time, we did the orchestra-only pieces in one session, followed by the works with piano in the afternoon. That way, Marc would not have to reset mikes with breaks of just ten or fifteen minutes. Yes, we did have the piano technician waiting in the wings, and she would adjust the instrument at every available opportunity.

For the *Cuban Overture*, we decided to take advantage of the four-channel technology, so we put the Latin percussion out in the hall and isolated them to the rear channels. When played back on two-track stereo systems, the sound "folds in" and it becomes part of the instrumental fabric. For the fifty people who maybe had a quad setup at home, it was heaven to hear musicians both in front and behind. This experience was new to us, but Marc kept us apprised each step of the way. It was fortunate that we had no electronic malfunctions.

As the final session was coming to a close, we were painfully aware that there would not be enough time to record and patch up the delightful *Promenade* (*Walkin' the Dog*). This was the one piece that we had never rehearsed or performed. Joanna urged us to play it once and hope for the best. The orchestra's principal clarinetist, George Silfies, delivered what could be described as a miraculous rendition, and the infectious nature of his playing inspired us all. What you hear on the recording is the only take we did of the piece.

Conducting for records is quite different than concerts, even when you play a work through from beginning to end. You always have to be aware of your tempi, keeping in mind the time when you will go back and re-record a passage. Often you might end a session and pick up the same piece the next day, trying to replicate what you did almost eighteen hours earlier. The producer will stop you mid-phrase at the most awkward moments, then have you back up about six or seven bars to correct the error in question. The repetition can be frustrating. Sometimes a player will freeze in a passage and you either have to keep trying to get it right or come back to it later. There is a stamina issue as well, but that is the reason there are breaks.

A couple of months later, the team reunited in New York, where Marc and Joanna had a studio called Elite Recordings. That is where we worked and edited. Ideally, it is preferable when some time has elapsed between the sessions and the postproduction. You can be more objective when the adrenaline rush is not a factor. Joanna had assembled what she regarded the best of the takes. When we heard something that we did not care for, we would ask if a better take existed Most of the time the answer was no, but in some situations we would listen to the three or four takes to see if any worked better. Jeffrey's solo sections had been added to the mix and we left feeling pretty good.

Vox Records was elated. This was about to become one of the best-selling albums in the history of the company. To this day, the recording has never gone out of print.

The Elite team would collaborate on several additional projects with Vox and us. Among them was a set of the complete works for piano and orchestra by Rachmaninov, with pianist Abbey Simon. At the very end of the last session, we had about ten minutes left and I suggested that we record the orchestral version of the composer's *Vocalise*. Abbey sat still and we put it down in one take. The folks at Vox did not know what to do with this individual item. It became the impetus for our recording the remaining six discs of Rachmaninov's orchestral and choral works: we embarked on the project just so the little *Vocalise* would have some company.

In 1979, another company approached the Saint Louis Symphony, the Cleve-land-based Telarc. This high-end audiophile label wanted to record in Powell Hall. Bob Woods was the founder and producer and Jack Renner the engineer. Their approach was quite a contrast to that of Elite Recordings—in some ways, not so detailed in musical structure, but paying much more attention to the actual sonics. They sure loved their bass drum thwacks.

The process was nearly identical: two full takes, then stop and start. One evening, we were doing the final section of Mahler's Second Symphony, with its huge orchestral forces, chorus and soloists. We finished the fifteen-minute epilogue, utterly drained. Bob asked if I wanted to listen to the playback. I said

no. Whatever I would hear could not match the collective feelings we experienced during that take. Like the little *Promenade*, the disc had just that one go
at it, including my stomping on the podium at a climactic moment.

The record executive Thomas Shepard was driving along in New Jersey in 1973
listening to a recorded concert on the radio. As he pulled into his driveway, he
sat with the engine running waiting for the announcer to inform the listeners
as to who had been performing. It was Saint Louis. That was the genesis of our
relationship with RCA. Our first disc was of the Prokofiev Symphony No. 5. A
new producer came on the scene for us: Jay David Saks. He was amusing and
also had tremendous ears, but was less direct in his criticisms than Joanna. He
always tried to say something nice even if what we had recorded was awful. His
most devastating line that I recall was, "What can I say?"

This first venture with RCA would earn us a Grammy. We had been nominated several times previously, never expecting to win. Ten years after our
initial recordings for Vox, we had a gold statuette. And it surprised the hell out
of everybody in the industry. How did this upstart orchestra from the Midwest
manage it?

European recordings followed for me, mostly conducting London orchestras—first the LPO, then the Philharmonia and last, the BBC. The producer for
the majority of these was Andrew Keener, a former music critic. In addition to
doing the best Margaret Thatcher imitation of anyone alive, he was similar to
Joanna in that his hearing was extremely sharp. We recorded in many venues,
including Abbey Road. I don't care if it is a cliché, but you really can see the Fab
Four in the famed crosswalk.

Most of the discs featured English repertoire. Lots of Elgar, Walton and the
complete Vaughan Williams symphonies. CDs were now in full sway, rapidly
supplanting the LP, and this required adding fillers to the discs to flesh out the
almost eighty minutes available. For the VW cycle, Andrew suggested that we
record that composer's *Five Variants of Dives and Lazarus*. I knew the work by
name alone, but Keener assured me I could sight-read it at the session.

I took him at his word and did not open the score until the red light came on.
This lovely piece for strings and harp cast a spell on me right from the opening
chords. When we had finished the first take, I told Andrew that I loved this piece.

"Was it all right?" I asked.

His gentle voice replied, for everyone to hear, "That was very nice, but you did it about three times slower than it is supposed to go."

Recording sessions in Europe varied slightly from those in the States. The three-hour sessions included only one fifteen-minute break instead of an hour. I thought this was wonderful until I learned of a restriction on the quantity of usable material that could come from a single session. Instead of taking a full break to listen to playbacks, I got off the podium, entered the booth to listen, then returned to the studio. The orchestra waited in their seats the whole time, reading books and papers, having coffee and tea, not caring much about the activities in the back room.

Marc Aubort had difficulty converting to the digital age, and so in Saint Louis we changed engineers. The symphony's soundman, Bill Hoekstra, who handled our broadcast work, now took care of the mikes. One year, when nominated for a Grammy, his name was announced as a winner, but this was in error and the award was rescinded. The group all felt so sorry that we had a replica of the golden gramophone made for him anyway.

His finest moment was during the recording of the Barber Piano Concerto with John Browning. We were having trouble getting the piano to sound just right. At that time, the recording booth had moved from the green room to the musicians' lounge downstairs. There was a pool table there. Bill picked up a cue stick, used it to prop the piano lid even higher than normal, and voilà, we had the right sound.

The '70s and '80s marked the closing years of the great recording boom. I was making five or six discs a year. Almost anything I wanted to do was recorded. Elgar's slightly obscure oratorio, *The Kingdom*? Sure, go ahead. A ten-disc series of American music? No problem. Operas? Of course!

And then it all came crashing down.

The German conglomerate BMG purchased RCA. After a few years, a number-cruncher examined the books and discovered—surprise!—classical music was not selling. Artists on most major labels were dropped. My own contract was actually bought out. With the National Symphony, I only made three discs, although the initial offering of Corigliano's First Symphony won two Grammys.

After a lull of about six years, I did some recordings with Chandos and the BBC Symphony. But more fulfilling was developing a relationship with upstart Naxos, an even more budget-conscious label than Vox. Our first project was the massive *Songs of Innocence and Experience* by William Bolcom. This piece, with forces of almost six hundred performers, garnered a record-setting four Grammys in 2006. To bring the size of this endeavor into some fiscal sanity, we recorded it with musicians from the University of Michigan. The chorus seemed to have almost anybody in Ann Arbor who could sing. What would have cost at least $1.5 million professionally, we accomplished for around $75,000. I wonder if listeners really would have noticed any difference if we had not put the school's name on the cover.

A couple of years later I won two more Grammys, this time for a disc of music by Joan Tower, recorded in Nashville. I am very proud that, so far, of the seven awards, six are for American music. And the head of Naxos, Klaus Heymann, forever seems one step ahead of the media curve. It may not pay much, but I have enjoyed every project with them.

To reduce expenses, an increasing number of orchestras are turning to self-produced recordings. This has advantages, but usually lacks the distribution power of a big label. I also still believe that handing someone a tangible manifestation of your labor is beneficial; the CD continues to be a powerful tool in promotion and fund-raising.

As far as identifying which are my favorites among my hundred-plus discs, I cannot. But the worst is easy: a completely wrong-headed partnership of the Saint Louis orchestra and the jazz/fusion pianist Deodato. He had a big hit recording with his riff on *Also sprach Zarathustra* and someone had the bright idea that he should record it with symphony orchestra.

We were taking the recording live from just one performance at the now defunct Mississippi River Festival. The band showed up an hour late for the rehearsal. By the time of the concert, a variety of aromas were wafting out of the dressing rooms. The trumpet player missed more notes than he hit. You can audibly hear the editing throughout the recording. I insisted that my name not appear on the jacket. You will not find any copies. I bought them all and burned them.

These days we have more avenues for reaching audiences than ever before. It remains to be seen how, and how well, orchestras and artists will use the technologies at our disposal. Certainly a number of issues will arise regarding funding for new media projects. Personally, I have never fully understood separate compensation for recording, especially if taken straight from the concert. Are we going to play better because we know this concert will pay more than last week's? I should hope this thought never enters the musician's head.

Maybe it boils down to a few minutes I spent at the Museum of the Hollywood Bowl. I asked the curator if she had all of my father's recordings. Her belief was that they were all there but, in fact, one was missing. I asked how we might locate them, and the two of us turned to the Internet. We discovered a site that offered downloads of my dad's discs for a dollar apiece.

My own thoughts focused on the proprietor: "Why should this guy make any money from my father's work?" Then I wondered what would happen if the website simply made them available for no fee. Actually, that would not bother me one bit.

The same would be true for my out-of-print recordings. As long as no one else is profiting from my work, I do not care. These days, anything we can do to get our message out there, while controlling the quality of the content, is paramount.

Still, there is nothing quite like returning to the studio, whether for concerts, films or radio. As far as classical music videos go, if I never see another shot of the poised flute player framed between the harp strings, it will be too soon. Somehow, we can listen over and over to an audio recording, but a visual version rarely elicits more than a single viewing.

Growing up on soundstages, it is surprising how little I have done in the way of movie music, at least for the big screen. In the '70s I was asked to do a couple of soundtrack albums, but that was about it.

Then in 1984, I received a message from Lionel Newman at 20th Century Fox. The studio was in the final stages of making a film called *Unfaithfully Yours*, a remake of a '40s classic. Besides an original soundtrack, the film called for some passages of classical music. For these segments, the studio decided to use the Los Angeles Philharmonic. The members were not seen on-screen, so I wondered what the point was, as classically trained freelancers did the remaining music and would have sufficed.

Nonetheless, Lionel thought it would be a nice idea for me to work on the same sound stage as my dad. He was right.

For a few moments in the film, a violin soloist, one of the main characters, is seen playing the Tchaikovsky Concerto. For this, they brought in Pinky Zukerman. Most of the excerpts were not very long, but we needed to coordinate with the visuals seen on-screen. The actors had been coached extremely well and did a good job following whatever prerecorded version was used.

The first thirty seconds or so of Beethoven's Fifth Symphony comprised one clip. We had to wait for the delivery of the canister of film so we could sync with it. After a while, I inquired about the recording Dudley Moore had used in the shooting of the sequence. It was a von Karajan rendition. I thought that if we simply played it a few times, one take was bound to match up. I worried that the same rules of overtime payment to symphony orchestras applied to the movie music industry.

Lionel pulled me aside. "How much do you do you think it costs the studio to pay for fifteen minutes of overtime?"

"I have no idea."

Lionel said, "Let's just say ten thousand dollars, even though that is probably high." He continued, "Now what do you think the budget is on this film?"

"I have no idea."

"Let's say about twenty million dollars. Do you really think the overtime is going to make that much difference to the studio?"

I got the point and we waited for the clip to arrive.

Television has played a role in my life as well, and not just with broadcast concerts. When I accepted the directorship in Saint Louis, the general manager of the local CBS affiliate had attended a concert that included the Shostakovich Fifth Symphony. He said that the program notes indicated some interpretive points that only recently had come to light. Asking me if I could explain this, I said that I could, but that the best way to comprehend it required comparing the differences from the more traditional viewpoint of interpretation.

The next day, he brought in a couple cameras, lights and a soundman. There was no director. I sat at the piano and tried to show what made this work controversial. After CBS viewed the demonstration, they proposed that I could have my own half-hour TV show. Its form would serve as a preview for the upcoming week's concerts. I could do whatever I wanted. The show would air at four in the morning on Mondays!

To generate a modicum of interest, advertising time was purchased on some very popular shows the preceding evening, in particular *60 Minutes* and *Murder, She Wrote*. Viewers were instructed to tape the preview, and watch at their leisure prior to coming downtown for the concert. They were also informed that if they had problems and the tape machines were flashing "oo:oo," a hotline with technical help would be available.

I have no idea how many people were up at that hour, but we did learn that on one morning, up to thirty thousand households had recorded the show. We never knew how this translated into attendance for the concert, but at least we had made an inroad with an audience that we may not have known existed.

The show aired for three seasons.

In my second season with Detroit, we came up with an unusual way to showcase the orchestra. Our goal was to humanize both the players and audience. The result was a ten-part series called *Making Music*. Each episode featured a topic that was then explored from different points of view.

One show had the title "Mommy, Do I Have to Practice?" We spoke with orchestra members, students, and musicians from the jazz and pop world, as well as some of our patrons. In the final scene, one of our percussionists gives a marimba lesson to an elderly lady who had never had any music instruction in her life.

We looked into what the musicians did in their off-hours. One episode was devoted to the staff working behind the scenes—librarians, stage crew and box office. In another, I even gave a conducting lesson to a security officer at one of the local malls.

With a tiny budget and just one person dealing with cameras, lights and action, this effort truly seemed a miracle. Perhaps some day it will be viewed nationally and maybe the concept will get picked up for another series. The show did win a local Emmy.

Interacting with the various media remains an important activity during current times, and has less to do with the question of being photogenic—I do not qualify in that category—and more to do with having some command of microphone and camera technique.

Most of us fail to think about preserving a legacy, as our principal desire is to make great music, but awareness of potential media outlets is helpful. The more ways we can reach our listeners and viewers, the better.

Audio and video reproduction can never replace the experience of the live concert. We must all play a role in assuring that audiences experience the distinctions.

21

Days and Nights at the Opera

*I don't think an opera house is ever a place that can make you
entirely happy.*

—BERNARD HAITINK

There was a time when virtually all orchestral conductors came from the world of the theater. Whether it was Wagner, Mahler, Toscanini, Walter, Reiner or Szell, people assumed that your credentials on the concert platform were only as good as those in the pit. For a number of reasons, this changed, probably beginning in the mid-twentieth century.

First of all, the orchestral repertoire increased substantially, whereas the operatic output diminished. Some conductors were beginning to prefer a career onstage for greater visibility and connection with their audiences. Motion pictures and television were mediums that placed their stars in front of the public, and conductors wished to follow suit. Record companies were searching for more glamorous figures as poster children, with wavy hair and dashing good looks.

I have conducted about two dozen operas, yet this part of my musical experience has been considerably more limited than my concert appearances. And repertoire is not the reason. The stage works that I have performed have consistently yielded the greatest of musical pleasures. Sometimes the antics of wayward stage directors and divas have been tumultuous, but the opportunity to realize masterpieces by Verdi, Puccini, Strauss and Mozart has outweighed any downside and provided more than ample rewards.

Growing up in the Slatkin household and listening almost daily to the finest string quartets and chamber music of, among others, Brahms, Schubert, Schumann, Mendelssohn and Bartók, it was impossible to imagine any other equally sublime music. It was as if each composer reached down to a special place deep inside his being and found the inspiration to transcend his already formidable output. Is there really a Beethoven symphony that reaches the heights of his Op. 132? Or an orchestral work of Brahms that aches as intensely as the slow movement of his C Minor Piano Quartet? Where is our orchestral equivalent of Schubert's two-cello quintet?

There is one further consideration as well. With the exception of Mozart and possibly Britten, no successful composer seems to have produced both opera and chamber music of the same high caliber. We have a vast output of masterpieces in the smaller forms by Schubert, yet his operas simply do not work. And what of the greats who never composed an opera? Brahms, Liszt and Chopin come to mind.

The reverse is similarly true, with Wagner, Verdi nor Puccini producing no substantive body of chamber works. What of those composers who avoided both idioms—not the least, Gustav Mahler, one of history's extraordinary operatic and symphonic conductors? You would think that he might have created for the stage. But it seems as if the realms of opera and string quartet have always been mutually exclusive.

My mother told me that she first experienced opera when she was taken to the Metropolitan to see *Parsifal*. She was nine years old. Was this meant as a punishment for something the child did at home? As for me, the first taste was *Madame Butterfly* at the cavernous Shrine Auditorium in Los Angeles. I was thirteen years old and enjoyed the scenery, but I dozed off midway through the opening act. The opera was sung in Italian and surtitles were nonexistent back then. There was not even an explanation of what was going on.

My two primary conducting teachers, Jean Morel and Walter Susskind, were men of the opera house. They instructed students by having us study some scenes from the operatic repertoire. With Morel, we learned *Carmen* and *Tales of Hoffmann*. Susskind asked me to do *La bohème* in Aspen as well as the American premiere of Walton's *The Bear*.

My professional debut in the pit was with the Opera Theatre of Saint Louis. When I became music director of the orchestra, I was invited to lead a production of *Ariadne auf Naxos*, by Strauss. I had watched Jimmy Levine conduct the work in Aspen one summer and had enjoyed its combination of chamber-like music and a mostly innocuous story. Now I had landed in unfamiliar territory with staging rehearsals, piano rehearsals, production meetings, coaching sessions and the like. It was far more time consuming than I could have anticipated.

Most of the singers had not previously done the work, so I was not alone. As I grew more comfortable with the process, I felt ready to insert some of my own ideas. The Saint Louis company performs its productions in English, but I had another idea for this particular work. As the Prologue is primarily conversational, our native tongue seemed suitable. Since the majority of the opera itself is so well set and the story so simple, it seemed impossible anyone could misunderstand what was happening. I suggested, and we performed, this part of the second act in German, then in the middle, when the commedia dell' arte troupe enters the scene to disrupt things, we reverted to English.

The initial plunge was not so bad, and the experience whetted my curiosity to explore the operatic repertoire, but very selectively. The Lyric Opera of Chicago invited me to conduct *The Magic Flute*, *Salome*, *Elektra* and Corigliano's *Ghosts of Versailles*. This is a fabulous company, with every employee, from the star singers to a lone chorus member, treated equally. This style came from the manager, Ardis Krainik, who had been a singer earlier in her life. Particularly satisfying for me was that I had achieved success with both the symphony orchestra and the opera company in that city.

This also marked my introduction to a spacious operatic venue. All of a sudden, the people onstage seemed far away. I didn't know, for instance, if I was covering up their voices or if we even coordinated in some spots. So I spent several days going to other, more experienced opera conductors' rehearsals and performances. Sometimes I sat in the pit to try to get a better sense of the technique and how it differed from orchestral conducting. I had to readjust my physical gestures, broadening them and compensating for the sonic delay between stage and pit. If I could get the orchestra's volume soft enough for the orchestra to hear the singers, everything should go along smoothly.

My European opera debut came in 1985, leading Massenet's *Werther* in Stuttgart. The production was under the supervision of Giancarlo del Monaco, son of the legendary tenor Mario. His somewhat unusual concept did not stray horribly from the intention of the composer, and the two of us seemed to get along well.

There was an unpleasant moment with the orchestra, though. At the dress rehearsal, I entered the pit and started the Prelude. Just before the protagonist enters, there is a little oboe solo, and the player did not lift his instrument to his lips. I stopped, and an audible gasp came from behind me. No one had bothered to inform me of two facts: an audience was in attendance and you were never supposed to halt the proceedings at the dress rehearsal.

I gave a slight reprimand to the oboist, explaining that the tenor really needs this cue for his first entrance. We got through the rest of the rehearsal with no further problems.

On opening night, when we reached the same place, the oboe player just stared at me, again not bothering to play anything. The first flute leaned over, played the oboe solo and saved the evening.

Shortly before the second performance, the flutist came to my dressing room. I thanked him profusely for his thoughtful and musical gesture. He asked me if I would write a letter of recommendation for him.

"Why?" I inquired. "Are you auditioning somewhere else?"

"Because I have been fired for playing the oboe part."

"That's ridiculous," I shot back. "If it wasn't for you, we might have had a train wreck. I will be more than happy to speak to the orchestra committee on your behalf."

"I am afraid that won't do any good. The first oboist is the chairman of the committee."

My debut at the Vienna State Opera occurred the following season with *Turandot*. I had done this popular work in concert version several times. The score is glorious and tremendous fun to conduct. We had a terrific cast; the highlight for me was the opportunity to work with Mirella Freni, singing Liù. There was just one rehearsal, and the sets were not fully mounted on the stage. I acquitted myself well enough that I was invited back a few years later.

This started a descent into Opera Hell.

The trouble was not with the work, *La fanciulla del West*. I was surprised to find myself in sympathy with Puccini. Much less so with a good deal of Italian composers including Donizetti and Bellini, but some of Verdi held appeal to me. Plácido Domingo was the main attraction, and the opera was billed as a new production, thereby attempting to justify the exorbitant Salzburgian ticket prices. In fact, the production was not new, merely a revival of a version last seen twelve years earlier.

Fanciulla is not exactly a staple in any opera house's repertoire. Performances tend to be infrequent, due to the demands on the soprano and the reputation of the piece as a curiosity, with its story set in California during the gold rush and with the libretto's Americanisms sung in Italian. We were restricted by the amount of rehearsal time, so I tried to be as efficient as possible. My hope for a session alone with the chorus was denied because they were busily preparing *Parsifal* for the company's Easter tradition. I repeated my request:

"You do it every year and the chorus knows the work. *Fanciulla* is new to them."

"You will just have to rehearse with them at the first orchestra/stage meeting."

That day started with the third act and it was abundantly clear that the men of the chorus had no idea how this music was to be sung. This portion of the opera is only about twenty-five minutes long, and after running through it, I thanked the orchestra, sent them home and asked for a piano to be wheeled onstage so I could rehearse the chorus.

There followed a heated exchange with the director.

"This is an orchestra rehearsal. You cannot do it with piano."

"The orchestra knows the music. There is no point to keep them here just to teach the singers the notes."

"We are sorry, but this is the law of the house."

"How can you tolerate this?!" I screamed.

"The law is the law."

"And you agree with this law?"

"It does not matter what I think. There is nothing I can do."

"Just tell me if you agree with it." By this time, my face was inches from his.

"No, but it cannot be changed."

He might as well have said he was just following orders.

The assistant conductor tried to calm me down and said that we should go up to the pursers' office, as it was Friday. We were paid in cash on a weekly basis. When I got there, a man behind the window said, "I see you canceled an orchestra rehearsal earlier this week."

"Yes, we worked quickly, and without the singers present, there was no need to go through the work again."

"I cannot pay you since you did not fulfill the number of services called for in your contract, but I can give you a loan for the weekend."

"No, thank you."

Next stop, the intendant's office.

He noted that there were apparent problems. After touching on the company's background and history, the intendant said that the Vienna State Opera has always been a tough place to work, dating as far back as when Gustav Mahler was the director, and it certainly was time that things changed.

I offered to speak to anyone during the remainder of my stay to help facilitate the changes.

"No, we will probably not get around to it for quite a while."

That night, I almost started packing to go home.

The shows went decently enough. Plácido and I established a rapport that has lasted to this day.

A memorable, amusing incident, or maybe not so funny on second thought, happened at the final performance. This was a benefit for the World Wildlife Fund. I was asked permission for a presentation to be made before the curtain went up.

For five minutes, three children and one adult stood at the edge of the stage in panda outfits and thanked the crowd for helping to protect the animals. I started laughing before I made my entrance into the pit.

When the curtain rose on the saloon in Sacramento, on the walls were . . . you guessed it: bearskin rugs!

Then there was the scandal in Hamburg. The opera was *Tosca* and it reunited me with Giancarlo del Monaco. The Stuttgart *Werther* turned out to be a big hit and everyone agreed that we would work well together again.

I knew something was wrong when we had the first production meeting.

"Everyone knows this opera," Giancarlo said. "We need to make it new."

All the traditions were tossed out. There was no church in the first act. No portrait of Tosca, just a blank canvas on a seven-foot easel, "because everyone knows what she looks like." During the great Te Deum, the chorus crawled like cats, while behind them a gigantic image of a crucifix morphed into a guillotine. Someone carrying a mirror angled it to reflect a laser beam at the audience. All this was supposed to represent the point of view that the story is seen as a nightmare of Scarpia. I tried to emphasize that people cannot dream of their own death, and if that happened, there would be no third act, but my logic fell on deaf ears.

By the last act, the spectacle had totally lost its way. No one was onstage other than Cavaradossi for the first fifteen minutes. The jailer was heard but not seen. The tenor was executed, but with the gunfire coming from the wings and the bullets magically invading his cell, the action managed to defy pretty much every law of physics. His body was finally put on a gurney and rolled to the opposite side of the stage where Tosca realized the horror of the deception. But did she jump off the parapet and kill herself? No, there was no place to leap from, and besides, in this version, Tosca did not die. An angel's wing appeared with an appendage, an obvious phallic symbol, and when she declared that she and Scarpia will meet before God, the curtain came down. I could not repress the fantasy that an announcement, "Coming next summer, *Tosca* Part II, *The Revenge!*" should appear at that point.

I now know how to spell *boo* in German. It is *Buh*. How did I learn this? Because the word was on the front page of the papers the next morning! A cultural difference I did not know is that in European opera houses, the conductor is considered a part of the production team, and after the opening night, whenever I took a bow, the audience regaled me with heckling and taunts. This was due not to my conducting but my association with this monstrous production. The last night, I was so scared that I did not even venture onto the stage.

Giancarlo would eventually admit that his intention all along was to create a sensation in Hamburg. He sure accomplished that goal. I facetiously suggested that if he could change things, why couldn't I do the same? After all, operagoers know the first two bars of the first act. Why not skim ahead and just start with the chase music? And the magnificent clarinet solo that precedes Cavaradossi's aria in the third act? Let's have it played on bassoon instead, an octave lower.

I truly do not comprehend why producers and directors can indulge in these kinds of liberties, but the musicians cannot. Most operas, from Mozart onward, are explicit as to dramatic intention. We have instructions from the composer and librettist. Recasting a piece is no problem as long as it does not contradict the text, but wholesale altering of the meaning in an opera or play seems cavalier at best. One day, if the economic gods would allow the fantasy, an opera house will offer two versions of the same work. One would be traditional in the stage concept and the other would be experimental. I wonder which would attract the larger audience, and which would bring the audience satisfaction?

Giancarlo and I would collaborate on one more production, this time at the Met. It was my debut at the house and when I heard who would direct, I almost did not accept the engagement. But assurances were given that this would be a normal version of *Fanciulla* and would not be set in outer space. Indeed, it was beautiful.

In general, the good experiences have outweighed the bad ones. But I still contemplate elements that trouble me. Perhaps it is the nature of opera itself. The form is bound by the story that is being told. Despite freedoms to enjoy in the music, the story must come through, although you never see the name of the author or librettist printed in the same size typeface as that of the composer. It is still Verdi's *Otello*.

But the world of concert music offers abstract pleasures. Listeners can be guided by the sound and create their own imagery. I might feel one way about a given piece, and the next day completely change my mind regarding its ebb and flow. This really cannot happen in opera. Once the show is in running, it is exactly that, a show. This term is not meant as condescension, just a perspective.

In some ways, I prefer doing operas in concert. This doesn't suit the whole repertoire, almost any Rossini opera, for instance. Having the resources of a first-rate symphony orchestra, without the sonic limitations of the average pit, is extremely gratifying. Semi-staged performances, where the singers act out their roles without sets or costumes, can be equally effective. The coordination between the various forces is more easily accomplished, but the conductor has to be more careful about balances. I know many singers who now prefer this method of presentation. Some are simply tired of boorish directors who make them do outlandish and unmusical actions. Others prefer the direct interaction with the audience, usually unseen from the operatic stage due to the darkness of the house and lights right on the vocalists' faces.

Recording opera is also gratifying but challenging. In reality, this is almost like doing a concert performance with no visual aids to move the story forward, only the words and music. So it is important that the works being committed to posterity are truly worthwhile. There have been three recordings of opera so far in my life. Just prior to doing *Fanciulla* at the Met, I participated in a studio production in Munich. We had plenty of time to prepare, but unlike the recording of most symphonies, for opera, the scenes are recorded piecemeal, utilizing whoever is available on a given day, then cobbled together.

It was a period of discoveries. We found a minute of music that Puccini excised after the premiere. It is not particularly consequential, but this is the stuff that musicologists love. It also served to clarify a textural discrepancy. The Hungarian soprano Eva Marton was the Minnie, and she had never sung the role. Teaching her Americanisms was delightful, and at one moment, she used a line from a Gary Larson *Far Side* cartoon. After a grueling set of takes in the second act, she told the group that she needed a break because "my brain is full."

It was back to Munich for Gounod's *Roméo et Juliette*. For this recording, we had Plácido Domingo, but only for three days. He was the consummate professional. If his voice was not in the right place for a passage, we delayed taping that particular line for a day. He omitted certain notes, aware that he would be able to return to the studio a few weeks later and drop in those missing pitches during the editing process.

On the final day, Plácido belted out a high C. It was amazing! The musicians erupted in cheers and applause. A few months later, when the first edit of the recording came my way, the top note had vanished. I called him and asked what happened.

"Leonard, I know it was good but if people heard this from me now, they would expect it every time I sing."

Of the three recorded operas I have done, the one closest to my heart was taped in London during my tenure with the BBC. Samuel Barber's *Vanessa* had been sorely neglected since its premiere in 1956. Only one recording had been issued since that time.

Mine was taken from a concert performance at the Barbican, and the cast was ideal. Christine Brewer and Susan Graham took on the main roles. Both were exquisite, as was everyone else. A patch session was scheduled for the following day. Both women had colds and could not really sing out, but the performance from the night before was so extraordinary, we needed only minimal repairs.

Concert versions and recordings of opera seem well suited to me, and I will definitely venture into the pit a few more times. However, I will always take care to maintain the musical integrity that the score demands. If push comes to shove, I will walk away if a major conflict arises between the director and me. When it works, opera is utterly absorbing and a true melding of artistic thoughts.

But opera does provide us with the best music lore.

Here is one more *Tosca* story, from a production I did with the Washington Opera.

There were two casts, quite different but both good. One of the leading sopranos was afraid to lunge headfirst off the tower, even though constructed so the fall was less than two feet into thick foam padding, and stagehands positioned to catch her. Instead, she faced the audience and fell backward off the wall.

Maybe patrons seated in the front row did not realize that the pit conductor could hear any comments they made. As Tosca left the platform, a person behind me quipped, "And the Hungarian judge gives her a 4.5."

I am not so sure that I conducted the final few bars of the opera, but that night I did know that somewhere the Marx Brothers were smiling. The boys would not have liked what occurred ten years later.

22

Everybody Dies

My God, who do they think I am? Everybody?

—LEONARD BERNSTEIN

We all knew that he was ill. It was October 1990. The previous summer, Leonard Bernstein conducted what would turn out to be his final concert at Tanglewood.

As it happened, I was in New York with the Philharmonic that fateful month. During the first of a two-week stint, Nick Webster, the orchestra's executive director, came out onstage at the first rehearsal. He read a statement that said Bernstein was retiring from the concert platform. Stunned silence greeted the announcement, and everyone seemed to know what this really meant.

But no one knew how few days it would be until the end.

During that week, my program consisted of William Schuman's "Credendum," the Barber Piano Concerto with John Browning and Saint-Saëns' "Organ Symphony." I also had a pension fund concert with soprano Roberta Peters.

On the Sunday in between the two sets of concerts, my then-wife, Linda, and I traveled to Cherry Hill, New Jersey, where a chamber music series was run by my longtime friend and member of the Philadelphia Orchestra, Herb Light. We had agreed to perform a couple of numbers on his program that night.

A car was sent to pick us up from the hotel in New York to make the not-quite-two-hour trip. The driver had his radio on and I got tired of listening to the news about shootings, robberies and how poorly the Mets were doing. He turned it off.

The concert seemed to go well. One of the pieces we did on that program was a song by Bernstein from *Songfest*. When it was over, Linda and I looked at each other. The performance was fine but somehow did not feel very satisfying. We sensed something was wrong but did not have a clue as to what it might be.

The ride back to the city was devoid of radio content. We stopped off, got a bite to eat and returned to the hotel at about two in the morning. A stack of messages awaited me at the front desk. I was quite surprised and asked the night clerk if there was a problem.

"Don't you know? The maestro is dead!"

The originally scheduled program at the Philharmonic would have to be changed, but how would we pay tribute and memorialize a man who was larger than life? And how could we assemble the right musical forces with barely twenty-four hours' notice before the first rehearsal?

Sometimes the Philharmonic plays the previous week's program on the Tuesday following the other performances, with the morning rehearsal devoted to preparing the upcoming program. That was the case in this second week, so we had to decide what to do for the audience during the turnaround concert. I suggested the Adagietto from Mahler's Fifth Symphony as an appropriate alternative; it would replace the Schuman. We already knew that an all-Bernstein evening would serve for the rest of the week.

In short order, management put together a chorus for *Chichester Psalms* and found a boy soprano to sing the solos in the second movement. Concertmaster Glenn Dicterow, who was scheduled to play the Beethoven concerto with me that week, quickly relearned the *Serenade*, in which he had appeared with the composer countless times. Mezzo-soprano Wendy White, who had also worked closely with Bernstein, was engaged to sing the final movement of the "Jeremiah" Symphony.

But how would we open this memorial?

It could have been one of the Meditations from the *Mass*. Perhaps it could have been "Lonely Town" from *On the Town*. Even something from the "Kaddish" Symphony. Ultimately, there seemed only one perfect choice, the *Candide* Overture. Bernstein needed to be celebrated for his joy, as well as remembered in solemnity.

At the commencement of the Tuesday rehearsal, Nick addressed the musicians. He reported all he knew about the circumstances of Bernstein's death and the arrangements being made beyond this week. There would also be a visitation at the maestro's apartment.

Then he did something unexpected.

"If there are any of you who would like to share your thoughts about Lenny, please stand and tell us."

Several orchestra members related tales of working with Bernstein and how much he meant to them. Some of the stories were funny, some sad. All of them were heartfelt. This moment was very moving and unforgettable.

Then my turn came. I knew how difficult this rehearsal was going to be, but reminded the players that he lived for them and for music. The podium would forever be empty, no matter who stood on it, and I was humbled to be present at this time.

We launched into *Candide*.

Originally, I had not planned to rehearse the Mahler, just sight-read it at the concert. After all, this was a piece closely associated with Bernstein and the New York Philharmonic. But Carl Scheibler, the personnel manager and former horn player in Saint Louis, said that I really needed to play it at the end of the rehearsal.

He was right.

No more than halfway through, a number of orchestra members broke down in tears. It would not have been possible to perform the piece that night if we were seeing it for the first time at the concert. Although I have conducted the Adagietto often, that evening, the orchestra performed Bernstein's interpretation, slow and stately, filled with emotion. The whole orchestra sat onstage, even though the movement is scored only for strings and harp. I tried to stay out of the way as the instrumentalists poured out their hearts to the audience.

As the next two days progressed, the orchestra settled in to its routine. We worked as hard and quickly as possible to ensure that everything would fall into place. By the time of the concert, we all felt that the program was just right.

Bernstein's family attended, as did many dignitaries from the musical world and New York. An atmosphere of stillness filled the evening. The concert itself seemed to go well, with the orchestra already having grieved Tuesday morning.

The end of *Psalms*, which concluded the program, was met with more than the sound of silence. You could hear people in the audience weeping as the Amen floated across the stage. The experience was completely overwhelming.

I cannot really tell you about the performance. Perhaps it was good, maybe not. I do not remember. I have a recording from that evening. I will never listen to it. The memory of the man, his music and the spirit of that night will suffice.

The Kaddish had been said.

23

Hitting the Road

Being on tour is like being in limbo. It's like going from nowhere to nowhere.

—BOB DYLAN

Presenting concerts on your home turf is relatively unproblematic. Things can go wrong but are in your control. You know everyone, the stagehands are on your side, and the orchestra can figure out a way to get to the hall.

It is a whole different ball game when you leave home.

For the conductor, there are two kinds of touring. The first is guest conducting, where you are responsible only for yourself. In some respects, it is the easiest part of a conductor's life, but in other respects the most challenging. The second is hitting the road with your own orchestra. There is a third kind of touring, an in between, where you might be guest conducting an orchestra and it schedules a tour with you.

Let's start with the conductor as guest.

As opposed to the solo instrumentalist or singer, the conductor will typically spend at least a full week in one town. Other musicians generally have a series of one-nighters, and I have the utmost sympathy for them. I find it plenty difficult to stay in a different hotel, sleep in a different bed and see another orchestra week after week. I cannot imagine enduring this routine on a daily basis.

Assuming that the agent has made the contractual arrangements, here is what needs to be understood. Most of the time, the artists have to pay the transportation, lodging and food costs. When you factor in the commission and taxes, it may be stunning how little compensation you earn. As I got older, I tried to persuade the presenting organization to cover as many of these costs as possible, even if it meant a slightly reduced fee. The fewer the headaches, the better.

You pack accordingly, sometimes for a one-week visit and sometimes for a couple of months in various climates. Your choice of suitcase becomes important, especially if given weight restrictions. I try to keep one bag for clothes and another for the scores and peripherals. Sometimes, if I am lucky, my librarian will send not only my score in advance, but a whole set of parts. It is up to me to decide how much I need to reacquaint myself with the music to be performed. With the availability of full scores online, some of this burden has been lifted, but most conductors still prefer to have their own editions.

Anyone who might have come across my website will know two things I really hate: travel and photo shoots. Travel means delayed and canceled flights, missing luggage, turbulence and awful food. Conducting is, among other things, about keeping time. Airlines seem to be about losing it.

Once, going through security, the officer noticed a baton in my carry-on. She asked what it was. I tried to explain.

"Can this be used as a weapon?" she inquired.

You have no idea how close I was to saying words that probably would have landed me in jail.

Baggage claim is a great leveler. Luggage loss and mistaken identity have no discriminatory factors. I arrived in Los Angeles for my first rehearsals as the principal guest conductor at the Hollywood Bowl, and for the occasion, I had bought a fancy Tumi bag. As the luggage bounced around the carousel, I reached for what I presumed was mine. A voice behind me boomed, "That is mine, sir."

I did not turn around but did say that the bag was mine.

Another similar remark from the gentleman as I lifted the bag off the wheel of misfortune. "Once again, if you look closely you will see that this is not yours."

This time, I spun around to confront my accuser. It was William Shatner.

I was on the verge of absconding with Captain Kirk's suitcase!

We settled our difference, both having the same bag with minimal identification attached. The next night, at a reception following my debut, Shatner was in attendance. It seems he loves classical music and is a supporter of the Bowl. We had a good laugh before he beamed me out of Southern California.

The next phase on tour is to settle into the hotel, learn the location of its restaurant and find out if the facility offers Internet access. The last can be a major expense on the road if the hotel charges for this service. And when you are a music director, it is imperative that you be in touch with your office a couple times a day.

It was a little different in the prehistoric days of the telex and fax, not to mention telegram. In London, I arrived at one hotel and asked if they could telex a message to Saint Louis. I was told yes, as long as I gave the information to them before five in the afternoon.

"Why, does the telex machine stop working then?"

"No, the post office closes and that is where we send them from."

The personal calendar becomes the most important non-musical tool you have ever used. Your life depends on knowing when you arrive, what time and where the rehearsals are, and the proper attire for a performance. It becomes excruciatingly embarrassing if you miss a concert because you neglected to check what time it began.

Usually upon arrival, a representative from the orchestra will meet you at the airport. Sometimes it is the artistic administrator or his or her assistant, sometimes a driver hired by the orchestra, and once in a while, but rarely, the orchestra will have its own car. Or you simply might need to get to the destination on your own. This is a bit tricky when you do not speak the language and have not acclimated to the new environment. Even though you might have the hotel name correct, and the name of the venue where rehearsals are held, it helps to know which entrance to use. Most drivers in any country do not understand the notion of the "stage door," and inevitably bring you to the front of the building.

It's helpful to know a few words in the language of the country you are visiting. Certainly a greeting to the orchestra in that language helps, even if it is only to say, "Hello. I am sorry I do not speak Korean." One finds that almost every group has members who speak English, and they will let you know that right away. All musicians understand the usual instructions that will clarify what you want in the music. In many ways, one of the most useful experiences for the conductor is learning how to get your ideas across using fewer rather than more words.

Foreign heritage played a large part in shaping the musical voice of the United States. Toscanini's English was barely understood, Mahler spoke little, and Nikisch was almost exclusively Germanic. The arrival of Asian conductors meant a whole new lexicon had to be mastered. Of course, English is pretty much the universal language, controlling our air traffic and most international business affairs, and Italian musical terms are universally understood, but the conductor's art goes well beyond language and remains mostly unspoken.

To start with, we have our own special vocabulary. Musicians can get away with the basics of *long* and *short*, *fast* and *slow*, *louder* and *softer*. But that only goes so far. When one is practicing piano or violin, there is no need to speak to yourself. It is virtually impossible to rehearse what you are going to react to when it comes to seeing the orchestra.

During my years in high school, I took basic French. Not basic enough, as our class was highly inattentive, and by my first trip to Paris, whatever managed to pierce my brain had now disappeared. The first orchestras I saw, where the language issue would become paramount, were in Austria and Germany. My agent at the time, a spritely West Coaster named Mariedi Anders, had arranged my Vienna debut. She was Austrian and assured me that I would have no trouble communicating with the Wiener Symphoniker. My plane was delayed and when I arrived six hours late, there was Mariedi to meet me at the airport and escort me into town.

Prior to the rehearsals, I did something that developed into routine when on foreign soil: I wrote out the numbers in the score, utilizing the language of the country where I was performing. Learning the equivalents of *before* and *after* was easy. All I would have to do is say, for example, "*Sechs nach Eins und Zwanzig*" or "*Vier vor Sieben*," and everyone knew the measure where I wanted to begin. After that, the basics of "*ein bischen langer*," "*Schneller bitte*" and Mahler's favorite, "*nicht schleppen*," came into play on a regular basis. However, after a few attempts, some of the musicians chimed in, "We all speak English here." Although discouraging, I still gave Deutsch a shot once in a while and perhaps the effort was appreciated.

Sometimes a psychological barrier, not the language one, can stand in the way. Here is an extreme example.

For my German debut, I had been asked to do a set of concerts in Hamburg with the Nord-Deutsches Symphonie Orchester. This group had a distinguished pair of music directors, Hans Schmidt-Isserstedt and Klaus Tennstedt.

I was quite young and did not know of the orchestra's reputation for being very hard-nosed.

The program was strange, as two of the works were to be recorded live for Teldec. These featured the fine pianist Rudolf Buchbinder and he was playing the Ravel G Major as well as the Strauss *Burleske*. The bookend works were *Benvenuto Cellini* of Berlioz and Debussy's *La mer*. Not an ideal program for a German debut. At the first rehearsal, where I had decided to run through each of the pieces, it was clear that this repertoire was not terribly familiar to the orchestra.

During the famous chromatic octaves in the first movement of the Ravel, the principal oboist simply sat there, not playing a single note. I looked inquisitively and he continued to just stare straight ahead. After asking him if we could do this passage again, he said, "It cannot be played." I responded that it could be performed freely, but he would not budge. He suggested that the English horn player could play the low note, then he would play the upper, but that was hardly a credible solution. After intermission, I consulted the concertmaster about what action to take, and he said I needed to request another oboist. Apparently, as a civil service employee, the musician maintained this position until retirement and could do what he wanted in the meantime. Considering that we were recording, we needed the work performed correctly. I agreed that bringing in a new player was fine. Indeed, another oboist arrived; however, he merely played for the bar and a half of that passage!

Rehearsals plodded along. It was obvious that chemistry between the orchestra and me was lacking. The original concept was to make the disc based purely on two performances. I knew after the first one that we would not have it properly done, and asked for a session between concerts so we could make sure that we had every spot covered. At this "patch" session, the Ravel was up first. We managed it in about an hour, and the producer thought we had sufficient time to play through the whole of the Strauss before fixing it up.

After the twenty or so minutes of the *Burleske*, the orchestra members rose and started to leave. I exclaimed, "We still have an hour left of recording time! Where are you going?"

"We did not know you were going to play through the whole thing without stop. We are finished for the afternoon."

I was flabbergasted! Folks know that I keep my temper pretty much in check, but on that occasion I yelled, "I came to Germany expecting to learn of the great respect that you have for music. Clearly this is what you think." And I snatched up the scores, threw them on the floor, then stomped on them!

I stormed back to the dressing room, ready to pack my bags and go home. A good friend, the tenor Walter Planté, had attended the session. He had been singing at the house in Krefeld and was quite versed in the German system. His advice was that not only did I have to stay and do the final performance that evening, I needed to strive for the best concert I had ever conducted. Most likely the latter did not occur, but when it concluded, I headed straight to the producer of the recording and told him that if they wanted to issue the recording, the company would have to replace my name on the album as its conductor. I would not be associated with this orchestra.

Since then, I have worked with the NDR on many occasions and we have had a wonderful relationship.

A lot of conductors tell similar stories. We can never know exactly why it works and why it does not. In some cases, the language barrier could cause miscommunication. In other cases, the personality of the conductor just fails to sync with the orchestra. I had a less than successful debut with the Concertgebouw Orchestra and twenty years passed before I was invited back. The second time was a charm; then I returned on a regular basis.

It is always helpful to know the rules. Each orchestra situation has differing rehearsal schedules and break times. Usually, it is two and a half to three hours for the first session and sometimes a bit less for the second. Other orchestras will break up a five-hour rehearsal with two pauses and intermissions of thirty minutes each. Rehearsal orders are frequently determined in advance. In Madrid, you get three hours between the first half and the second, allowing for lunch and siesta. Still other orchestras rehearse in the morning and then do not commence again until the evening, convenient for those who teach or spend the afternoon at home.

Most Asian and European orchestras have a canteen where everyone gathers for lunch breaks and coffee. In Berlin, at the Philharmonie, the canteen is right off the stage. I guess it still bothers me to watch players drinking beer and other alcoholic beverages, knowing that in fifteen minutes they need to play the *Fantastique*. And despite the regulations changing overseas, be prepared for music and stage personnel smoking. On one occasion for a set of concerts with Kathleen Battle in Madrid, the position of her dressing room required her to pass through Nicotine Gulch on each trip to the stage. She complained, I switched rooms with her, and all was well.

Protocols for concerts vary, too, starting with the entrance of the orchestra. In the States, a majority of orchestral musicians gradually walk to their chairs onstage, tune and warm up with excerpts. As the concert begins the lights dim, the concertmaster makes an entrance, then the conductor comes onto the platform. A "European" entrance has the stage completely bare and then the members come in, en masse, to the applause of the audience. Normally, the concertmaster is one of the group, but sometimes he or she is accorded a separate entrance.

The reason for this is quite logical. As the figurehead representing the ensemble, the leader, as the principal position is known in the United Kingdom, accepts the applause on behalf of the orchestra. The conductor is a separate entity. In fact, in England, it is the assistant concertmaster who gets the tuning A from the oboe. When the leader enters, he or she simply bows and sits down, awaiting the conductor.

Business structure and management of an orchestra outside of the States are other elements different from what Americans are used to. First of all, the title *music director* is not consistently used. Sometimes it is *conductor*; other times, *chief conductor*; and sometimes *principal conductor*. The majority of musical decisions are left in the hands of the orchestra itself along with an intendant. This uncommon title refers to the person in charge of just about everything except the music taking place onstage.

During my four-year tenure at the helm of the BBC Symphony Orchestra, not only were my responsibilities fewer than expected, I was under the supervision of the general director of the orchestra as well as the head of Radio 3. Some of the repertoire was preordained and I was to conduct works that fit into the scheme of the planners. In my wildest dreams it would not be possible to imagine my choosing to do what they had in mind for me: the Piano Concerto by Alan Bush, featuring a tenor soloist and male chorus intoning pro-communist rhetoric. Or being part of the Schnittke weekend, where I conducted his unmemorable Third Symphony along with the very inventive *Faust Cantata*.

Interestingly, an idea that I had proposed a few years prior to the London gig actually materialized with another BBC Orchestra, the one in Manchester. The concept was based loosely on Aaron Copland's book *What to Listen for in Music*, and consisted of ten one-hour shows. We had the use of the orchestra to demonstrate points of melody, rhythm, harmony and the other fundamentals of music-making. I loved this project and hoped that a video component could be created.

For some reason, I got it into my head that honoring the American composer Leroy Anderson on the occasion of his centenary would be a splendid idea. Over the course of two years and five discs, we committed his complete output for release on Naxos. The BBC Concert Orchestra specializes in light music, but for these sessions, we were putting down a number of Anderson pieces that no one had ever recorded or published. Since most of the works ran no more than three or four minutes, the read-through was recorded, and often that is what wound up on the discs.

Another experience was a very bizarre recording of excerpts from *Porgy and Bess* made in East Berlin. I am confident that the Philips label knew what it was doing, but listening to the gentlemen of the chorus singing "*seben komm eleben,*" trying to imitate "seven, come eleven," was truly off-putting.

Audience behavior is a component of performance to familiarize yourself with when preparing for your first encounters abroad. I am continually asked about the distinctions between publics, and my answer inevitably describes the degree of attention felt emanating from the assembled masses. In general, with the exception of the radio orchestra populace, overseas audiences tend to be even more conservative than their American counterparts. When I submit programs, most of my new or unusual concepts are rejected. I have probably done the "New World" Symphony more often in Europe than in the "new world." Unless for a special theme or festival, I hardly presented American composers beyond the usual suspects, Copland, Bernstein, Gershwin. Every so often I would try to sneak in a newer piece, and if balanced on the rest of the program by Beethoven or Brahms, I got my way. The seasons at the BBC worked well, as I have a love of the English repertoire and for the most part, none of the other orchestras was doing a lot of Basically British during this particular period.

The applause ritual also varies from culture to culture. Overseas, concertgoers rarely award standing ovations, but they certainly do stomping ones. At the conclusion of a performance, the audience might stamp and clap in appreciation, often in rhythm and together. How they know when to do this, and in what tempo is a custom beyond me. In Germany, there have been occasions when the applause is so prolonged that the players exit the stage and leave the conductor to acknowledge the ovation alone.

Whistling is a no-no, an international equivalent of booing. And in the land where this form of derogation is prevalent in the opera house, the scandal of *Le sacre* no longer exists in the concert hall. Only once have I encountered it, for a piece by Joan Tower, a composer who really does not engender controversy. I presented a work of hers in Berlin with the Radio Symphony and there was a smattering of jeering when it ended. Neither Joan nor I could figure it out. Evidently, some people from the academic world of Donaueschingen came fully prepared to show their dismay for a conservative female composer.

The radio orchestras can afford this type of programming luxury due to the fact that they depend on neither fund-raising nor ticket sales to establish their budgets. To that end, the musical heads of these organizations do not have the overflowing social calendars mandated for music directors in the United States. The lack of this obligation has compelled more than one major conductor to abandon positions with American symphonies. It is all well and good to believe that music can exist without financial boundaries, but when you are the titular head of an orchestra, it is practically impossible to be disassociated from the responsibilities that come with the territory.

It has been most fascinating to see how orchestras have evolved, or not, in various parts of the world. Who would have believed that China would be producing world-class ensembles as well as outstanding soloists and conductors? Or that Venezuela would become the paradigm for music education? On the other hand, I am forever hearing accounts about the deterioration of music programs in the schools, even in Germany and France.

A story from my very first appearance in Madrid illustrates one sign of change. *Ein Heldenleben* by Richard Strauss was the main work scheduled. The orchestra was not very good; perhaps I was not, either. In any event, at the first rehearsal, I ran through the whole piece without pause. When we got to the moment where the trumpets are supposed to leave and play two fanfares from offstage, no one got up. They simply performed from their orchestral positions.

I did not say a word at the time, but when we got to the same passage during the next rehearsal, the same thing occurred. I asked why they did not leave and was informed that they never do.

"But the composer tells you where to depart and when to come back."

"We are sorry, but this is our tradition," he politely explained.

It turned out that the real problem lay in a concern over musicians walking off the stage in the middle of the performance. The audience might perceive that the trumpeters were fired on the spot. Our eventual decision, at least in order to get the desired effect, was to hire three more trumpet players who would only play the few bars of offstage music.

Strangely, in 2009, the notable Spanish conductor Rafael Frühbeck de Burgos was conducting the same work with my orchestra in Detroit. When this moment in the piece arrived, the trumpets simply put in mutes and the passage was played from onstage. I had dinner with the maestro after the concert and recounted my story. He said that keeping them onstage was a holdover from his youth and that he found it less disruptive.

Other small differences in conducting abroad involve matters of music terminology, even in English. In England, a quarter note is a crotchet; an eighth is a quaver; and a half note, a minim. *Viertel*, *Achtel* and *Halb* are the German. *Intermission* in France is *intervalle*, *Pause* in German. In a London rehearsal, if you stop and ask the orchestra to begin at "T," they get up and leave.

When you are with your own ensemble, the road seems a bit easier. Most of the musical preparation has been done at home. Performances have taken place so you have a good idea of how both the musicians and audience react to a given program. The staff takes care of itineraries, transport and accommodation. Some conductors prefer to travel separately from the orchestra; others will hop on the plane or bus with the rest of the gang. One part of traveling together winds up feeling awkward to me. The orchestra usually sits in the economy section of the plane, with perhaps a few members allowed to move up. The conductor goes business or first class, which means he or she is among the earliest to board the aircraft. Thus, most members of the orchestra pass by as they inch their way to the cattle car. I greet them with appropriate friendliness but keep a book handy in case I want to bury my head.

A side benefit of traveling with the hometown team is the personal trunk in which to pack your clothing for the performances. Mine has been around for almost thirty years and has almost as many frequent-flier miles as I do. I typically bring two outfits for concerts, including shoes, cufflinks and shirts. If you are leading five or six concerts in a row, there is no time to go to the cleaners. Once in a while, transit may jostle the tux or tailcoat to the bottom of the trunk. Conductors need to have a portable steamer for removing the new creases, as well as a brush for dusting things off.

The union establishes separate orchestral rules for touring, at least with American orchestras. Some limit the number of hours you can travel before either rehearsing or performing. Rehearsal time is quite restricted, with only a few venues getting a sound check. Playing a hall "blind" is part and parcel of the touring regimen. For that reason, it is usually a good idea to open with a short piece in which the players can gauge how well or poorly they can hear one another, how much volume is too extreme, and the general balance or orchestral sound. Even if there is a full rehearsal, there are still questions, simply because no one knows how the hall will sound when the audience is in attendance.

There is a philosophy that claims an orchestra adjusts to the venue in which it will play. I don't agree. To me, a genuinely good ensemble will measure the hall, then set out to replicate the sonority of its own home. The truly superb groups retain their individuality because they carry this characteristic sound with them. It becomes a matter of how the musicians achieve the sound. If the orchestra is used to a "dry" acoustic, one with minimal reverberation, then it might use a bit less bow if the new venue resonates more than at home. Conversely, if the hall on tour is rather sterile, then more bow and vibrato might be applied to compensate.

Sometimes I have contemplated the importance of a particular venue or concert. It is wonderful to succeed where other orchestras have triumphed. Appreciation by the cognoscenti is naturally an ego boost; however, you cannot overestimate the value of performances in out-of-the-way places. A lot of potential audience members do not have the luxury of experiencing a magnificent orchestra in their hometown. Reaching those first-time listeners is, in numerous ways, more gratifying than connecting with concert veterans.

There are times when a certain naïveté is amusing. On tour with the National Symphony in Florida, we were performing Ives' *Three Places in New England.* The second of these has an abrupt and loud ending, but nonetheless indefinite. When the orchestra pounded out the final note, a lone voice from the audience was heard to exclaim, "Oh, my God!"

It was, in a sense, precisely the kind of reaction Ives would have wanted and that only seems to happen on the road.

24

Summertime and the Livin' Is Complicated

Life is a festival only to the wise.

—RALPH WALDO EMERSON

Hot and humid. Bugs everywhere. Wine bottles clanking. Babies screaming. Ah, there is nothing like the sights and sounds of summer.

The alfresco concert has been with us for centuries now. Tribal drummers, troubadours and rock stars, even classical ensembles have enjoyed a place in the great outdoors. Handel must have loved the *Royal Fireworks Music* as he stood at a safe distance away from the barge that carried the musicians and explosives.

We don't know when the formally organized, professional, outdoor concert series was conceived. Major orchestras in America lacked summer homes until both the Chicago and the Boston Symphony moved out of town in 1936. The vision of Serge Koussevitzky helped forge Tanglewood, a bucolic venue in the heart of the Berkshire Mountains. The first concerts were played in a tent, but in two years' time, the famous Shed was dedicated. The BSO plays and resides in the Lenox area almost all summer. Although located in Massachusetts, it amounts to a second home for New Yorkers who flock to the area, families in tow. This seasonal music center includes a well-known school for very dedicated young musicians, who play with master conductors and soloists. It is arguably the go-to place for serious music-making during the summer months.

Teaching, from its inception, has been fundamental to the Tanglewood ethic. A number of fine conductors have emerged from the program, and for most years, this class was held in Saranac, the original residence of Koussevitzky. All the greats have taught there and that history is so palpable, you can feel it oozing from the walls. Everyone respects the festival's traditions, no doubt a factor in why it remains at the top of every music lover's list for summertime listening.

Ravinia, which claims to be the oldest music festival in the nation, was founded in 1904. The New York Symphony Society played an inaugural concert the next year. Not until 1936 did the Chicago Symphony establish permanent residence there. Over the decades, Ravinia has built a substantial following as the only major summer outlet in the Midwest. There is a train station nearby and the sounds of the engines on tracks can make and sometimes add an additional sonic punch to a piece of music.

Throughout its existence, there has been a gulf between the conductors who appear downtown and those who head out to Highland Park. Each institution has its own board and thus tries to be proprietary when it comes to those on the podium. Therefore, regardless of my Chicago engagements, my regular appearances in Ravinia did not begin until the mid-1990s, as my city time was growing limited.

The outdoors subjects everyone to the whim of the elements. As with so many summer festivals, Ravinia does not provide a lot of time to practice, so each minute is valuable. One particular afternoon when I was conducting, the skies turned black and the wind picked up quickly. A tornado alert was issued and all of us were hustled to an area downstairs. It took about twenty minutes before we could get going again, and the soloist, Manny Ax, was due to rehearse a couple of pieces with the orchestra. We opted to simply read them at the concert, as time was now running out. As is usual with summer fare, all went well, but Manny was a nervous wreck.

Like many orchestras, the Minnesota Orchestra (formerly the Minneapolis Symphony) was searching for a way to fill out the newly negotiated fifty-two-week contract obligation to its musicians. Pops concerts helped a bit, but a series at the old home for the orchestra, Northrop Auditorium, was not doing well. By 1974, the city's Orchestra Hall came into existence and finally, the Minnesota Orchestra could control its own destiny. I was thirty-one and asked to create a novel summer project.

We decided to use part of a model that was in place with the New York Philharmonic. These were under the direction of Pierre Boulez and were called Rug Concerts. The idea was to cover the seating area with platforms, and the audience was encouraged to bring pillows and spread out. The programming was eclectic, to say the least. Each first half usually had new, electronic and experimental music. Varèse, Xenakis, Erb and likeminded experimentalists were presented. We even performed Ligeti's *Poème électronique* for one hundred metronomes. The audiences were not nearly as large as we had wished. The '70s were coming to a close and we needed to pursue some other ethic.

We considered a French festival, then thought that the theme would too soon become boring. An exhibition of Picasso was on its way to Minneapolis, so Spain seemed like a good idea. Again only fleetingly, maybe for a week but no more. Eventually the orchestra's program annotator made a suggestion. Why not center a festival on the city of Vienna? After all, the bulk of the repertoire had originated in this corner of the musical world, and with Mozart, Schubert, Haydn, Beethoven, Mahler and almost every composer of stature spending time in the Austrian capital, we could continue indefinitely.

On July 17, 1980, the Viennese Sommerfest was born, transforming downtown Minneapolis into a lively marketplace and concert venue. At first, the festival ran just three weeks, but would later expand to four. Concerts ranged from traditional evenings of waltzes and polkas to new music. Ensembles performed daily, outside on the newly created Marktplatz in Peavey Plaza, adjacent to the hall. Beer and brats mingled with Mozart and Strauss.

The festival kept a select group of guest artists busy, as they would be in residence for the whole time. Benita Valente, John Browning, Jeffrey Siegel and Walter Klien agreed to everything I suggested. As the years progressed, we would blend other nationalities and concepts with the Viennese traditions. Concert opera would become an annual visitor, as would evenings of multi-piano extravaganzas. Who could ever forget the sight of ten pianists pounding out "Ride of the Valkyries" as a pair of ladies decked out in horned helmets and dirndls pranced down the aisle? Not to mention the stagehands who tossed a football around onstage during this spectacle?

Friday nights were devoted to chamber music, but we decided to set them as if held in a salon. The stage was decorated appropriate to the evening's theme. For example, we created a program in the manner of a Schubertiade. Members of the staff dressed in costumes of the period and some of the audience did likewise. On another memorable evening, upon hearing a piece by Karl Stamitz,

Walter Klien, an incredible pianist and gentleman, declared that anybody could write this music. Beginning at ten that night, after the performance, he and I settled in the conductor's room improvising an imaginary four-hand sonata by the Mannheim master. We almost mustered the courage to play it the next night and pass it off as a "world premiere of a major minor discovery."

These summer happenings even gave me the opportunity to create a film festival. Following the concerts on Friday, a screen was erected outdoors on the Marktplatz. It was my job to select the movies to show, each connected to some musical theme. We watched old classical music biopics, including *A Song to Remember*, horrid campy films such as Charlton Heston's *Counterpoint*, and movies that featured phenomenal artists such as Jascha Heifetz in *They Shall Have Music*. A cartoon, usually Bugs Bunny or Tom and Jerry, with a musical theme, preceded each film. It was tremendous fun.

So much music, so little rehearsal time. Never has that been so true as it was for the decade of Sommerfest. Several members of the orchestra wore T-shirts that read, "I survived the Minnesota Orchestra Summer Sight-Reading Festival." Who would have dreamed *Salome* or Mahler's Eighth Symphony in just three rehearsals? One program included some difficult contemporary music on the first half, and we put everything together in a single rehearsal. Beethoven's Seventh Symphony was the concluding work, and there were barely five minutes left to rehearse it. I scanned the faces in the orchestra and said, "We know this piece. Here is where I would like notes longer and here is where they should be shorter. These are the repeats we will do. Trust me on this."

They did, and that night we gave an utterly magical performance without rehearsing one note. Flying by the seat of our pants was not always the best idea, but when it worked, it was incredible. The ten years flew by and I look back in great fondness at this time in my musical life.

For the next two years, I presided over the Pittsburgh Symphony at the Great Woods Festival in Mansfield, Massachusetts. It had been founded a few years earlier with Michael Tilson Thomas leading the way. Neither of us made enough of a noise to transform this into a true summer home for the orchestra. It was thought that the location, a little under an hour away from Boston, would see a natural flow of music lovers attend this charming venue, but only the rock concerts could ensure decent houses and the orchestra's participation came to an end.

I moved on to lead the Cleveland Orchestra at the Blossom Music Festival. To say this invitation surprised me would be an understatement. Even though I had conducted the orchestra on several occasions, both downtown and at its summer home, ours was not exactly a predictable musical partnership. My own way with rehearsals and concerts was rather more spontaneous than the orchestra of Szell and Dohnányi. The administration of the orchestra was hunting for more spice in its summer programming and hoping to attract a new audience.

Blossom itself is a wonderful venue. It rests on what seems an endless expanse of land. The natural slope of the audience seating somehow makes the cavernous four-thousand-person interior intimate. The sound is extraordinary and natural, possibly the best outdoor facility in existence.

For nine years I had the privilege of leading this great ensemble through repertoire its players probably would never see again. Certainly we still relied on the standards, as that is what most summer music-making is about. And we drew very good crowds, especially for baroque marathons and evenings with artists other than the traditional symphonic soloist. As at Minnesota, we did concert opera, multi-piano concerts and chamber music. Our collaboration with Kent State University and other educational aspects of Blossom never really took off.

This most disciplined of orchestras did provide a few moments of amusement. One evening, we were performing the Dvořák Cello Concerto with Cleveland native Lynn Harrell. During the slow movement, I noticed that the lone percussionist, who only plays the triangle in the last movement, had fallen asleep. As I was the only one who could see this, I frantically tried to signal to players in the vicinity but to no avail. It turns out that you can still get through the piece without the dinner bell.

After my stint with the BBC inside at the Albert Hall, a couple of years would pass before I took on another outdoor facility. This time it would return me to where so much began.

In 1922, the first concerts at the Hollywood Bowl were presented. This iconic structure, seemingly carved out of a hillside, would be the summer home of the Los Angeles Philharmonic, although that formal relationship did not commence until the '60s. It was at the Bowl where I received some of my earliest musical training.

When I was sixteen years old, my application to become an usher was rejected. You can imagine what it felt like, in July 2006, to walk out on that stage as the newly appointed Principal Guest Conductor of the Los Angeles Philharmonic at the Hollywood Bowl. Quite a mouthful and the longest job title I had ever heard in the music business. At least until someone appended "former," when I relinquished the post.

There are two orchestras which perform at the famous amphitheater. The LA Phil does primarily the "classical" evenings on Tuesdays and Thursdays. On the weekends, the Hollywood Bowl Orchestra takes over, made up of an entirely different group of musicians. Once in a while, the two ensembles overlap or trade nights, but this has been the routine for about the last twenty years.

My duties at the Bowl were to oversee just my own concerts and programming concepts. I conducted three weeks of the ten scheduled. Since the facility seats more than seventeen thousand people, part of my job was to keep attendance at six thousand or so for the classical evenings. Somehow we managed this, and during one week, we outdrew the weekend appearances of Queen Latifah. There was a fine presentation of Peter Shaffer's *Amadeus* with the play interspersed with music by Mozart. An evening of serenades proved to be quite popular.

A conductor has to get used to the aesthetic of the Bowl audience. Should a wine bottle come clinking down the aisle, you must ignore it. Even though the music comes as no surprise whatsoever, the audience customarily lets out a cheer when the first four notes of Beethoven's Fifth Symphony are sounded. And you must be prepared for applause not only between movements, but also in the wake of a showy cadenza in a concerto, despite the possible several more minutes before the concerto is over.

Still, there is no place like the Bowl. The acoustics on the enormous stage are not nearly as awful as its appearance might suggest. The instrumentalists can hear themselves quite well. These days, amplification techniques are so sophisticated as to seem natural in these surroundings. Cameras project images on two large screens on either side of the stage. Normally I do not care for this type of multimedia display, but it succeeds in such a huge space. Every performer and the conductor must be aware of their facial expressions and gestures. You never know what those cameras will catch!

For the last few years, I have spent summers working with young people. Conducting and teaching in Aspen and Breckenridge, Colorado, and Santa Barbara, California, has been deeply rewarding. Coupling this with my position at Indiana University, I feel I have a nice balance of professional appearances and educational activity. Perhaps the time has come for me to take more time off and enjoy what I have worked to achieve. On the other hand, who is to say I am not enjoying myself now?

25

9/15

Unending was the stream, unending the misery,
unending the sorrow.

—KARL AMADEUS HARTMANN

On September 10, 2001, I was nearing the end of my first season as chief conductor of the BBC Symphony. That evening, we performed Ralph Vaughn Williams' *Sea Symphony*. The next few days would be spent preparing for what is known as "The Last Night of the Proms." For 106 years, at least as of this concert, the festival, founded by Sir Henry Wood, has offered a variety of concerts at low prices, intended to attract a general public. The programs are presented at the Albert Hall, which seats about five thousand people and stands one thousand more, even if they have to last through a full act of Wagner's *Ring*.

Traditions associated with this night go back more than sixty years. It was Sir Malcolm Sargent who began to address the audience, offering humor along with thanking everyone for coming to the concerts. So among my assignments was a speech that would contain statistics, jokes and puns. I was the first American, and only the second non-Brit, to lead this special event. In addition, it was televised worldwide as well as broadcast on radio and the Internet.

Usually, I do not prepare remarks in advance. For me, because of the radio work I had done in Saint Louis, I got used to speaking unscripted. But for Last Night, the BBC insisted that it have a copy of what I was going to say, most likely for the sake of television and the camera angles. With a free day on the eleventh, I decided to head down to the Maida Vale studio, where the orchestra rehearses, and use an office to work on the speech.

On September 11, because the performance the previous evening had been long and a dinner followed, I planned to write in the afternoon, after lunch. This was about two o'clock, British time. As I was leaving the restaurant, I passed a newsstand selling *The Evening Standard*. A man was inquiring as to availability of the latest edition, and any news about the plane crash. I did not pay much attention to this and got in a cab. The driver had the radio on and I could decipher isolated words: "Twin Towers," "terrorist attack," "second plane." Then, I asked him to turn up the volume.

For the next fifteen minutes I listened in shock, as the events of the day were unfolding. I tried phoning home. No service. I called my office in Washington DC. Same story. What I had heard over the radio could not be happening.

Arriving at Maida Vale, it was clear that no one knew how to react. Some were in tears. Others were wandering about aimlessly. Not yet accepting what was going on, I asked for a desk and computer to write my speech. The televisions were on and I finally saw the horror. Once again, I tried calling, thinking maybe that only cell phones were affected. But still no answer.

My wife did not use a computer at this point in her life, so I could not get in touch with home. Then, the third plane hit, this time at the Pentagon. My son went to school near where we lived in Maryland, and this was a school day. So I assumed that he was nowhere near the downtown area, but my office was, and I could contact my assistant via e-mail. For some reason, she was still at work, perhaps waiting to hear from me. I asked her to check on my family. On this day, technology had its pluses and minuses.

The managing director of the orchestra, Paul Hughes, said that the head of the Proms, Nicholas Kenyon, wanted to come by to discuss the Last Night. I was determined to give my speech and made more attempts at writing, but every time I punched a key or tried to start a sentence, I simply could not continue. A feeling of total helplessness had come over me.

As soon as Nick arrived, I suggested that another conductor take over the concert. To know why this thought occurred to me, it is necessary to understand the nature of this unique program.

The Proms is a huge festival, the largest in the world, with an orchestral performance virtually every night for eight and sometimes nine weeks. In addition, there are ancillary events, late-night concerts, talks and much more. The Last

Night is based on what has gone on before, summing up some themes of the season and presenting a couple of big-name soloists.

It is the traditions, comprising the final half hour or so of the concert, that really draw in the public. Most obvious is the attire of the audience. After queuing up for almost twenty-four hours, those who stand in the arena area come in all manner of clothing. Some wear silly hats. Others wave Union Jacks and flags of their homeland. And some even arrive clad in formal tails and gowns. Celebration fills the air, though some feel it borders on jingoism. This never bothered me. It is like a Fourth of July concert and picnic, the only nationalistic event of its kind in Britain.

Every year there are articles galore decrying the Last Night. Does Britannia still rule the waves? Is Hubert Parry's "Jerusalem" anti-Semitic? If the concert is seen and heard across the globe, should the program be so insular? Maybe it should be more inclusive, especially with Ireland, Scotland and Wales right on the doorstep.

Those questions aside, the atmosphere in the Albert Hall is supposed to be festive. There are inside jokes, usually entrusted to those who stand in the middle of the arena. For example, when a piano is brought out to the platform, just as the stagehands are about to raise the lid, one half of the audience cries, "*Heave!*" and when they get it on the stick, the other half answers, "*Ho!*" A couple of nights before my concert, I had attended a performance of Beethoven's Ninth Symphony. Some concertgoers spotted me in the audience and, prior to the beginning of the concert, yelled out, "Arena to Leonard! Have you written the speech yet?"

The "traditional" part of the program follows a particular format that has hardly changed over the years. Musically, it gets off to a start with Elgar's *Pomp and Circumstance March No. 1*. This is the processional that accompanies high school students in America as they walk down the aisle at graduation. However, in the United Kingdom the piece is known as "Land of Hope and Glory." The audience sings along with the familiar tune, at first softly, then with full gusto. After prolonged cheers, the final verse is reprised, even louder than before. The conductor inevitably shouts out something like, "I couldn't hear you the first time."

After that comes the controversial part, a performance of arrangements made by the Proms founder, Sir Henry Wood, of British sea songs. Most of the tunes are familiar to all audiences, but for this night, the audience joins in with whistling, stomping and Klaxon horns. As a hornpipe gets faster and faster, audience members are exhorted to try and keep up with the dance. This part ends with "Rule Britannia." Sometimes a prominent singer will come onstage, dressed in full-flagged regalia to lend an operatic or oratorical twist to the lyrics. Frederica von Stade was the scheduled soloist for my concert and she had agreed to try something special for this occasion.

Then come the speech, "Jerusalem" and the national anthem. Anyone can view videos of past concerts and get the idea.

But not the one from September 15, 2001.

The original program was scheduled to contain, among other works, John Adams' *Short Ride in a Fast Machine*, obviously inappropriate on this occasion, eerily similar to the work's planned performance a few days following the death of Princess Diana. There was a rarity, *The Rio Grande* for piano, chorus and orchestra by Constant Lambert, which seemed too lighthearted. Also for this evening, Flicka was slated to sing a few Auvergne songs and show tunes. She was coming from the United States but with all flights canceled, she would no longer be available.

We postponed the rehearsal on the twelfth, as too many decisions lingered. At noon, I went to the American embassy, now under heavy guard. I witnessed a memorial service just outside. No one really had words to adequately express our shared feelings.

The first issue was to decide what was to be kept and what was to be omitted. Verdi's *Forza del destino* Overture seemed fine, as did a work by Gerald Finzi, whose hundredth birthday was being celebrated that season, but the rest on the program simply would not do. Again, I mentioned that I would be perfectly happy to withdraw from the concert, but Nick said that I was the director and that we should all work together to make the appropriate changes.

Bach's Passacaglia and Fugue in C Minor replaced the Lambert. Adams' companion fanfare, *Tromba Lontana*, was substituted. The finale from the Beethoven Ninth, heard just two nights previous, was inserted. The only remainders from the patriotic pieces were "Jerusalem" plus the national anthem, and even that evoked some discussion.

This is normally performed at the close of the program, but I preferred it at the beginning, preceded by "The Star-Spangled Banner." At first, there was resistance, not because of the placement, but because the audience would not know the words to the American anthem. There was even talk of eliminating both. Instead, we put the text into the program book, and I have to say that I have never heard this sung with greater passion in my whole life than on the evening of the London concert.

We also made one very creative nod to the British-American relationship. I remembered, as a student in Aspen, hearing a performance of Sir Michael Tippett's oratorio, *A Child of Our Time*. In place of chorales, as you would hear in a Bach oratorio, Tippett uses Negro spirituals. We performed four of the five.

On the thirteenth of the month, we gathered at Maida Vale to begin rehearsals. A moment of silence began the morning. I am not sure what I said, but it included this quote by Verdi: "Words cannot do justice at this time. Our expression is in our music." It was a reminder that the Congress of the United States also used music to express solidarity. When they gathered on the Capitol steps, they sang "God Bless America." Rehearsals progressed in a surprisingly normal manner.

On September 15 we paid our tribute. The audience did not come dressed in party attire. There were no flags, other than British and American banners that dotted the edges of the boxes. Ann Murray substituted for von Stade, but only retained some of the Canteloube, with the show tunes Flicka planned to sing eliminated.

The emotional heart of that night was the piece that Americans use in times of grief and tragedy, Barber's *Adagio for Strings*. I said a few words to the audience before playing the work. At the conclusion, I do not remember anything. I simply left the stage, went into the dressing room and started crying. There are several videos of this performance, some taken directly from the BBC broadcast, and another, wrenching version, which cuts from us to police officers, military and firefighters, standing in stunned silence as the tragedy unfolded. In the parks, where there was a simultaneous relay of our concert, one couple, draped in an American flag, is seen weeping.

With the end of "Jerusalem," which now concluded the concert, I returned to the dressing room. My cell phone was ringing. Daniel and Linda had heard the broadcast, which NPR carried live. Hearing their voices was a reassurance of how close loved ones can be when you are far away.

And the reactions to this concert?

> Slatkin's role . . . was crucial. It must have been desperately difficult for him, and his remarks were finely judged. But it was a strangely unsatisfactory occasion, certainly not the mindless jamboree of tradition but then not a fully fledged memorial concert either. (Andrew Clements, *The Guardian*)

> I have never sung the American National Anthem before, but was somewhat amazed to find myself singing about "The rockets red glare / The bombs bursting in air / Gave proof thro' the night / That our flag was still there." It seemed somewhat incongruous that we were singing such belligerent words in honour of a devastated country that had just been on the receiving end of such violence. Perhaps "God Bless America" (sung, of course, to the tune of "God Save the Queen")—even in the originally programmed Charles Ives/William Schuman version—would have been more appropriate. (Nick Breckenfield, *Classical Source*)

I received a death threat. Another person wrote to me saying, "Now the United States knows what the rest of the world feels like" and "Shame on you for taking away what little tradition we still have."

But most responses were positive. Since that night, the Proms have indeed undergone transformations. The three other constituents of the United Kingdom are now represented when the sea songs are played. Alternate versions of "Jerusalem" are performed. The controversies do not go away, and perhaps that is a good thing. Music can still be a hot topic in some circles.

On the day following the concert, I flew home with my good friends Geryl and Frank Pearl. How they managed to get a private plane into US airspace, when no aircraft were allowed, is beyond me. When we approached the coastline, I stared out the window. We were about twenty-five miles south of the World Trade Center site. Now nothing but plumes of smoke was still highly visible five days after the tragedy. When we touched down at Dulles Airport, I realized that I had not returned to the same country I had left ten days earlier.

I conducted a memorial concert at the Kennedy Center a week later. This was to honor those whose lives were lost at the Pentagon, victims sometimes neglected. This performance, too, was a moving event. There will always be tears, but the music affirmed that there will also always be hope.

26

Two More Weeks at the Opera

"La traviata" last night a fiasco. Was the fault the singers' or mine?
Time will decide.

—GIUSEPPE VERDI

In 2010, I was scheduled to lead performances at the Metropolitan Opera of *La traviata*. Under most circumstances this should have been a routine job. After all, even though I had not conducted it, it was the second-most-performed opera at that house, *La bohème* taking top honors. I had plenty of time to prepare the work and knew that with an internationally renowned cast, there should be no problems. At the time, I thought it would be nice to keep a journal of what happened, partially to help me write for my website, but also with the idea of eventually letting readers in on exactly what goes on when putting an operatic production together.

Here is a chronological accounting of events, lightly edited for clarity, as written on my website in April of 2010.

March 15

Every week, the Met posts a schedule for the artists, stagehands and virtually everyone involved in any production that will take place. There is one for the whole week and daily updates that are given out at the stage door when you depart. We were slated to begin piano/staging rehearsals two weeks prior to opening night. That is about normal for a standard repertoire opera. A new production might begin four weeks or more before the first performance.

There were greetings at the stage door, which was harder to find this time, as there is a great deal of construction going on at Lincoln Center. Twelve years ago all I had to do was walk past the stage door of Avery Fisher Hall, enter a garage and the entrance was easy to spot. Now I had to either go down Amsterdam Avenue or enter the front door of the Met, go down a couple of flights of stairs, outside again and then finally arrive.

After being welcomed, given a security pass and a packet, shown the conductor's dressing room and given a little tour, I arrived at the orchestra rehearsal room. This is where most of our staging rehearsals will take place. Every day starts at 11 for us, with the printed schedule being followed almost to the letter. If we are doing Act 1, Scene 4, it is written exactly how long this will take and who is needed.

At this point, we learned that Tom Hampson had bronchitis and would not be around for several days. Seems that he was ordered by his doctors to stay in Vienna until he was better. But Angela Gheorghiu is in town and expected a bit later in the day. The Alfredo is James Valenti, making his Met debut. There are also covers, those people who will take over if someone is ill. In most cases, they get to sing one performance but it is a really a thankless role.

I have a staff of two other conductors, a prompter, in this case the redoubtable Joan Dornemann, and a pianist. We have a lot of time on our hands while the director positions and places the cast in various spots on the stage. Good stories abound.

It seems like I am the only person who has never performed *Traviata*. This causes some raised eyebrows but Joan assures everyone that a fresh view of the piece is what is needed. As we progress, it is possible to discover what traditions make sense and which ones might be subject to debate. An accent here, dynamic change there, tempo shift in this place, even the occasional questionable note. It is all very instructive.

We decided not to do an outright musical rehearsal, one that would simply be a run-through of the work with piano and no action. It seemed more efficient for me to listen as we did the staging. Sometimes the nature of an action will alter the tempo, breathing or phrasing of a particular passage. For example, there is a moment in the second act when Alfredo picks up Violetta and spins her around while he is singing. Clearly there must be some adjustment to allow the voice to cut through while his back is to the audience. And it was also important to listen to how the voices interacted with each other. With Tom out of the picture we did not get a chance to do certain crucial moments in the second act. But as the day ended, I was starting to get a good idea of where we were all headed.

March 17

Another day in the orchestra rehearsal room. Another day without Tom Hampson. We are told that he will arrive tomorrow and come to the sitzprobe the next day. For those of you unfamiliar with that term, it translates as "seated rehearsal," one in which the orchestra is present and the singers simply go through it without stage action. Kind of a concert performance.

In place of Tom we have Dwayne Croft, another veteran of the house and a person who also would have been in *Ghosts*. So now at least, we get to see and hear some of the music in the second act that was not done the first two days. Dwayne sounds terrific and if somehow Tom does not make it, we will still be in good shape.

These rehearsals went quickly and they ended early. During the second one, we got around to the last act and here was where trouble with Angela probably first started. As in *La bohème,* the heroine dies of consumption—tuberculosis. In Verdi's case she belts out a high B-flat before expiring. Zeffirelli has Violetta cling to Alfredo and then collapse on the floor. None of us liked it. It did not seem to convey the aristocratic nature of her courtesan life. We could not decide if her head should wind up in his lap, which side of him she should be facing, and what his reaction should be. It is critical that this moment, done without singing, be tremendously powerful. I pointed out the moment we hear the chord when Alfredo actually realizes that she is dead, and thinks about his character. He has been through a lot of turmoil during the course of the opera. But he is young and clearly does not understand what is going on. I felt that at one point, with him holding Violetta's head, he should look up, asking God why this has happened, and then look back down. Yes, a little bit cheesy, but that is probably what he would have done in the play. Not sure how this will turn out.

March 18
Another beautiful day out there. We all thought that the rehearsal should be public and done around the fountain in front of Lincoln Center. Still no Tom. Angela was tired and decided not to come in. So we just worked a bit with the alternates and smaller roles in the cast. Afternoon rehearsal was canceled.

March 20
It is the first rehearsal with the orchestra, and I will only see them two more times before opening night. Upon arrival in the orchestra rehearsal room, one finds that most things are set up as close as possible to the actual way it will be when we get into the auditorium. The podium is quite elevated, the orchestra is seated in the same configuration as when they will be in the pit, and the singers are located behind to approximate the distance between them and me.

I recognize only a few musicians from my previous appearances. Why is it that as I get older, the players get younger? After an initial greeting, we start right from the top. I always have a game plan for each rehearsal. In this case the idea was to play through each scene and only comment on a few things. During the Prelude to the first act, many of the details that I had noticed on recordings were present. Realizing that my credibility as a Verdian might be questioned, I decided never to reveal that this score was new to me. There were no references similar to "I know this is what you usually do but I would like it played this way." It seemed better just to say what I wanted and sometimes explain why.

So no extended fourth beat or strong accent in the third bar. The main section accompaniment does not start loud. Same thing for the tune. The score says *ppp* and *con espressione,* so why not play it that way? Joan Dornemann was smiling during some of these moments and I think that was a good thing.

Most of the time, I felt quite comfortable with the work. But every so often, I forgot about a ritardando or a spot where the singers might need a bit more time. Tempi seemed right and the dramatic flow felt good. We had been informed just before the downbeat that Angela would be filling in the next day for Anna Netrebko in *La bohème.* The Russian star had become ill. Talk about luxury casting! It would be fun to be at the show when General Manager Peter Gelb walks out and tells the audience that the soprano they all came for is not here, but Angela will take her place.

Fully expecting that she would not be at our rehearsal, we were all surprised when she bounced through the door, all bubbly and happy to be with us. Tom Hampson arrived as well, fresh off a plane from Vienna and looking quite well.

As wonderful as it was to have the whole cast, I still had not seen the chorus and today was no exception. Earlier I was told that in some cases they did not show up until the dress rehearsal. It is still not clear to me when we will have them with us. The same goes for the "banda." For this rehearsal, the parts were played on the piano.

In performance, the work is in three acts with two intermissions. At rehearsal, there is only one half-hour break in the middle. We had decided to do the first act, jump to the second scene in the second act and then take the interval. After snacks, back to the top of Act 2 and then the last one. We did not stop too often, just enough for me to make some points and rehearse what I felt was needed. The last bar sounded with three minutes to spare. Now I was trying to figure out how long the show actually runs. Checking the Met schedule, I noted that when we start at 8 p.m. we are supposed to finish at 11:05! I will try and end at the three-hour mark.

Last week, Alex Ross delivered a lecture in London. He advocates applause during the course of a concert, not just at the end of works. Of course, this is what was done for most of music history before the mid-twentieth century. And it has always been the case in opera. For this set of performances, I will need to know where to expect an interruption and when to just keep going. Most of the time, it is fairly easy to guess, but with all the musical stops and starts between scenes, one can never know. However, there are many places where the drama could come to a grinding halt because of the audience. Clearly, Verdi built in where he thought applause was appropriate. We just don't know where he did not want it.

Since Angela was now involved in a performance tomorrow, and all we really had to do were the scenes with her and Tom, it was decided to cancel the remaining rehearsals for the day as well as Saturday. The weather was still cooperating and we were all happy to agree. So nothing until we get on the stage Monday morning.

There is one week and four rehearsals left before the opening.

March 22

It was a dark and dreary day in Manhattan. The beautiful spring weather of the past week is a thing of the past. Rain and wind took its place. This did not forebode well for the second week of *Traviata*.

Today's rehearsal is the first of two that will be with piano and most of the stage sets. The singers are not quite in costume but some are trying on the outfits to see if they fit. It is also helpful for them to get used to moving around while wearing the costumes. The schedule only has us down for two and half hours, rather than the usual three. And the break time will be thirty minutes, as opposed to the twenty we took when we were in the orchestra rehearsal space.

We started with the second act. It had not yet been staged, as Tom Hampson only arrived for the sitzprobe last Friday. Since most of the action revolves around the three principal singers, there was not too much to do. So we were able to get most of it finished in a short amount of time. It feels strange to be in the pit, have the entire set and all the soloists, but just have a piano. That instrument is amplified so the singers can hear it onstage. At one point, Angela Gheorghiu asked me to make sure that one of the numbers begin a little louder than usual as she will be upstage (*downstage* means near the pit) and might not be able to hear the strings clearly enough. The orchestra is not amplified.

However, there are video monitors on either side of the stage as well as in different locations. The singers use these when not able to see me directly by looking in the pit. It is also how the offstage conductor of the "banda" receives the information about tempi and coordinates it with my beat. I had not planned on conducting these spots, but now I will, to help keep everyone together.

The chorus master stopped by to check on how things were going. They will be around tomorrow, the only chance I have to work with them prior to the Wednesday rehearsal with orchestra. We spoke about the beat patterns that I will be using. The vocal forces need to know whether I will conduct in two or four in a couple of spots. There is one tempo transition that is difficult because of the placement of the chorus onstage. Not much I can do until we actually try it out.

After the break, we have just thirty-five minutes to do the last act. This portion is divided into two parts, with a scene change coming about twelve minutes in. There is a mechanism that involves elevators, making it possible to do the switch in less than a minute. Today, the machine was broken and the stage crew had to do it by hand. It was an amazing sight, watching these guys move huge, bulky pieces of scenery so quickly. We finished right on schedule.

It dawned on me that tomorrow is meant primarily to rehearse the parts that we did not get to this morning. Since we have the orchestra on Wednesday and one final rehearsal on Thursday, there is no "piano dress." This would normally be where we go through the whole opera, costumes and all, but without the orchestra. In effect, I will only have one opportunity to go through the work from beginning to end.

As we ended today, I felt very good about how everything was progressing. Verdi is starting to feel like a good friend now, and I found myself humming tunes from his other operas. All of a sudden, this composer has captured my imagination. During one of the pauses for stage direction, the musical staff and I discussed portions of *Traviata* where the influence of Brahms might be felt, how Verdi moves through the different keys, and which words are highlighted with a musical punctuation. Could *Trovatore*, *Otello* or *Falstaff* be next? Would I finally succumb to the lure of composers for whom I previously had little sympathy, such as Bruckner? How wonderful to be reminded that music is a never-ending learning and growth process.

March 23

It is day two in the pit, still with piano. But lo and behold the chorus is here! Most of the sets are in place, at least the part that the actors stand on, with the area above them still needing to be filled in. Above the first act parlor are the sets for *The Nose*, an opera that will be presented that evening. One can see the wear and tear that years have taken on the Zeffirelli production of *Traviata*, but nothing a little bit of paint wouldn't cure. And the size is very impressive.

Most of the rehearsal focuses on the portions we did not do yesterday. For the first time since we began, the bulk of the cast is onstage but they have the least time to get familiar with the production. Several of them have done it in the past, especially the dancers. Ballets in opera are a long-standing tradition and it was only a clever composer, such as Verdi, who could figure out how to insert this without disrupting the story line. In the case of the second act, which takes place at the home of Flora, Violetta's friend, the occasion is a party. So she has all kinds of folks around.

One very good thing about piano rehearsals is that it gives me the opportunity to really see what is happening. Our pianist is terrific, and much of the time, I don't have to really "conduct." Giving the singers cues, setting tempi and shaping the phrases are enough. We do not have the sixty-five or so musicians in the pit, so eye contact downward is not needed.

At the end of the rehearsal, one of the music administrators, Craig Rutenberg, came down to talk to me in the pit. "Are you planning to stop during rehearsal tomorrow?"

"Well, it is my only chance to fix things, as the dress rehearsal is the day after," I reply.

"You know that there are only three and a half hours of rehearsal. You cannot go overtime. And we tend to clock the show in at a little less than that."

"So, you don't want me to stop?"

"That would be greatly appreciated."

For the first time so far, I get a little apprehensive.

March 24

Uh-oh! Guess who did not come to the rehearsal today?

I left my residence, which is all of two blocks from the Met. On the way, I was sure that I saw Angela in the distance walking away from the Met. And it was only thirty minutes before rehearsal was scheduled to begin. Upon arrival, I checked in with the musical crew. About seven minutes before we were to start, Craig came over to the pit, grumbling about problematic sopranos, only not in very nice words at all. The rest of us did not understand what was going on and it was then that we were informed that Angela said she was too tired to sing and act today.

Now what were we supposed to do?

This is why there are covers, although when there are more than a few hours notice, stars are brought in. Last Saturday, when Anna Netrebko bowed out of *Bohème,* it would have come as a severe blow to those who purchased tickets, with the expectation that they would see the Russian diva. There were almost two days' notice and Angela filled in. So I guess it is understandable that she is a bit frazzled and wants to take it easy right now.

In our case, we are very lucky, as the Korean soprano Hei-Kyung Hong is the understudy. She made her Met debut twenty-five years ago and actually sang in this production for the opening of the season in 2007. So she certainly knows her way around the piece. She is also slated to sing the final performance in April.

But last week, she was ill and not able to do the rehearsals with us. As of today, no one in the cast had worked with her, and the first time I would see her was when the curtain opened. Frantically, I asked my crew what I could expect that might be different, and they said, "Everything," but it would be solid and more than dependable.

This was supposed to be a working rehearsal. It was also the first time everything would be in place: sets, costumes and even the "banda." The orchestra tuned, the house lights went down and we were off.

No problems with the Prelude. In fact, it was very beautiful and understated. Up went the curtain and the party was on. After a few moments, Violetta makes her entrance and I felt like stopping, just to introduce myself. Everyone was right. She is excellent, but quite a change, both musically and dramatically, from what we had been used to. More than likely hers is a performance that stems from a more traditional school of seasoned Verdi singing. Always in tune, perhaps a bit more *rubato* in some of the phrases, but always with a fine sense of style.

After the first act, I asked my assistants, Steve White and Robert Morrison, to give me details, especially those places where I misjudged a tempo or did not hold a fermata long enough. Balances were fine throughout, with the orchestra never covering anyone. The chorus master came over to tell me that I needed to make sure that my beat, even when the music is soft, always is high enough for the full group to see. Good advice. He also thought that the "banda" music was a bit fast. This caused a bit of disagreement with the musical staff as it was no different than the way we had done it previously.

In the orchestral world, we get used to very limited rehearsal time. With instrumental soloists, it is a luxury to get them for two sessions before a concert, something that I usually insist on. And with people I know well, we rarely meet before playing with the ensemble. Most passages get worked out as you go along, in front of everyone. It is one thing to play through a work with the piano, and another when the full orchestra is there. There have been other times when there was no rehearsal at all and we just showed up for the concert.

It is no different at the opera.

But this was a different matter altogether. Not only was the work new to me, but also I had never even met the soprano! It is a very good thing that the orchestra is used to changes such as this. They negotiated every turn with an amazing ease, saving me in a couple of critical moments. I apologized just before Act 2 and thanked them.

"Welcome to our world," was the response.

And so it went for the rest of the rehearsal. No major problems and I started to feel very comfortable with Ms. Hong. Tom and James Valenti, the Alfredo, did a great job, and as we progressed I started to take more of a leadership role. Everyone went with it. The critical transition between having the piano and the orchestra was now going smoothly.

We finished ten minutes ahead of the deadline. Usually, at the end of rehearsal, notes are given to the cast by the director. If I have anything to tell the orchestra, this is also done at this time. The musical assistants tell me about any balance problems or tempo issues and I pass those along. The question of who would be singing at the dress rehearsal came up, and most everybody was sure that Angela would be there. I was not so certain.

March 25

There is an axiom that says that if the dress rehearsal doesn't go well, the performances will be good.

If this is true, we should have a hell of a show.

In actuality, most of what we did went fine, but there were a few glitches. First of all, as in many big houses, what you see one day is not necessarily what you get the next. Looking at the orchestra, which I had only seen twice before, there were some faces that were not familiar. With a standard rep opera this is not uncommon. Everyone is supposed to know the music backward and forward. *Traviata* is performed every year at the Met.

But what I might have said in rehearsal to one player, or a section, may not have been put in the music. And so there were a couple of minor traffic accidents. The players always caught themselves, but it still seemed awkward at certain moments. The concertmaster of the NY Philharmonic, longtime friend Glenn Dicterow, refers to these incidents as "premature articulations."

There was an audience at the dress rehearsal, which helped me understand how the performance would flow. For the first time, I knew where the applause would occur and for how long. This is particularly helpful when I have to give a cue for the next section to begin. However, this crowd was a bit noisier than I expected. The first couple of measures in the Prelude, on which we had worked hard to get a simple and soft sound, were drowned out by nervous expectations in the gallery. Somewhat unexpected was the burst of applause for the scenery.

Since Angela had not rehearsed with us yesterday, there were some shaky moments. We will need to go over a couple passages just to make sure that the coordination between stage and pit is solid. One surprise for me was how little I referred to the score. Not that I could do the piece from memory, but once a scene has begun, it is possible to focus almost exclusively on the stage. Having two complete run-throughs back to back helped me understand the physical and emotional demands of the work. Both the first and last acts are short, lasting around thirty-five minutes each, but the second act is quite long. We all have to keep the tension alive in order to avoid sagging.

It all went by quickly. There were a few friends in attendance and all of them thought that it moved very well. The singers could be heard throughout. We never had to stop for any reason. All the technical devices worked, but there were a few places where lighting was still being adjusted. It is possible to be overly critical and I have to remind myself that we remain human. I also realize that even though this is my first *Traviata*, I have made numerous trips to the opera pit, including three other Verdi masterpieces. Mistakes happen, but in this work, even the dead rise to take a bow.

There are three days remaining until we open.

At this point I concluded writing for my website as things began to spiral out of control. Here is what I wrote in my journal that did not make it into my blog.

March 24

The dress rehearsal was the next day. By now I had heard through the grape vine that Angela was very unhappy with me, and said so onstage to members of the cast.

March 25

The excesses increased and it was impossible to stay together with her. The orchestra expressed their displeasure with her and told me that I was doing very well. The same sentiments were uttered by Peter Gelb and other Met administrators. There was not one word of complaint spoken to me by anyone, including Angela.

We debated about whether or not I should speak to her privately, and upon advice from some, I decided that I would see her just prior to the opening on Monday.

March 29

It rained all weekend. And the temperatures went back to winter levels. I have no idea if any of this affects attendance at the Met, but I do know that we have been sold out for quite some time.

There is no particular regimen that I follow for any performance day. Most of the time, I try to eat a bit of lunch, no later than two in the afternoon, and then hang out either at home or where I am staying as a guest. My hotel in NY is only two blocks from the Met, so it is not very complicated.

Most of the day was spent reviewing *Traviata*. It is certainly possible that some in the audience for the dress rehearsal secretly taped that event, and since we are broadcast live on opening night, most likely there was a trial run from the satellite company. I prefer not to listen to what I have done, but rely on the notes from the staff and my own intuition.

I went over the places where I believed we had a few problems on Thursday, and got those firmly imbedded in my head.

The performance begins at 8, so I thought it would be a good idea to get there early, around 7:30. I visited Angela in her dressing room, and she mentioned two spots in the opera where she wanted to move ahead a bit more. She could not have been nicer.

Back in my dressing room, the telephone rang and a voice informed me that we were at the five-minute mark before curtain. But in our case, the curtain doesn't go up until six minutes or so after we start. The conductor can wait until the actual start time, but I prefer to hang out close to where I will make the entrance into the pit. In fact, I get right to the place that is closest to the podium, rather than make a dramatic long walk.

The lights come down, the orchestra tunes and I quickly make my way through the maze of players and music stands. Taking a bow in the pit is a little tricky. When you are in a concert hall, the door opens and the audience sees you right away. In the opera house, most people don't know you are there until you get to the podium. But those in the balcony can see what is happening and the applause commences.

After everyone settles down, we begin. As opposed to the dress rehearsal, the audience is quiet for the Prelude. But the response to the set is met with oohs, ahs and more applause. Everything seems to go smoothly. Angela tosses off "Sempre libera" with the ease she exhibited at the first rehearsal. Lots of cheering when it is over, as this also ends the act.

After the thirty-minute intermission, we start up again. James wows everyone with his aria, earning the longest ovation of the evening. There are a few coordination problems but they are quickly resolved. Tom is great, as usual. The lengthy duet between Violetta and Germont has the tension and beauty one would expect with these two artists. But there are moments when it appears that Angela is simply not going to follow what the rest of us are doing. It becomes frustrating as the scene comes to a conclusion.

The second act has a five-minute pause to allow for a major set change between scenes. It seems silly for me to just stand around waiting, so I descend from the podium and chat with the first stands of the orchestra. We tell stories, and I am reminded of Berlioz's book, where he pretends to be a musician in the pit with a lot of time on his hands. The lights dim again and we start up.

This set is just amazing! I agree with the audience when they vociferously applaud, but wonder who would take a bow. The ballet sequences go very well. Again there are a couple of minor lapses but nothing that most people notice. But now Angela starts causing trouble.

I am considered one of the best accompanists in the conducting world. This is not a boast. Ask virtually any singer or soloist who has worked with me in the past. However, this time I was at a loss. Angela distorted phrases to the point where no one could anticipate what she would do. She would hold notes longer than her colleagues onstage, disrupting the ensemble. In critical moments where we needed to make eye contact, she would turn her back to the pit. I do not know how all the others managed it. I do know that I became more frustrated with every passing minute. My timing and concentration were thrown completely off. Of course, one of the roles of an opera conductor is to follow the inflections of the singers, but in this case, at least for me, it was simply not possible.

After another thirty-minute intermission we start the final act. This time when I arrive at the podium and ask the orchestra to rise, there is quite a prolonged ovation for the great work they have done during the evening. The Prelude is absolutely ravishing and the mood is sustained into action onstage. I am totally into this and having a very good time.

The curtain comes down and I shake hands with all the front stands of strings. It is not necessary to race anywhere for the bows, as it will take some time for each of the singers to do their own. You have to leave the pit, go up a flight of stairs, make your way to the stage and then wait behind the curtain. As each soloist comes out, the ovations seem to increase. I go out and am pleasantly surprised with the audience approval of what we have done in the pit. It is then my turn to call out the principals and we take a long collective bow.

Were we perfect? No. Could we have done things better? Yes, we always can. But no one criticized me that night. In fact, administration members praised me for holding it all together as well as I did.

Am I pleased with how it went? Mostly, but I know that I will replay the entire opera in my head tonight, recalling the spots where I can improve. This is the nature of every performer I know. But overall, it was an exciting evening of theater.

I wish we could do it again tomorrow, but our next performance is not until Saturday night. A lot can happen over the five days off.

And it sure did!

March 30

A day passed with no communication of trouble ahead. Then the reviews came in. I read them, knowing that no one can be more critical of my work than me but these were downright mean. Opera blogs had appeared, clearly written by people within the Metropolitan Opera organization or at least leaked to them from inside. My own words were being used against me, even though at no point had I written that I was unprepared. The word learn was taken completely out of context.

That afternoon, I got a call from my agent, saying that I needed to walk away from this production. At first I thought that this was a reaction to what had been written in the press. A cast member told me that Angela had insisted that I not conduct. It was fairly easy to understand what happened. The conductor was expendable, but the soprano was not. After two and a half weeks of work, this was the first time anyone had expressed dissatisfaction as to my own contribution. At least directly to me.

March 31

The stress and aggravation were not worth the effort. I decided to walk away from the opera. The Met issued a terse, one-sentence press release, saying that I left for "personal reasons." That would be true but misleading.

It was time to clear out my dressing room space. I ran into a couple of people from the Met musical staff. They did not yet know I was departing. When I informed them, there were looks and expressions of shock and dismay. Three different conductors will take over the next three performances, each having no rehearsal other than some piano work with the singers. I wish them all the very best, and am sure that Angela will behave.

Will I give up working in opera? No. Will I continue to write about my musical experiences? Yes. Did this change my life? Certainly not!

When it was all said and done, this incident was just a small part of a very rich musical life for me. I have always considered my work in the opera pit to be secondary to the orchestral stage. Much of the repertoire does not suit my temperament but there are still pieces that I wish to perform. Some of the singers I have had the pleasure of working with are very good friends and colleagues.

As it turned out, I had another operatic appearance a few months later in Santa Fe. This was the world premiere of Lewis Spratlan's Pulitzer Prize–winning *Life Is a Dream*. In some ways, the atonal world that inhabits this score was even more foreign to me than the Verdi, but with a lot of work, it came off well. Overnight, it seemed like the travails of Violetta were more than a century old.

27

Heart and Sole

Health food may be good for the conscience but Oreos taste a hell of a lot better.

—ROBERT REDFORD

It is difficult to estimate the number of times I have heard, "Conductors are among the longest-lived people in the world." It is thought that the simple act of moving ones arms around for a couple of hours is enough to keep the blood flowing. To put it in a different context, here are longevity figures for some very distinguished conductors.

Gustav Mahler	51
Wilhelm Furtwängler	58
Dimitri Mitropoulos	64
Leonard Bernstein	72
Fritz Reiner	75
Sir Thomas Beecham	82
Sir Georg Solti	85
Bruno Walter	86
Arturo Toscanini	90
Carlo Maria Giulini	91
Leopold Stokowski	95

Perhaps there is a correlation between the profession and good health. Of course, other conductors expired at younger ages, and some on this list did not conduct toward the end of their lives.

There is no question that conducting is an aerobic activity. Professional athletes will acknowledge that necessary, constant motions for a steady length of time will, in some cases, exceed that of, say, a football player. We only get time-outs between movements or at intermission, if there is one. In each piece, the orchestral musician has the occasional rest or two along the way. If the conductor is lucky, a concerto may include a nice long cadenza.

For the most part, our job is to keep going. Some conductors make the mistake of expending huge amounts of energy early on in a performance, and then have little left for the home stretch. Others use minimal gestures, which can have an adverse effect of making the opening moments seem too casual. Each person on the podium has his or her catalog of physical gestures.

With more women entering the profession, actual physiognomy deserves more attention. When I teach, inevitably I see students who try to mimic their idols or mentors. It might be through their personal appearance, posture, facial expression or the gestures they use to communicate with the orchestra. I always wind up offering the same advice: "Be yourself. You are built uniquely. Go with what you have, and do not add anything that alters your basic makeup. Do not imitate what is good but do avoid what is bad."

Starting in the 1980s, women have become increasingly prominent on the podium. Their bodies are uniquely built and they should not necessarily try to imitate their male counterparts when conducting. Each needs to adjust the beat and expressive gesture to fit the physical demeanor of the body he or she was born with. To do otherwise simply imitates and does not represent the singular presence of the individual.

Just as the composer must have a distinctive voice, so must the conductor have a personal physical profile. Some of us are short, others tall. A few have very long arms. We can control our weight but that is about it. Range of motion, the ability to stand still or move around and the manner of eye contact with the players comprise part of what must be considered when mounting the podium.

A tall person does not need a long baton and also sometimes chooses not to use a podium. However, even a tall conductor standing on the floor forces some players in the back of the sections to look very hard to find a beat. Conversely, shorter conductors can heed the advice of Teddy Roosevelt, when he wrote,

"Speak softly and carry a big stick." Perhaps speaking softly is not the best tactic, as those same people in the back of the section need to hear you, too.

Obviously, the more assertive and aggressive the conductor, the more he or she will perspire. One cannot assume that this leads to weight control. I would lose almost two pounds of water weight per program. It was quickly made up at the post-performance dinner. We all know the perils of heavy eating late at night, but the conductor has very few options.

Unlike some wind players or singers who sometimes prefer to dine fairly close to curtain time, conductors will usually have a lunch around mid-afternoon. Dining soon before the commencement of the concert makes concentration difficult and can be a little uncomfortable. Besides, the big meal tends to be saved up as a celebratory gesture. It can last well into the wee hours of the morning.

Americans have heard time and time again about the importance of a good breakfast, but most people do not have to exert the high degree of physical activity required to get through a couple of rehearsals. It's the same on concert nights. If I eat even a "normal" meal in the morning, I get sluggish and start to feel uncomfortable when conducting. I might grab an apple, or maybe a bowl of cereal. Another part of the Western regimen of which I do not partake is drinking coffee. Never liked the taste or smell. Plus, I usually pop out of bed ready to go without the need for caffeine.

Problems of weight rarely come to mind when it comes to conductors. Once again, there seems to be a correlation between the aerobics of conducting and health. Huffing and puffing through a rehearsal or performance is not good. Generally, conductors are trim enough, and of the ten mentioned earlier in this chapter, only Bernstein seems to have had a problem belly. And that, likely due to overindulgence of items other than food.

Perhaps the lower back is the area of concern shared by every person standing in front of an orchestra. I do not know of a single conductor who has not experienced spinal trouble. Whereas instrumentalists might complain about the tailcoat or other concert attire, conductors might speak about shoes. For some, back problems start right away. Imagine standing on a solid platform, giving a strong downward gesture, and not getting the spring back from the floor. Those conductors who are especially physical subject the spine to an abnormal amount of pressure.

Although it might sound like a luxury, massage is almost crucial in this profession. Identifying the problem areas is not as easy as it might appear. For some conductors, the first signs of trouble might come in the form of tightness in the arms. Others experience difficulty in turning their heads from side to side, relying more on gestures and less on eye contact with every orchestra member. There are conductors who can never find a comfortable place to stand on the podium and whose backs are constantly in agony.

The podium itself can be to blame. A few conductors have had one custom made, often with a material that cushions the feet and minimizes the impact on the lower back. When there is enough spinal pain involved, the body will not allow you to leap or jump as you might be used to. On one occasion with the New York Philharmonic, I had *Le sacre* on the second half of the program. My back was killing me and I asked the whereabouts of the orchestra doctor. Fortunately he was around and recommended I take Motrin. When I asked, "One or two?" he replied, "Four! You don't have a headache!"

Dependence on drugs, even of the mild variety, can have adverse effects. If there is one thing more important than the physical capacity to actually conduct, it is the mental ability to concentrate. As much as the news reports about drug abuse in the pop and jazz world, it is still an unspoken subject in the orchestral strata. Overuse of alcohol and controlled substances certainly takes place.

Arthur Fiedler needed to have a bottle of Scotch waiting as he came off the stage. The illustrious big band leader and arranger Billy May actually had a glass of booze on the music stand as he was conducting recording sessions. Some orchestra and jazz musicians claim they play better when a bit high. At least they think they do. The use of beta-blockers to combat shaky nerves is becoming prevalent among classical performers.

It is a fine line between insecurity and nervousness. I once asked my father why he did not seem to have any anxiety when performing.

"I practice, study, work hard and feel prepared. Most of the time it comes out fine and once in a while it does not, but I can never say that I was not ready.

"On the other hand," he continued, "if I have not practiced, did not study, did not work hard and am not prepared, not only should I be nervous, I shouldn't be onstage in the first place!"

Tough words for a young musician, but ones that I kept to heart.

The only times I have ever felt even the slightest hesitation about onstage performances were those where I knew that I could have done more. Of course that can apply to any appearance, but there comes a point where it is fine-tuning as opposed to lack of knowledge. There is also a fine line between anxiety and excitement. Adrenaline can be a powerful agent and it is perfectly all right to have a degree of apprehension, but it must never override the joy of walking onto the concert platform.

Another physical ailment that afflicts many conductors is plantar fasciitis. I had never heard of it until my feet started to give me trouble. This was in 2007 and I had arrived in Tanglewood. All of a sudden, walking was painful. The soles of my feet seemed to be in constant agony. Getting up in the morning was the worst and I had no idea what was happening.

Upon my return to Detroit, I was sent to a foot specialist who made the diagnosis. Charts and diagrams were trotted out and I was given a set of exercises to stretch out the afflicted area. There was still not much improvement. A few weeks later I was in Taipei.

During this tour, a relative of the violinist Cho-Liang Lin had contacted me. She invited me to dinner with some friends and family. When they picked me up, they asked about my impressions of the city.

"It is wonderful. I love the museums and have enjoyed the foot massage parlors, especially since I have plantar fasciitis."

The reply was, "Are you all right? We should take you to the hospital."

"No, I am fine."

"But I am a doctor there and we have a whole section devoted to this problem."

So off we drove to the Taipei Hilton Medical Center, which was more like a small city rather than a hospital. Indeed, there was a place devoted to the construction of implants for shoes meant to ease the problem. In ten minutes, I had been x-rayed, examined and fitted. This would have taken two weeks at home.

It took a little while but the pain went away.

At the outset of this chapter, I listed the ages at which some distinguished conductors had passed away. Here are the official causes of death.

Mahler   infectious myocarditis
Furtwängler   pneumonia

Mitropoulos	heart attack
Bernstein	progressive lung failure
Reiner	heart attack
Beecham	stroke
Solti	heart failure
Walter	heart attack
Toscanini	stroke
Giulini	not reported
Stokowski	heart attack

In 2009, my own bout with mortality took place. The following is what I wrote for the monthly column on my website.

December 2009

No complaints this month. In many ways, I am lucky to be writing anything at all. But with the enforced vacation due to a heart attack on November 1, I have had some time to reflect about many matters, most having very little to do with music.

Here is what happened.

During my week of rehearsals and concerts in Rotterdam, I had started to feel a bit out of breath, especially walking over to the hall. Being somewhat overweight, this was not out of the ordinary, but once in a while, I actually had to stop. This should have told me something.

There were four concerts all together. During the first three, I got a bit winded and dizzy but got through the programs easily enough. At the first performance I felt I might actually fall forward off the podium and attributed this to simply not getting my balance. There were even moments when I knew I was losing concentration, but again, I ignored the signs and thought it was jet lag.

The final performance was on Sunday, at 2:30 in the afternoon. I had brought my luggage to the hall, as my flight to Prague for the next set of concerts was due to leave at 8:30 p.m. It is about an hour's drive from Rotterdam to Schiphol Airport in Amsterdam. Again, I got quite out of breath walking to the hall, but this time the feeling did not dissipate, at least for a while.

When I got to my dressing room, I was already huffing and puffing. The first piece on the program was the Third Piano Concerto of Beethoven, not a particularly physical work for the conductor. As it progressed, I began to feel much better. However, during intermission, I started to experience the out-of-breath symptoms that had occurred an hour earlier. Someone asked me if I was okay and I said yes. Then things started to change.

The moment I got to the podium for the Rachmaninov Second Symphony, I started to feel tightness in my chest, almost like someone was standing on it, trying to prevent me from breathing. I really did think that I should leave the stage for a few minutes and get some water. The reason I did not suspect a heart attack at that point was that there was no tingling in either the jaw or left arm, symptoms which I have always thought were the signals of a coronary event.

I am not sure what it was that made me believe I could get through the almost hour-long work, but somehow, I did. At that point I was perspiring profusely and the pain in my chest was unbearable. Collapsing on the couch in the dressing room, I asked for the door to be closed while I caught my breath. A few minutes later, Frans, the head of the stage department and a very fine fellow, came back in and called the medical team. Each European house has such a group on standby and they rushed into the dressing room.

By this time, my shirt was off, and I was desperately trying to find a comfortable position. Cold towels were pressed on my forehead. All that was on my mind was that the pain was increasing and I needed help. The medical assistants then uttered the magic words, "You are having a heart attack but will be okay. An ambulance is on the way."

I called my girlfriend, Cindy McTee, who was in Dallas at the time. At first she did not believe that there was anything wrong, but after the phone was taken away from me, it became clear that all was not well. She caught the first flight out and arrived in Rotterdam, staying on to take care of me.

Much of the next hour is a blur. I remember being hoisted onto a stretcher, being taken outside in the rain to the car and arriving at the hospital. We raced down a hallway and into an operating theater. I think there were only a few questions, like what I was allergic to, name, age and so on. Insurance never came up. The angioplasty progressed with me somewhat awake and able to see the wire going up my artery.

At some point I started to feel better and woke up in the hospital's intensive care unit. There was much fussing and constant monitoring. A medical unit came in to tell me what had happened and what they had done. The angioplasty was successful and I now had three stents and a balloon pump in my body. Uncomfortable? Oh, yes! But better than the alternative.

My job now was to just listen and follow instructions. So for the next ten days, I stayed put with occasional forays into the hallways, attempting to get some motion back. This was not so easy and often I used a walker to get around. Eventually I managed on my own. It was even possible to survive the rigorously bland items that passed as food. Jell-O never looked so good.

It was initially thought that I might get back to the States in six or seven days, but then the doctors decided that pushing it was not a good idea. So on the Monday nine days after the heart attack, I took a stress test on a stationary bicycle, passed and went to Miami. Many years ago, in DC, I had seen a cardiologist who would later move to Florida and become the dean of the University Medical Center. I decided to stick with a doctor I knew for the next phase of evaluation.

After three days, it was determined that my heart had not suffered very much damage, but that I needed a few more weeks of rest and recovery. At first, my own thoughts were that I could easily conduct one half of a program, probably doing just the concertos that were scheduled, maybe one rehearsal and then perform the concerts sitting down, not expending too much energy. But it became clear that even this was not possible, as I grew fairly tired as the day progressed. I also tried not to do very much paperwork either, with just a little time spent moving program ideas around for next season.

It was awfully good to get back to my home, where I could enjoy cooking in new and different ways, do a bit of low-impact exercise, and catch up on DVDs that have been lingering on shelves for months on end. At one point I was surprised at how easy it was to let go for a bit. Not similar to a vacation, but much needed after all I had been through.

What did I learn from this?

Perhaps not quite as much in life-changing experience as I thought. No major revelations, as almost everything I had thought about this past month was something that had been on my mind earlier. Slowing down? Probably a bit, with more time off. Obsessing about details? I am not sure that I am capable of letting go of the control issues that face almost every conductor. It is part of our being. But maybe more delegation of certain aspects of the job can take place. It truly was no problem letting substitutes fill in for me. After all, this was how I got my start, jumping in for indisposed conductors way back in 1974.

I was reminded of a trip to Milwaukee that I made almost forty years ago. At the time, I was assistant conductor in Saint Louis and spent a great deal of time flying up to Chicago to hear concerts there. This was during the period when Sir Georg Solti was music director and Carlo Maria Giulini was principal guest conductor. The orchestra used to play a series of concerts in Wisconsin, on Monday nights, and I would go in a car with the conductor, giving me a wonderful opportunity to speak with the maestro in a calm environment.

Giulini very rarely spoke about music itself. He was mostly concerned with the philosophy that underscored a piece or even a note. He told me about a time in his life, when he was not quite fifty years old and had to undergo a serious operation. It was possible that he might not have survived the surgery. When he awoke from the procedure, he made a vow to himself, and these were words I would never forget: "You must make music a part of your life and never make life a part of your music."

Maybe experience of a life-threatening situation is necessary to fully comprehend this. That it took this long for me to act upon his wisdom

is unfortunate. Perhaps others can follow the advice sooner and not
wait until it is almost too late.

In retrospect, it appears that the actual episode was exacerbated by the physical
act of conducting. The aerobic activity definitely caused the clogged artery to
be pushed to its limit. There are many examples of athletes who have collapsed
in the midst of their own performance. Still, the active lifestyle probably kept
me around longer.

The level of exercise does not determine a person's physical fitness. Plus, there
are mental and emotional factors. These can lead to more disruptions and may
cause a loss of concentration, something no conductor can afford.

In addition to the responsibility for personal conditions, the music director
must be alert and sensitive to each and every performer on the stage. At a rehearsal in Atlanta, the second trombonist collapsed and was writhing onstage.
I quickly shouted for someone to call 911 and in five minutes a team was on the
way to take care of what had been an epileptic seizure. With all the anxiety, it
seemed best to cancel the remainder of the rehearsal, and the orchestra understood that we would have to make up lost ground the next day.

Over two successive performances, a pair of audience members suffered heart
episodes during concerts I was conducting with the Bamberg Symphony. It was
best to leave this in the hands of the medical staff in attendance and continue
with the concert. By bizarre coincidence, both incidents took place at the same
moment during the fourth movement of Schumann's "Rhenish" Symphony, a
piece depicting the great cathedral of Cologne.

The conductor needs to grasp any problem immediately and make an in-
stantaneous decision. If it is your own orchestra and you know the personalities involved, most likely you will have a good idea of what to do. If you are on
the road, your main contact will be the personnel manager. Do not wade into
something on your own here. Practical knowledge and common sense will
dictate what must occur.

In one's life there are certainly matters that do not rely exclusively on physical well-being. The conductor's life is somewhat solitary, and being on the road
only amplifies that status. It takes a toll on most musicians' personal lives. I envy

those who have been able to maintain solid relationships. One can go looking for pleasure or escape. Likewise, it can find you.

I am not so sure that my inability to sustain a stable personal life was due to roadwork, although there is no question that this played a key factor. My first two marriages were brief, lasting one and two and a half years. The third lasted over twenty years, and during that time, I became a father. When your life is devoted to music, you will be apart from family for weeks at a stretch, sometimes months. This requires an unbelievably strong will and extraordinary patience from your partner.

That partner who enters into a living arrangement with a conductor, and in particular a music director, has a significant role to play. In the past, this person was meant to represent and be subservient to her husband. Yes, I know this sounds ridiculous nowadays, but back then, only men held the job and the wife was the social butterfly, advocating on behalf of her spouse. She traveled constantly at his side, and somehow managed to raise a family. After the conductor died, she inevitably wrote a book.

Physical and mental health are important issues to consider. It is not so much that conducting is beneficial because of the aerobic activity involved. Conducting also provides a physical outlet for virtually every emotion. If the music is tender we can show that. Violent, passionate, serene and every other feeling you can imagine all exist in most pieces of music. Being able to convey these to the orchestra and audience makes the rehearsal and concert experience special. Feeling them on the inside makes it unique.

Perhaps conductors are long lived after all, but not because they move around on the podium. Instead, it might come from being moved by the nature of the music itself. The connection with the past is very powerful. Every day, the musician gets to do what doctors can only dream: bring the past to life.

28

One Strike and They're Out

It is not he who gains the exact point in dispute who scores most in
controversy—but he who has shown the better temper.

—SAMUEL BUTLER

For more years than I care to remember, a certain piece of advice has stayed with me: "If your orchestra goes on strike, get outta town."

It was uttered during my very first season as music director of the Saint Louis Symphony. That year coincided with the hundredth anniversary of the founding of the orchestra, so there was much at stake in the negotiation of a new contract.

Labor strife seems to have been with us for a long time, and it surfaces almost annually in contract talks between management and symphony orchestras. Hard to believe that a little over half a century ago, unions did not have much to say where orchestral musicians were concerned. Seasons were shorter, the pay was low and the players were regarded as servants or slaves to the conductor.

Stories abound as to mistreatment by music directors in those days. The conductor could literally toss out somebody just because the player was not looking at the podium constantly. Individuals could be asked to play a passage in front of the whole orchestra. If they did not pass muster, they were dismissed.

George Szell once confronted a member of the Cleveland Orchestra, asking him to purchase a new instrument. The musician said, "I don't make enough money for that." Szell replied, "You had enough to buy a new car," and promptly fired the musician.

To properly understand today's situation, it is necessary to go back. Here are five orchestras as they existed in the 1952–53 season. These were the minimum sizes, length of season and weekly wage.

Orchestra	Players	Weeks	Weekly Wage
Boston Symphony Orchestra	103	46	$125.00
Cleveland Orchestra	95	36	$98.00
Detroit Symphony Orchestra	102	34	$100.00
National Symphony Orchestra	86	26	$100.00
Saint Louis Symphony Orchestra	85	23	$96.25

In 1958, not one orchestra offered full-time, year-round employment. Few had the right to ratify their own contracts. Seven out of twenty orchestras surveyed offered a basic pension plan and only one provided paid vacations. Players had to stand in line to receive their weekly paychecks. Relations between orchestra members and the union were strained, with negligible support for the workforce.

Strong union bosses held sway, with power being the ultimate tool. James Petrillo, head of Local 10 in Chicago, best exemplified the old school. His preferred method of negotiating was to put a gun on the table. Finally, in 1962, the Chicago musicians said, "Enough," and after years of wrangling and fighting, Petrillo was defeated. What followed was a revolution among orchestras and recording artists.

Just look at the changes in numbers for the five orchestras cited earlier, slightly more than fifty years later.

Orchestra	Players	Weeks	Weekly Wage
Boston Symphony Orchestra	103	52	$2,465
Cleveland Orchestra	101	52	$2,219
National Symphony Orchestra	96	52	$2,327
Saint Louis Symphony Orchestra	85	43	$1,786
Detroit Symphony Orchestra	81	40	$1,975

There are, of course, variables: seniority, additional revenue from broadcasts and recordings, as well as different health and retirement benefits. But it is easy to see that in some cases wages from 1953 to 2010 have jumped more than twenty-five times higher in those fifty-seven years!

With a diligent and organized union machine to support them, orchestral players gained much ground. What was a part-time job is now one of the highest-paying professions in the United States. Competition for a position can be fierce and many experienced musicians find themselves in the awkward position of having to prove themselves yet again.

I was but a young man in 1979, hardly attuned to the ways of the negotiation world. Considering that when I began in Saint Louis eleven years earlier as the assistant conductor, I made the princely sum of $8,000 for the year; running the ship seemed like pure fantasy. Now I was the captain and leadership was expected.

The disputes were the usual suspects: salary, health benefits and pension. As it was an auspicious season, there was an assumption that management would not risk forgoing any performances. The opening-night gala was to include many of the heavy-hitters in the music world, and had potential for raising a great deal of money. Excitement had been building in the community; someone started a "Slatkin's back!" campaign.

The board made an offer and presented it to the musicians as the final one. The orchestra's attorney, Leonard Liebowitz, did not believe it and told the orchestra that there was more money to be had. A six-week strike followed. All the hard work that had been put into the opening went for naught. Public confidence eroded and contributions declined. When the orchestra came back to work, it accepted the identical deal that had been presented six weeks earlier. Everyone lost.

For the duration of the strike, I did as told and left town. There is no more frustrating feeling for a conductor than to be without an orchestra. Some pressure was put on me to say a few words, but I kept my promise and did not open my mouth. I received updates relayed by telephone, as this happened during the prehistoric era devoid of computers. Most of the news reached me about a day after any discussions.

The previous season, there had been a work stoppage by the National Symphony Orchestra in Washington. It garnered much publicity when the music director, Mstislav Rostropovich, joined the orchestra on the picket line. The impetus for this extraordinary gesture had to do with the threat by the police to arrest the musicians for marching where they were not permitted. Slava's actions were viewed as a sign of support for his players who fiercely adored their maestro, but it did not influence the position of the board and the strike continued for five more weeks.

A lot of the time, music directors stay out of the fray. After all, the board of directors hires them, but at the same time, they do not want to offend the players with whom they must make music. It is a tough balancing act. You want to support the musicians, as they are the heart and soul of your professional life; however, you understand the position of the board as regards fiscal responsibility.

It was more than thirty years later that I would be placed in a similar position. Among the questions most prevalent in 2008 when I became music director was, "Why Detroit?" My answer was consistent: "It is a great orchestra playing in a great hall with a great tradition."

Everyone warned me of the dire financial times the DSO faced. The organization carried a lingering debt to the banks approaching $60 million. The impact of the recession was just being felt, and Detroit looked like the economic black hole of the United States. Some portions of the city resembled Berlin in 1945. Orchestra Hall was just a bit north of the downtown area and seemed an anachronism. Here was an elegant concert venue with little connection to its constituency in the neighborhood. The same could be said of any number of major orchestra's halls in this country.

In an effort to show my support of the management, I was asked to speak to the orchestra about a freeze on hiring. For over an hour I rattled on about how I was trying to "protect" them from an even worse scenario. Little did I know how true that would be.

Attempts to renegotiate the current contract were futile, with everyone pinning hopes on an upward spike in numbers that might enable a more positive outcome. Talks between management and union were going nowhere fast. I was once again brought in, this time at the request of the orchestra, to sit in on a bargaining session. My conditions were simple: Lenny Liebowitz, representing the DSO musicians, could not attend. I still held him responsible for the Saint Louis strike.

After I carefully reviewed the proposals on the table, I made a few recommendations, nothing severe. Those were rejected and that marked the last time I would ever get involved in the negotiations.

As the summer of 2010 progressed, very little movement was palpable from either side. Management would put an offer on the table and the orchestra would turn it down. Each side accused the other of not negotiating in good faith. I am never sure what that term means, as all parties come to the sessions with his or her own agenda. The board needed to dramatically slash the budget, and the orchestra wished to stay in the same economic ballpark with at least nine other top-paid ensembles.

For most of my career, the elite number was five. They included the New York, Boston, Philadelphia, Cleveland and Chicago orchestras. The Holy Quintet. When someone decided that a top ten was in order, the numbers game went into full court press. In the past, the big five also referred to the consistent quality of symphonic performance week after week. As the expanding pool of available musicians made its way into the workforce, great concerts were heard nightly from at least fifteen different groups. In 1984, *Time* magazine declared the Saint Louis Symphony the second-best orchestra in the country. And in 2010, Alex Ross wrote that the Minnesota Orchestra had earned first place.

Arguments abound as to the relationship of salary to quality, with the strongest that high pay ensures a high caliber of musician. In some instances that applies, but that notion does a tremendous injustice to those outstanding talents in orchestras that do not rank in the top ten. My experience tells me that many highly qualified musicians would be happy to land a job in a fine orchestra, even if the pay was not among the privileged.

Another hotly debated topic in Detroit was whether the musicians of the orchestra should appear in any other guise than onstage with the full ensemble. Should the DSO contract ask them to participate in chamber music, teaching or outreach? The orchestra members contended that they were hired just to play in the band and that is all they should be required to do. Management announced that it was impossible to sustain a full symphony orchestra and leave musicians idle for weeks simply because the repertoire did not demand their specific services.

One fascinating aspect was that a number of the players already fulfilled these other duties on their own, but did not consider them as part of the orchestra business. Board members wondered why they were paying big bucks for musicians who only played on a part-time basis. Inevitable analogies to sports were made, citing the placekicker or relief pitcher who might not be used at all in some games, but is invaluable when needed. Of course, the big leagues are about making money, whereas the orchestras are about trying to lose as little as possible.

A few orchestras have tried to implement some form of what is referred to as service conversion. This can get cumbersome, as no one can quantify the relative rehearsal demands for a Beethoven trio versus a symphony. An ancillary and rather paradoxical situation is that chamber music tends to be far more difficult and require longer rehearsal time, but pays far less than an orchestra job.

There is no arguing that the orchestra, as we know it, is evolving. Now there is less demand for what we do, the competition for concertgoers' attention is greater from all media, and the arts education models of the past no longer exist, so building an audience is much more difficult.

Part of the problem is the simple definition of an orchestra. Here is one of the most frequently found definitions:

> A group of instrumentalists, esp. one combining string, woodwind, brass, and percussion sections and playing classical music.

Fine, but a crucial part is missing: How many instrumentalists?

Each orchestra contract defines the maximum and minimum number of musicians in the group. If a piece of music is written for fewer than the maximum, the musicians who do not play are paid anyway.

This raises all kinds of questions when it comes to choosing repertoire for the season. If a piece calls for nine instruments and is conducted, does this nonet count as chamber music or orchestral? What happens when a work requires each player to perform a solo part, such as the Strauss *Metamorphosen* for twenty-three solo strings, or even Ligeti's *Atmosphères* where each member of the full orchestra has a separate part to play?

Another major issue under negotiation was the fifty-two-week season. This concept was a rarity until the 1960s. A few orchestras had summer homes, notably in Chicago, Philadelphia, Boston and Los Angeles. The competitive nature of negotiations changed the picture and several others hopped on the yearlong bandwagon. It worked for a while. Festivals sprouted up and provided lots of options for musicians as well as audiences.

Population bases shifted and diversions were ubiquitous. The public, in a good number of metropolitan areas, seemed not to want so much music all year long. Yet the contracts stayed in place. One economic rule that I do not completely understand: it turns out more fiscally viable to lay off the orchestra for a week rather than to have it play to a smaller crowd. In a job that included between eight and ten vacation weeks per player, more were added because no one was out there to hear the music.

Are there easy solutions? No, but each orchestra has to decide what is best in its own community. Comparisons with other institutions simply do not apply. Considerations include cost of living, needs, and most important, what kind of orchestra the city wants. In addition, one overriding factor dominates the others: Can the city afford it? We have always played to a small percentage of our entire population base: roughly 4.5 percent. This can be expanded if you include one-off concerts that are targeted at a specific audience, or even a wide-ranging pops season. Educational programs and initiatives can broaden the horizon. The bottom line is that symphony orchestras do not appeal to a majority of the public.

The music director is the face of the orchestra. He or she is the person most identified with the group. That is why I believe it is crucial for the conductor to be an integral part of the community. Some of my colleagues prefer to jet in and out, staying in hotels as needed. My own philosophy is that if I am expected to help fund-raise, I need to know my supporters. Seeing them in the markets, at dinners or attending ball games is still the best way to establish relationships.

That is precisely what I did during the course of the Detroit strike. Rather than get out of town, I toiled behind the scenes. Meeting with board members, patrons and orchestra members, my goal was to discover if any hope existed for immediate funding. The overwhelming answer to my questions about recovery for the DSO was, "As soon as there is a contract, we will come forward."

Obviously, the orchestra would prefer this action in advance of a settlement. Many in management shared this feeling but were encumbered by a very rigid stance by some key board members. This work stoppage epitomized a rock and a hard place.

The music director must sympathize with his or her musicians. Many people think that orchestral players are overly compensated for their work, especially in light of a declining economy. But it must be pointed out that these artists are highly skilled and trained specialists. Many have worked their entire lives to achieve a place in a fine orchestra. So it could also be argued that orchestral players are currently underpaid. But because of the tremendous gains by the musicians and union, it is getting more and more difficult to raise salaries above their current scales.

There was much talk of the "reinvented" orchestra. No one was sure what this meant but everyone felt that some fundamental changes needed to occur. Perhaps it was hinted at in a speech given in 1987 by Ernest Fleischmann, then executive director of the Los Angeles Philharmonic. At the Cleveland Institute of Music, he argued for a new "community of musicians," one that would be more flexible and cover almost every aspect of musical life.

At first, I thought it was a terrible idea. Visions of smaller community orchestras being eaten up came to mind. If a large ensemble was suddenly split into several groups and sent to outlying areas, what would happen to the local orchestras? Didn't this idea move away from the basic definition of the symphony orchestra?

Now, more than twenty years later, I think not only was he right, but also very much ahead of his time. Here are a couple of examples he proposed.

> First of all, we need to rid ourselves of the idea that an orchestra consists of fixed numbers of strings. Winds, brass and percussion, adding up to around one hundred players. The ideal new musical community should include some 140 to 150 musicians: a large string complement, based on twelve double basses, plus six each of woodwinds, trumpets and trombones, two tubas, ten French horns, eight timpani and percussion, a couple of harps and a couple of keyboard players . . .
>
> We've got 144 terrific musicians. They'll still need a music director, of course. That's always a problem, whether you have a conventional symphony

orchestra, or this pool, this new community of musicians. Too many orchestras are constantly chasing too few good conductors. Anyway, in addition to the music director, we also need a director of new music programs, who can also conduct and who specializes in music of our time. Ideally, and additionally, there should be someone to lead the pool's chamber music activities and this person must also be a good chamber orchestra conductor. Now, with the music director at the head, and with really competent people directing new music and chamber music activities, we can dip into this golden pond, this precious pool of a community of musicians and come up with an infinite variety of activities over just one season . . .

Then, too, when you get a community of some 150 musicians, plus an expert staff, it's highly likely that there will be among them a number who are skilled at other important aspects of audience service and development: adult education for example (this is too often overlooked)—our audiences are so much more receptive and attentive when they come to a concert well-prepared as a result of lectures, discussions and written materials . . . And then there's ethnic music, folk music, jazz—the possibilities are endless. It should be possible for every single member of our community of musicians to practice those forms of musical and ancillary activity that allow each and every one of them to express themselves fully. And that's how we can perform a quality and range of cultural and educational services for our audiences that the traditional symphony orchestra is just not able to achieve.

And there it is! More or less the Detroit debate, a quarter century earlier. For me, the critical part of the equation is to ask the musicians of the orchestra to participate, rather than demand that they do these new tasks. To that end, what makes sense is to "grandfather" in these new options, with a different model for auditioning. This would include a set of questions that help define the strengths and weaknesses of incoming members.

Under this new paradigm, it would be possible to have a group of, say, sixty musicians play a standard symphonic concert in the main hall. A baroque ensemble specializing in historically informed renditions of Bach could perform at a local church. The Detroit New Music Ensemble might hold sway in the lounge of Wayne State University. Another group could be in the pit for *West Side Story*. Remaining musicians not involved in these activities could work in educational forums, helping to create music programs where none may currently exist. This scenario could actually take place, not over a week, but in a single day. Fleischmann's ideal community makes it not only possible, but also probable.

Why am I bringing up this subject in a book mostly devoted to what the conductor is supposed to do?

Because in most cities, the music director is the first person the public looks to for leadership and vision in the fine arts. Also, any restructuring of the current division of labor within the orchestral ranks will fall squarely on the music director's shoulders, at least for the time being. As the artistic head of the institution, the music director is the person who calls the shots.

The consequences of labor strife involve a lengthy healing process. No one will have received everything he or she is seeking. Both sides will claim some sort of victory, simply as a face-saving gesture. Everyone will be happy to have left this bitter time behind them. Now the reality of putting Humpty Dumpty back together again begins.

In Detroit, to salvage the remaining nine weeks of the season, a series of low-priced concerts was put on. These produced many sold-out houses. The association now had the right to both video- and audio-stream its concerts. The concertmaster resigned abruptly without informing the management or music director. Several members of the orchestra either retired or left for other positions. The orchestra started playing concerts in venues throughout the metropolitan area, beginning the process of building audiences outside Orchestra Hall.

When work resumes after a stoppage, it is vitally important that the music director establish the necessary professional tone at the first rehearsal. Therefore, the choice of words at the start may be the most crucial utterance that you will ever make. It is not your job to comment on the negotiations. I do not remember what I said when the strike ended in Saint Louis, but for Detroit, this seemed appropriate:

"Welcome home."

PART
THREE

God is in the details.

—**LUDWIG MIES VAN DER ROHE**

God may be in the details, but the goddess is in the questions.
Once we begin to ask them, there's no turning back.

—**GLORIA STEINEM**

29

Ten Essential Decisions

*As soon as questions of will or decision or reason or choice of
action arise, human science is at a loss.*

—NOAM CHOMSKY

As stated at the outset, it was not my intention to write a textbook about
how to conduct. That is best left to others. However, nearly every aspect
of the conductor's craft requires some type of decision-making process. Here
are ten musical passages that exemplify problems common to a large amount
of the repertoire, with commentary illustrating a majority of problem-solving
devices the conductor must have at his or her disposal. These are not intended
as technical exercises, but rather as an introduction to what faces anyone who
wishes to step onto a podium.

Beethoven: Symphony No. 5

Here they are—probably the most famous five bars in music history! (See Ex.
1.) Look at them carefully. First you see the notes. We all know them. But nine
out of ten musicians who have played this passage for years cannot tell you what
instruments are in use and which are silent during those measures.

Some think the horns are blaring, others believe the timpani is being hit
and some believe that everyone in the orchestra is bowing, blowing, striking
or scraping something. Amazing, isn't it? Just the strings and two clarinets.

Why are the clarinets there? Surely no one will hear them. Maybe we are
not supposed to. What was going on in Beethoven's head when he wrote this?

I do not pretend to know the answer to the last question, but I do know
that if the clarinets are omitted, or other instruments added, the characteristic sound of this opening is altered, and not just on the page. The ear notices

Example 1. Ludwig van Beethoven's
Symphony No. 5, first movement, mm. 1–5.

something different, even if not sure what that is.

What decisions does the conductor have to make with this first page?

For our purposes, we will not get into the discussion about Beethoven's metronome marks. You can agree or disagree, but one thing is for sure: the composer wants the feel of one beat to the bar. Does this mean that a phrase is just this single measure, or is it longer? Does the pattern of the baton indicate a series of single downward strokes or perhaps a larger beat gesture, as if the passage really was in four?

In his insightful book *The Compleat Conductor*, Gunther Schuller spends a great deal of time analyzing the movement and structure of the opening in particular. He gives a clear-headed approach to the meaning of the second fermata's being one bar longer than its predecessor. If you want to know every possibility for this opening, pick up Gunther's tome. But that is not what I am going to write about.

You stand in front of the orchestra, ready to pounce on the first bar with a vengeance. What goes through your mind at this time? I believe that first and foremost, you must have the feeling of the tempo already coursing through your body before you lift your arms. However you envision this outburst, it must be instantly clear to the orchestra. Whether you think of the eighth-note rest at the start of the first measure as the ictus of the beat, or you think of the first three notes leading to the fermata as the high point, it does not matter.

What you must do is to be clear so the orchestra cannot misinterpret your conception. Do not start until you are absolutely sure of what you want. If, after a while, you still cannot make up your mind, perhaps you are not ready to conduct this piece.

Practice over and over in front of a mirror, pretending that you are the second clarinet player, performing under your own direction. Where and when will you breathe? What kind of sound should be produced? How short or long are the eighth notes? How much time passes between the second and third bar? Now place yourself in the violist's chair. Are the first three notes on open strings? Do they start on an up- or down-bow? How fast will the conductor take this? And how long or short will the fermatas be?

The process is the same for essentially every bar of this movement: questions about length, short versus long, where to change bow, even where the string players need to take a breath.

Yes, once you have figured out how to manage these five bars, you have it made. Uh-oh! There are 497 more measures to go, with decisions for all the notes and rests. Still sure you want this job?

Brahms: Symphony No. 1

This shouldn't be too hard. First, examine the scoring (see Ex. 2). Woodwinds in twos with a contrabassoon; four horns, two in C and two in E-flat, so that all the notes of the C minor scale can be covered; trumpets, timpani and strings. Fairly conventional for a mid-romantic work.

Three things are going on simultaneously. One line moves upward, one moves down and the other stays static with a steady pulse of Cs. Let's look at this last item first.

Obviously those hammered notes are supposed to help us determine the tempo. But what is the tempo marking? *Un poco sostenuto!* A little sustained. What is that supposed to tell us? Is it fast, moderate or slow? And can you really hear the contrabassoon with the timpani pounding away? The length of these notes becomes paramount as you grapple with the balance issue as well as striving to create clarity for whatever tempo you choose. "Why couldn't you have given us a metronome mark?" you ask of the absent Brahms. It would have made the transition at the end of the movement much easier to decipher.

Example 2. Johannes Brahms' Symphony No. 1, first movement, mm. 1–7.

Next, we have to decide what to do with the double basses. On the instruments of Brahms' era the player could not get to a note below E. Would the composer have preferred the opening C lower if he had had a more contemporary double bass with an extension lowering the string's pitch? Or would this have altered the sound too much and made it less characteristically Brahms? You will have to deal with this dilemma time and time again.

Now let's look at the line that moves upward. Just violins and cellos, no violas. He could have added the alto voice with the others, but chose not to. Why?

Texture, perhaps? Could the strings be too overwhelming if the majority of the section carried the line that goes up? We know that ascending scale patterns get louder even if no crescendo is indicated, just as they get softer when descending even if no diminuendo is marked.

But we also have to wonder about those slurs. Surely Brahms did not intend the players to play two bars to the bow. This would take away the intensity of the growing turmoil. So the conductor must find a way to get around this without losing the tension inherent in the phrase structure. I usually divide up the bowing so that some instrumentalists change bows an eighth note after the others. This helps create a more seamless flow, and minimizes the stress at the bar line, already under attack from the timpani and others.

The line that moves down has its own problems. You will notice that the flutes fall out of the pattern by bar three. Even if Brahms had the highest C available, he would not have wanted this note squealing out, so he had to decide where to move the flutes upward to continue as subtly as possible to play the descending scale. As the instruments approach the lower part of the system, they must make a crescendo, as the upper line will have taken over.

This brings us to a significant issue. Breath.

Just as it is mandatory for the conductor to have a working knowledge of the string bowings, it is equally, maybe even more important, that he or she know when to breathe. This applies to the strings, too, not just the winds and brass. Sometimes you want the musicians to breathe in unison and sometimes you want to stagger this so that the sound appears to have no breath at all.

As with every piece, the conductor's job is to convey the essence of the mood right from the upbeat. That first gesture must contain tension, motion, tempo, mood and sound.

What looked simple at the outset has become complicated indeed.

Mozart: Symphony No. 40

On the surface (see Ex. 3), the instrumentation seems quite clear and simple. Winds mostly in twos, only two horns (but in somewhat unusual keys) and strings. But it brings us to a question that must be asked with pretty much any repertoire prior to, say, Brahms.

How large should the orchestra be?

Example 3. Wolfgang Amadeus Mozart's Symphony No. 40, first movement, mm. 1–7.

History tells us that Mozart, along with most of his contemporaries, used however many he could get. His visits to Paris confirm that he enjoyed a large body of strings. We also do not know whether he heard this particular symphony in his lifetime, or what he had in mind when writing the work.

The second half of the twentieth century has provided us with useful insights into the manner in which music was performed in earlier eras. A whole industry was founded on the basis of "historically informed" performance practice. Yet this approach instills a slightly false sense of historical perspective. We know that composers welcomed the progress that instruments underwent during their lifetimes. So what do we do now that so many changes have taken place? What would Mozart have wanted?

Halls are substantially larger. Audiences do not arrive in horse-driven carriages. The performers play without candlelight. Most important, we have the advantage, or disadvantage, of having heard works written after so many masterpieces were conceived. This accumulated knowledge alters our listening perspective. We simply cannot ignore where we are at this moment in our lives. In other words, although it might be possible to play a work as audiences heard it two hundred years ago, an audience cannot listen to a work that way.

So a major portion of the conductor's job is to decide how he or she wishes to interpret music from an earlier period. This takes years of research and study. Many examine the score and try to determine what it says to us in the present day. Others make decisions on how it might have sounded in earlier times. Either approach can be considered correct.

The first three bars of the Mozart 40 show a real problem, no matter into which camp you fall. The writing is clear enough, but take a look at the viola part. *Divisi* means, in this case, that half of the section plays the upper part and the other half plays the lower notes. Should they be divided in equal numbers? How many players will it take to balance with the other strings? Should the upper half be assigned to the first couple of stands or should the violists divide the part on the stand, with one player taking the top and the other the bottom?

Most conductors just starting their careers do not have to deal with the size of the orchestra. Their first jobs will probably be with smaller ensembles, so every member plays every composition. If you are the head of an orchestra of one hundred, not all those players are needed, or even appropriate, for this classical symphony. One of the first decisions the conductor must make for almost any work from the baroque period through the early romantics is the size of the orchestral workforce.

Ultimately, the decision comes down to three things: taste, study and who is available. Our job is to preserve the integrity of the composer's wishes, not impose our will. If we are good musicians, then we will come up with the right solution.

Dvořák: Symphony No. 9

In this excerpt from Dvořák's "New World" Symphony (see Ex. 4), we are concerned only with the very last bar, not that what comes before is so easy, as there are countless decisions to be made. This ending is extremely difficult to pull off and has prompted some conductors to drastically alter what is written. What we are talking about are the *diminuendo* and *ppp* markings.

The obvious predecessor is the "Great" C Major Symphony by Schubert. For many years, the work's rendering was based on the assumption, as notation seemed to show, that a diminuendo takes place over the course of the last note. Scholarship now tells us that in Schubert's case, this was not a marking

Example 4. Antonin Dvořák's Symphony No. 9, fourth movement, mm. 345–348.

for getting softer but an accent to be sustained throughout the whole measure. Dvořák is quite clear in providing an actual dynamic marking, all the way down to *ppp*, pretty much the softest possible sound. Audiences new to this symphony are somewhat perplexed when the energy seems to drop suddenly from what has been a most exciting coda. In some cases, a few conductors have chosen to ignore the diminuendo and simply stay *fortissimo* throughout the measure.

A couple of reasons can almost justify this rationale. First, the chord is scored just for the winds, which do not really have the ability, especially those in the upper registers, to play at the specified dynamic. Second, and somewhat presumptuous, is the feeling that the composer erred in his judgment. All conductors try to get into the head of the creator, but inevitably we cannot know exactly what he or she had in mind.

Perhaps in this case, Dvořák does not want a feeling of exhilaration with the bright-sounding E major chord. Given that this symphony is a postcard from a slightly homesick author, it needs to be imbued with a bit of longing. At least that is how I view it.

So how do we achieve the right balance?

First of all, remember these words: "*Diminuendo* means 'loud'!"

The chord has to begin full and any relaxation should not take place immediately. Wait a moment before starting the lessening of the dynamic. The reverse is true as well. When the marking of crescendo appears, don't increase the volume right away. The famous "Rossini crescendo" only succeeds when the passage starts as softly as possible and gradually works its way up.

How long should we hold this final note in the "New World"? The composer says *lunga*, but the lungs can only hold so much air. It is easy enough to hear when the instrumentalists are running out of breath, much less waiting for the majority of them to turn beet red, but the practical solution is to stop when you believe the sound cannot get any softer.

How do you know when that occurs?

At a rehearsal, hold the chord and ask the players to get as quiet as possible. Get that dynamic into their head so they know the sound when it has been achieved. There are also matters of intonation, which change as the dynamic is lessened. It is all much harder than you would think.

The ideal solution, I am afraid, can only be accomplished if the conductor has the luxury of doubled winds, or two to a part. This way, everyone can begin the last note very loudly and as the diminuendo takes place, the doubling instruments gradually drop out, leaving half the numbers that started. Plus, it allows the solo players to make subtle adjustments to the intonation as they hear the chord fade away.

If you have reached the point in your conducting life where this is an option, most likely you don't need advice from this book.

Debussy: *Prelude to the Afternoon of a Faun*

This simple opening (see Ex. 5) should be an easy problem for any conductor to solve. Perhaps the best example of a symphonic piece starting with a solo instrument, Debussy's exquisite miniature, some think, represents the break-through piece as the twentieth century dawned.

Example 5. Claude Debussy's *Prelude to the Afternoon of a Faun*, mm. 1–4, flute solo.

The question is quite obvious. Do you conduct the passage or just stand there?

Clearly the flutist (Jimmy Galway rejects the term *flautist*—"I don't play the flaute") must have some input, if not all. It is the conductor who must determine the overall tempo and feeling of the piece. After all, if these first three bars are done in a manner that is different than the remaining ten minutes, then the structure of the work is damaged.

Psychology must figure into the decision-making as well. A conductor does not want a clash, over how the passage should go, to be brought in front of the rest of the orchestra. What if the principal flute player, who has no doubt per-formed the work more often than the person on the podium, is equally strong willed? No one in the orchestra or audience will praise or criticize the conductor's interpretation of this opening. It is all about the flute.

Assuming that there is time, the first thing to do is to request a few minutes alone with the player in question. Together the two of you determine how this will go. The conductor speaks about the choice of tempo and the flutist will respond either in accord or disagreement. If the result is the former, then there is no issue, but if you are on different wavelengths, it jeopardizes the conception for both of you.

It is in fact rare that the actual tempo of this Debussy passage is in question. If anything, the soloist might want to go a bit faster than the conductor, if only to get through the phrase in a single, smooth breath. The conductor, citing the slurs, could argue that a bit of time, and therefore a breath, can be taken before each measure, thus maintaining a slower tempo. Far-fetched? Not really. I have heard it done this way a couple of times.

Let's say that both parties come to an understanding about the tempo. That original question still stands. How do you start the piece?

In general, passages like the opening of the Sibelius First Symphony or *The Rite of Spring* are not physically conducted. It makes no sense to lift the baton when the player is not ready, and equally no sense to wait forever when the soloist is raring to go. A discreet nod to the instrumentalist should suffice after ensuring the crowd is silent, the coughing and program shuffling abated. Then the work can commence.

What if the flute player at the concert chooses to go faster than you agreed, unlike the way you rehearsed? Here is where a bit of musical diplomacy comes in. Don't do anything for the first two bars, but bring your arms up gently, leading the third bar and quietly indicating the tempo. This motion is not visible to the audience, but enough so you create a bond between you and the flutist. Keep in mind, you have to shape the whole work ahead of you and a basic tempo is crucial.

In decades past, chances are the conductor would have given every beat from the first measure. We would hope that nowadays, much more of a cooperative spirit exists between the podium and the orchestra. However, the conductor continuously controls the ebb and flow of any piece in the repertoire except a concerto, so make sure you have properly established your speed credentials during the rehearsal process.

I might add that this Debussy comes up often for audition purposes when orchestras are hiring assistant conductors. The first thing the members of the ensemble want to see is how the conductor acquits him- or herself during this opening. In this case I usually advise that eye contact is established between the two of you, and you give a discreet upbeat in the tempo you prefer, then let the flute play the rest of the passage without your assistance.

Rimsky-Korsakov: *Scheherazade*

This masterpiece remains one of the most complex works in the standard repertoire for any orchestra and conductor. There are myriad decisions on virtually every page, but here is the one that is most commonly spoken about.

Example 6. Nikolai Rimsky-Korsakov's *Scheherazade*, second movement,
free clarinet solo (continued on next page).

Example 6 (continued from previous page).

There are several pieces where the concept of at least two different tempi occurring at the same time appears. You can find examples in Ravel, Stravinsky and Bartók, among others, where the conductor must make a choice about which element to lead. There are some these days who easily can conduct one tempo with one hand and a different one with the other. I am not so physically ambidextrous, so it is important for me to figure out which set of forces I will actually lead.

As you can see (see Ex. 6), the composer lets us know that the sixteenth notes in the strings are to be played at an equivalent tempo as the ones that precede this passage. He further instructs that these notes are to have neither an accelerando nor ritardando, so there is no change whatsoever in tempo. The clarinet solo (later in the movement the same thing will happen with the bassoon) is free. It looks fairly straightforward.

Not so fast. Once the pizzicato reaches what looks like a whole note, with the sixteenth-note lines, any sense of rhythm for the strings vanishes. Add to that, the clarinet, because of the rubato, may or may not wind up together with the strings at the end of each phrase. There are numerous solutions for this. Some simplify the problem and some possibly distort the composer's intentions.

Let's deal with the strings first. We know that the sixteenth notes have to be in a pre-determined tempo. Some conductors simply think of four-note groups, almost accenting each of the first of these groups. Others will actually conduct this discreetly, keeping strict time and hopefully keeping the pizzicati together. Others will let the strings listen to one another and not conduct at all until the downbeat of the next measure.

All of these solutions are certainly plausible.

The trouble is that no indication shows that the sixteenths move in groups of four. It could be that they should sound indeterminate, blurring any real rhythm. Many conductors have put accents on the moving notes in the second bar to emphasize the pattern. This causes a new dilemma, perhaps, as it locks the clarinet player into a potentially unnatural phrase ending, due to waiting for the group of four notes to be completed.

Here is what I do, and this is by no means gospel. When we get to the first bar, I conduct the notes of the strings in tempo until the fermata. I stop beating, make eye contact with the clarinetist, and the musician starts more or less at will. There is no feeling of pattern. The rhythmic motion has moved away from a beat pattern of any kind. As he or she nears the end of the phrase, we look at each other, and I follow the lead of that phrase and signal the start of the second measure. There is no waiting for a second, third or fourth sixteenth note to occur. Then I conduct the first two beats of that second measure, again stopping on the fermata. No incidental accents are added. If Rimsky had wanted them, he certainly could have put in accent marks.

In past decades, the work was so well known and often played, that next-to-nothing needed to be said to an orchestra at this point. Yet today, many of the younger entrants in the orchestral field have not seen this composition before, so it can be said that for them, this is truly a piece of new music. As such, you must include rehearsal commentary to accommodate those unfamiliar with the piece, and ensure you are not boring those who have done it countless times.

Mahler: Symphony No. 1

This example (see Ex. 7) brings us to a critical argument that has surfaced in the latter part of the twentieth and early part of the twenty-first century. The debate is not about any conducting technicality. But before we contemplate it, let's examine the violin parts.

Example 7. Gustav Mahler's Symphony No. 1, first movement, mm. 335–344, violin parts.

The first violins have sustained notes played with a crescendo and the second violins have the same exact notes but with a tremolo and a specific instruction from the composer, *without crescendo.* That is blatant enough to understand what Mahler had in mind. It also brings up a vital decision-making subject: the physical position of the musicians onstage.

The matter of orchestral setup has varied over the centuries. Most scholars, backed up by sketches and photographs, have shown us that the second violins were placed to the conductor's right, directly opposite their counterparts in the first violins. No one is positively sure when the practice of placing together both violin sections began. We can deduce from two recordings made by the Chicago Symphony under Fritz Reiner that their switchover occurred sometime between 1954 and 1960. In an early stereophonic version of Strauss' *Also sprach Zarathustra*, the antiphonal violins are clearly audible, but the remake six years later has the whole violin sound on the left. There are photographs of orchestras that hint that conductors used this arrangement long before, perhaps dating to the 1940s.

Every conductor must determine what setup suits the orchestra, hall and music. Mahler certainly divided violins when he wrote his compositions, and the effect this example demonstrates works to full value only when the violins are antiphonal. If the instruments are seated side by side, no one can hear either the tremolo or that one section makes a crescendo while the other does not.

So why would any conductor not split up the fiddles?

The twentieth century has a lot to do with it. Up until that time, composers tended to keep divisi in the violins to a minimum. However, some works simply could not be performed as effectively with the antiphonal violins. The divisi in the slow movement of the Shostakovich Fifth or the single violin section in the Concert Music for Brass and Strings of Hindemith are two problematic works in the historical setup. Many works of Penderecki and Ligeti would lose their cumulative power if the upper registers were separated.

In his invaluable book *The Grammar of Conducting*, Max Rudolf advises, "The historically justified separation of first and second violins, on the left and right of the conductor's stand, should be preserved for the performance of music of the Classical era." The Mahler example would seem to refute that limitation, merely on the basis of what we know the composer wanted.

This is not to claim that the music of Mahler, or any other romantic composers, has been harmed by amassing the upper strings. On the contrary, there is an argument that asserts the sound produced by the unit of violins is richer and the ensemble is tighter.

Other factors influence setup decision-making as well. One of them, at least for me, outweighs historical precedence: acoustics.

Each venue has its own auditory characteristics. In Saint Louis, after much experimentation, I found that the mid-twentieth-century seating of massed violins to the left with violas right center and cellos on the outside worked best in Powell Hall. The National Symphony in Washington fared better with the antiphonal seating, placing the double basses on either the left or center, behind the winds. And in Detroit, the hall was optimally served with the violas at the edge of the stage, switching positions with the cellos. An auditorium is to an orchestra what the instrument is to the instrumentalist. You have to find the right combination to produce the best sound. The conductor shapes the overall sonority of the orchestra, and to do that, he or she must know the hall inside and out.

I am not sure that there is a uniform solution to the dilemma of orchestral setup. Leopold Stokowski spent much of his life as a conductor wrestling with alternative placements, including putting the string section at the rear of the stage with winds and percussion to the fore. Other questions for us include: Should the horns be part of the woodwind or brass section? Are the timpani separated to play with the low end of the orchestral force or as part of the percussion section?

It makes no sense to move things around physically piece by piece on a given program just to satisfy the way each might have been performed long ago. The conductor must devise programs that are practical in terms of stage considerations. Just moving a piano on and off can take up to five minutes.

Ultimately, it comes down to a matter of taste and, to a lesser degree, comfort. Some conductors simply are used to their gestures going one direction or another and cannot adjust to new habits. Others contemplate the sonority they wish to achieve, and some strive for historical and musical accuracy. All are valid approaches if one has truly studied the text and come to conclusions that make sense.

One has to wonder, though, how Mahler would have reacted if he had seen the violins seated together. Maybe another set of revisions?

Beethoven: Piano Concerto No. 5

Every conductor hates this place (see Ex. 8). You can be the most insightful interpreter of the Bruckner Eighth, the most poetic in Brahms' Third, the cleanest in *Petroushka*, but if you miss this Beethoven run, orchestra members will think less of you.

That may seem harsh, but it points to the distinction between the conductor's art and his or her craft. Imagine that a violinist has wonderful ideas but cannot technically bring them off, or a vocalist imparts a fresh approach to a major

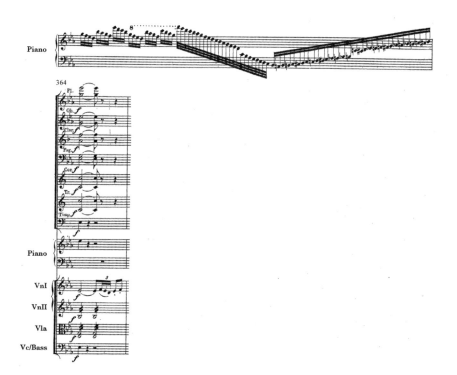

Example 8. Ludwig van Beethoven's Piano Concerto No. 5, first movement, mm. 363–364.

operatic role but sings out of tune. Of course we can all name musicians who have shortcomings that limit their ability to be accurate. In some cases, they are truly great artists. In a maestro, an orchestra wants to see someone who is in command of accompanying skills as well as shows the leadership that comes from a strong musical personality.

George Szell and Carlo Maria Giulini are two examples of conductors who, through opposite means, could coax an orchestra into precisely what they wanted. The first could frighten the daylights out of the players and the second called on his generosity to get results. Both could communicate each small detail with a combination of stick, body language and eye contact, but few mortals are blessed with their skills or God-given talent.

The role of the conductor in a concerto, or any work with a soloist, is a perennial subject for discussion and debate. Who decides matters of interpretation?

Does the soloist have the last word? What if the two fail to agree, as was so infamously on display when Glenn Gould and Leonard Bernstein duked it out publicly over the Brahms First Piano Concerto?

I personally have never run across a work entitled Concerto for Orchestra and Violin. The solo instrument gets top billing, and as such, implies that this is the dominant part. The soloist has spent a tremendous amount of time with a specific piece of music, far longer than the conductor. We might have a repertoire of, say, a couple hundred pieces that we will conduct in a given season, including the concertos. The soloist may offer two or perhaps up to ten such works. Conductors are expected to know the ins and outs of the concerto as an equal.

Once in a while, a young conductor will ask, "How do I adjust to a soloist?" My answer is, "You don't." The conductor must get into the mind and heart of the person who has spent more hours contemplating a single line of that one piece than most podium masters have time for. The key to the collaborative process is using your ears. Develop the strongest listening skills possible. Anticipate every variable, but remain objective enough to understand what is about to happen. Know the solo part as thoroughly as the orchestral writing.

As for this Beethoven passage, as well as countless other traps in the accompanying canon, there is more than one way of approaching the problem. You can watch the pianist's hands and try to physically see where the last note will be placed. This can be risky, especially if the pianist stumbles along the way or you cannot figure out how to give the appropriate upbeat in the correct place during the run. Some conductors discern a rhythmic pattern in the run itself. In this case, use the B-flat at the bottom and count the number of times it appears. At the last one, give a quick upbeat for the orchestra.

If you are lucky, your soloist will have already explained how he or she is going to do the passage. And if you are luckier still, the person will be very musical and you will not have to do anything except listen to the phrasing and inflection. This will give you the best indication of what action to take. Meeting in advance with the soloist can help as well. Know where all the danger spots are, ask for the soloist to play them through for you, and actually conduct at this conference to get the physicality into your arms and body.

And if all else fails, there is prayer.

Beethoven: Symphony No. 9

Somehow we always keep coming back to Beethoven to help us with our problems. This excerpt from the second movement (see Ex. 9) was forever a source of discussion among conductors when I was a student. The issue involved the orchestration of this passage.

But first, we must deal with a fundamental priority of the conductor's job, here in the form of a question.

When, if ever, are we allowed to change what the composer wrote?

If this were a matter of the actual notes and pitches, the answer would be simple: never! Unless the composer might have made a mistake, or the

Example 9. Ludwig van Beethoven's Symphony No. 9, second movement, mm. 93–100.

publisher did not accurately transfer some detail. You would think that nowadays, errors like this would not appear. If so, how can one account for all the "new editions" of masterworks that keep popping up? As Raymond Leppard wrote, they "often reflect the foibles of an academic or a printer with little or no real intuitive understanding of the manuscript, the composer or the process and circumstances of performance it represents." I rehearse and perform numerous pieces of contemporary music, some of them several years old, and usually with the composer present. We are constantly changing things, and if the composition is examined under the microscope, we inevitably discover something that can be made better or more accurate.

If we can alter Corigliano, Rouse, Tower and so many others, why not Beethoven, Brahms and company? Just because they are not on the scene to approve does not mean that their texts are beyond reproach. Experience and familiarity with a given work often suffices to spot either an egregious error or at least raise a question in the mind of the interpreter.

Let's take a look at the first eight bars of the excerpt. Nothing is wrong with the notes or rhythms. Assume that the orchestra has just two players in each woodwind section, as indicated by Beethoven. Clearly, they have the tune. We can also assume that the string section has about fifty or so players and there are four horns as well. None of them is playing the melody. Therefore, the woodwinds are outnumbered by at least six to one. In addition, the bassoons are in a register that can be easily swamped by the others.

There is one more factor that makes this, and almost anything else in the classical and romantic canon, problematic. Block dynamics. What this means is that the entire ensemble simultaneously has the same indication, in this case ff. However, if everyone plays full out, there is no way the melody will be audible.

It was with shock, during a lunchtime discussion at Juilliard in my student days, that one conductor wannabe said, "Have you heard what Toscanini did with this passage?"

"Yes, he was faithful to the score and did not change anything."

"Wrong! He adds horns and has them doubling the melody!"

A number of us rushed to the library phonograph to listen to the offending moment, and sure enough, we could hear what our colleague was talking about. You can imagine the kind of argument this triggered in 1965, just prior to when the period-instrument boom began. The disagreement pitted the purists against the revisionists, with no common ground.

Almost forty years later, I performed a series of concerts in Washington that explored the Mahler *Retuschen* of several symphonies by Beethoven. Among the things I learned was that the convention of the era allowed the conductor to make alterations. In fact, it was expected. After all, here was Mahler, a distinguished composer and conductor, taking on the master and basically saying that if Beethoven were alive and working in this context of different instruments, orchestras and halls, this is what he would have changed.

During the course of the Beethoven/Mahler festival, I chose to make an example of the eight measures in Example 9. Here are a few of the versions and retouchings as done by Strauss, Wagner, Szell, Bernstein and of course, Mahler. Some are subtle and some are drastic. Even period specialists must confront some flexibility. The moment the conductor says to the horns, "I know it is written *ff*, but could you change it to just one *f*, just so we can hear the woodwinds more clearly?" That is a change from what the composer wrote.

Here is Wagner, with only lines that he alters (see Ex. 10). The oboe, clarinet, and bassoon sections now each play in unison for the first four bars. In addition, Wagner has the four horns play the melodic line (not shown).

Example 10. Beethoven's Symphony No. 9, second movement, mm. 93–100, Richard Wagner's alteration.

Richard Strauss is a bit more conservative and only changes the horns (see Ex. 11).

Example 11. Beethoven's Symphony No. 9, second movement, mm. 93–100, Richard Strauss' alteration.

George Szell was regarded, like Toscanini, as a textually faithful conductor, but he too made changes in orchestration. In this spot in the score (see Ex. 12), Szell uses four players in each woodwind section to add strength, manually writing in two clarinet lines underneath the printed horn parts.

Leonard Bernstein takes the Toscanini route by having only one horn play the quick notes (see Ex. 13), giving the illusion that the instrument is playing the whole line. However, it must be said that Bernstein frequently doubled the woodwind parts.

Finally, we look at Mahler's version (see Ex. 14). He essentially puts in as much as possible, with not only the horns and doubled woodwinds playing the melodic line, but the trumpets as well. In addition, he appears to have the brass instruments separating the quick notes as opposed to slurring them, resulting in an even more startling spin to this passage.

Regardless of your score-reading skills, it is easy to see what each conductor has done. And in every case, these men are trying to enhance the phrase, not inject their own personality. As instruments continue to evolve, so must orchestral practice. With judicious study and experience, we can reach conclusions for problems without sacrificing the intent of the creator. We will never know what the composers might have thought as regards how their music would be played in one hundred years. We do know that the greats tended to welcome evolution and embrace change.

Example 12. Beethoven's Symphony No. 9, second movement, mm. 93–100, George Szell's alteration.

Example 13. Beethoven's Symphony No. 9, second movement, mm. 93–100,
Leonard Bernstein's alteration.

Example 14. Beethoven's Symphony No. 9, second movement, mm. 93–100,
Gustav Mahler's alteration.

Johann Strauss II: *On the Beautiful Blue Danube*

Tradition and style are inextricably linked. Typically, a composer's intentions are clear, with the notes and musical text providing a roadmap for the conductor to follow. But there are many examples of a sort of indigenous flavoring that is assumed and apparently supposed to be followed, despite the lack of written directions.

Nearly every composer has such moments, and this excerpt (see Ex. 15) is arguably the best-known example. Leaving aside any rubato in the melodic line, it is the accompanying figures that drive all but the Viennese crazy.

Most conductors have been told how this is supposed to go: "The downbeat is in tempo, the second beat is slightly rushed and the third beat is somewhat elongated."

All well and good. But by how much? How short or long are the notes, are the bows positioned on or off the string, and is every waltz from the period executed the same way? The list of questions goes on. In Vienna on one occasion, I had the opportunity to perform the "Donner und Blitzen" polka by the same composer. At the start of the rehearsal I told the orchestra which repeats we would take, and that was met with a collective sigh. "No, here is how it goes," I was informed by at least half of the orchestra. On the same program was the "New World" Symphony and when I said that we were taking the first movement repeat, there was another outcry, with members replying, "We never do that." It must be remembered that Dvořák's homeland is just across the border from Austria.

There are definite national characteristics in every country's music, but how they translate from region to region varies wildly. I suspect, as have others, that this variation is rooted in spoken language—where accents are placed and which syllables are emphasized. It is easy enough to attempt to replicate the Viennese waltz outside of its place of origin, but most of the time, this comes off as a forced musical experience. In some ways, a straightforward interpretation seems a more natural expression for the non-Austrian performer.

The process can be reversed with intriguing results. It is almost impossible for me to count the number of performances I have given of Gershwin's *An American in Paris*. Most of the time, during the passages where I ask for a swing rhythm to be played, I pretty much get the response I desire when conducting orchestras in the States and the United Kingdom. Once, however, I had a set of

Example 15. Johann Strauss II's *On the Beautiful Blue Danube*, mm. 45–56.

performances with the New York Philharmonic. Initially, I thought the piece would be easy to put together, as the ensemble had played it quite often. But a previous conductor had made it raucous and, for my taste, unstylistic, so we devoted an hour and a half to the piece at the first rehearsal.

After one performance, Kurt Masur, then music director of the Phil, asked me to do the Gershwin in Leipzig. He said that I was the ideal person to teach it to his other orchestra, the Gewandhaus. So off I went and although I tried my best, it simply did not work. When you have to explain how the printed eighths are really relaxed triplets, you know you are in trouble. They did try but in the end, I doubt that I taught them very well. And I won't even get into what happened when I asked for a "Billy May" glissando from the saxes!

The dilemma is that a conductor cannot always communicate with gestures alone. Some of my most rewarding experiences have been with orchestras in countries where I do not speak a word of the native language. But once in a while, we need to find the exact way to explain something verbally. There are some concepts that defy description and can only be felt. But in the global marketplace, we do have the chance to hear a variety of renditions, whether right or wrong. Singing a phrase, even if horribly out of tune, can go a long way. The aim is to make the players feel the line or rhythm, not just imitate.

Whether the situation involves double-dotting baroque music, trying to distinguish a waltz from a ländler, or explaining why an English gigue is distinct from a French one, stylistic differences must be dealt with. As with almost every element of music, study and experience are the best teachers. You must be natural in every facet of music, and what is not comfortable should be left to others.

And when is the last time anyone actually saw the Danube *blue*?

30

Ten FAQs

It is better to know some of the questions than all of the answers.

—JAMES THURBER

Over the years, I have heard countless queries on all manner of subjects related to conducting. What follows are the most frequently asked of those questions with answers rooted in accumulated experience.

1. What does the conductor do?

Recently, I had the pleasure of judging a conducting competition. Normally, I avoid this display of music as sport, and only rarely sit on a panel, but in this case, I made an exception. The contestants belonged to the Pittsburgh Symphony Youth Orchestra, and six young instrumentalists had applied for the opportunity to lead their own orchestra in "Les toréadors" from *Carmen*.

Each musician had to submit a written response to the above question. After so many years of struggling to explain it, I could not have phrased it as well as those teenagers did.

Kemper Edwards: "The conductor is the lightning rod of the orchestra, focusing the energy and communicating it to the audience."

Daniel Orsen: "The role of the conductor is to guide the orchestra and make all of the major interpretive decisions for a piece, because a democratic approach like that used in chamber music would be impossible."

Yani Quemado: "The conductor imposes his interpretations and musical views upon the orchestra during rehearsal. This is where the conductor does most of the work with the orchestra. He must exhibit an innate skill of communication, conveying his focal point to the orchestra to convince them of his understanding."

Adam Janssen: "The conductor is the ultimate interpreter of the music at hand. It is up to him or her to make the audience understand what the composer was trying to convey in the music."

None of the candidates was older than sixteen. They seemed to know as much as I did, perhaps more.

2. What do I do when I get out of school?

Opportunities exist wherever you look, but most of them are not obvious. In earlier days, the budding conductor might have entered a competition, sought an assistantship with an orchestra or taken a job as répétiteur in an opera house. These are almost all long shots now.

If one has a real interest in a full-time professional career, the best way to learn is to attend as many rehearsals of others as possible. None of us likes aggressive people running up and trying to barge in after practice. However, there is a big difference between aggressive and assertive. Showing interest in those with more experience is always good advice. Seek out conductors who have a good track record of working with young people. Watch them, ask questions and do not push yourself upon them. If they can help, they will offer to assist in some way. If not, you will have still learned a great deal.

Keep your eyes and ears open for any vacancies. This can be done in the States through the conducting arm of ICSOM, the Conductors Guild. There are websites that post information as to openings. If your interests are in the opera world, it is de rigueur that you play the piano. Most likely you will get a foot in the door either in Europe or the States by serving as an accompanist and coach.

There are other options that most young conductors do not consider. Even though ballet relies heavily on prerecorded music, working in that field can be thoroughly rewarding. Great maestros are not commonly associated with dance, but Monteux made his initial success this way. Getting experience in musical theater is also a fine way to hone many skills. Forming your own ensembles can be another way to garner attention, which then leads to the next question:

3. How do I get a manager?

You would not believe how many people consider this to be the top priority of a conductor's life. Perhaps it is the age in which we live, but as far as I know, Berlioz, Wagner and Weingartner did not have agents collecting fees on their behalf, at least as conductors. It could be argued that Leopold Mozart was the first real manager, but the phenomenon of actual agents began in the early twentieth century.

The corollary to the question is, "Are managers necessary?" A lot of conductors will answer with an unqualified yes, but as we move along into the age of instant communication, we might now say, "Perhaps not." Because it is a complicated world, and matters of finances and taxes are involved, having specialists take care of these inconveniences seems prudent. I certainly know of several artists who have managed it on their own. Some conductors hire a personal assistant, pay the person a salary and let him or her do all the drudgework. For the most part, however, it helps to have the guiding hands of people who are in the business, at least at the outset.

When I was considering a change of management, a wise man, Sheldon (Shelly) Gold, the president of ICM Artists back in the '80s, asked me, "Leonard, what do you think an agent does?"

My response was, "Looks out for the welfare of the artists and guides them on a good career path."

Shelly then offered words I had never heard before. "No. The agent's job is to make money. The more we can charge for you, the more we make. You are in a business that is not for profit, but we are just the opposite."

A good manager will take care of your needs, as this affects his or her own livelihood, but in far too many cases, artists get pushed to the point where they are overworked and burned out. Most conductors would love to be in that position to start with, but as my current manager, Doug Sheldon, told me in 2004, "Now that you are sixty, your career can begin."

Artist's agencies are always looking for hot young prospects. In a market that values appearance as well as musicianship, there is a possible profit motive for a company that discovers the next attractive podium sensation. Ultimately it is talent that determines the staying power of a conductor.

Very few have managed to sustain a long career without the musical ability to back it up.

My suggestions usually focus on two things: creative ideas and who you know. It is not possible for every conductor to be seen in person by other maestros or managers. You can make an appointment to speak with any number of agencies, but words must be supported with strong recommendations. These days, conductors have videos of either rehearsals or concerts they have led. Try to get the best possible sound quality but do not overproduce your DVD. I have witnessed enough title sequences and endless voice-overs to embarrass Steven Spielberg. Your business is music-making, not post-production.

Think up projects and concert ideas that are unique. This makes you more saleable. Yes, we would all like to believe that our profound Beethoven Sixth is utterly unparalleled, but ensure you have choices to mold a true profile. I took a chance early in my career with scores by American and English composers not on the radar of many conductors. There are wonderful repositories of neglected, forgotten or new scores that can become calling cards. Unless you are a specialist in a certain repertoire, you will be able to present a wide spectrum of the musical canon, but as a start, keep a few pieces on hand that mark you as an individual.

Musical America is a handy reference book that is published every year in the States. This guide lists practically all the artists and their managers in the world. By checking who is with which agency, the young conductor can get sense of how each roster stacks up with his or her own goals and objectives. Some companies are larger and have a number of big names. My own feeling is that it is better to start with a firm that has few conductors. That way, there is a likelihood of more personal attention.

Do keep in mind that the agent will take a commission of anywhere from 10 to 20 percent of your earnings. Even if you secure an engagement for yourself, you must notify the manager. An agent is part of your team. Shutouts are frowned upon.

The manager will also be the person to negotiate the terms of all your contracts. The two of you will come to an agreement about your fee structures, many of which will last for a long time. Your agent works on getting you repeat engagements. Do not be upset if these do not come along for a while, or even at all. What you might have considered a success may only have been your opinion.

You must trust your agent! A manager is not there to constantly compliment you, but is your support when things are not so good. It will be a love/hate affair at times, the proverbial necessary evil. But most are good guys.

Perhaps this little story can help.

In 1970, Walter Susskind took me into the offices of the most powerful man in the classical music industry. His name was Ronald Wilford, the president of Columbia Artists Management, and he was a man of few words. Just getting in to see him took several months of effort.

After greetings were exchanged, Susskind waxed enthusiastically over my abilities and the good work I was doing as his assistant. Mr. Wilford thanked him for bringing me in but said, "I don't think Mr. Slatkin is at the level of conductors we currently have on our roster." We left somewhat dejected.

A few weeks later, the irrepressible Mariedi Anders, from San Francisco, came to hear a concert of mine in Saint Louis. She signed me the next day and we had a wonderful relationship for fifteen years. Eventually I moved to ICM under the watchful eye of Lee Lamont and then landed back at CAMI, some thirty years after that initial trip to Fifty-seventh Street.

4. Do I need a baton?

No. Just do whatever feels most comfortable. If the stick helps you in communicating to the orchestra, then use it. The baton, as every teacher will explain, is simply an extension of your arm. Many of today's conductors alternate between using it and putting it down, depending on the nature of the music, but you must be sensitive as to what aids the orchestra. Whatever you can do to illustrate the music physically is always welcome.

It definitely helps to know how to conduct without the stick. It is easily flung away in the heat of performance.

5. What if the orchestra doesn't like me?

Conducting is not a popularity contest. Sure, you want the musicians to do as you request, but patronizing commentary, shortening rehearsal just to curry favor and joking around does not get you a better performance. Orchestras sense the ability of the conductor within two minutes after the downbeat. We all have our insecure moments, but do not try to mask them with superfluous gestures and rhetoric.

Orchestra members do not want speeches. It is wise, however, to treat each person with respect. Remember that out of one hundred musicians, eighty of them think that they can conduct better than you and, quite probably, twenty of them can.

6. How do you pick the pieces you conduct?

For most of the early going, the programs were not always my choice. Naturally, at school I had no say in the repertoire. When my professional life began, I studied what other conductors put together. Sometimes you make a mistake. My debut program in Toronto consisted of:

Brahms	*Tragic Overture*
Mozart	Concerto for Flute, Harp and Orchestra
Delius	Prelude to *Irmelin*
W. Schuman	Symphony No. 8

No wonder I did not get asked back until twenty-five years later!
A famous example of horrendous programming was the following:

Gershwin	Piano Concerto in F
Bruckner	Symphony No. 5

Thank God it was not mine.

Sometimes you have a piece thrust upon you and have no choice.

In the middle of recording a Vaughan Williams symphony cycle with the Philharmonia, we presented a concert at the conclusion of the Brighton Music Festival. An American first half was planned and we also needed to include one of the English master's pieces, which would be performed in front of microphones the next day.

It was not until a few weeks before the performance that I was informed the Festival always ends with the "1812" Overture, complete with cannons and chorus.

So the program was as follows:

Bernstein	*Candide* Overture
Barber	*Adagio for Strings*
MacDowell	Piano Concerto No. 2
Vaughan Williams	Symphony No. 4
Tchaikovsky	*Ouverture Solennelle* "1812"

The Vaughan Williams is a highly energetic and difficult work. Nothing can come after it. The sheer physical stamina required for this half-hour is exhausting. I made a cut in the "1812." I think we got the work down to about eight minutes. It didn't help.

Common sense will usually guide you through the rigors of programming. Try to keep concerts under two hours. The order of the works is not as important as the content, but it does seem logical to do the biggest pieces last. Examine programs of earlier periods and you will notice that the idea was reversed, but these days listeners go for the big ending. I prefer contrasting styles within the traditional concert format, but many conductors are on a quest for new ways to invigorate concert life.

You must take into account the audience for whom you are playing. Challenging works and programs are fine, if you are confident that you can successfully take the public on that journey. All conductors try to incorporate new or unfamiliar music into the concert, but usually tempered with something familiar. Sticking with the overture-concerto-symphony pattern continues to work, but there are alternatives. Shaking things up a bit is welcome, although conventional formats remain viable options.

Be creative, play to your strengths and try to avoid doing pieces that you don't like. You might have no choice in your first job, but experience will teach you about the proper repertoire to match your tastes. With so much music available, limiting yourself at the start is not wise.

Unless you play the accordion.

7. Who gets solo bows?

Believe it or not, this is a very tricky question to answer. There are obvious bows, such as the flutist in *Daphnis et Chloé*, the trumpet and horn players in Mahler's Fifth or the principal cellist in the Brahms Second Piano Concerto.

But what happens when there are several instrumental solos? Or if the solo is short? What if you leave out somebody? And more critically, what do you do if the player messes it up?

Good examples of the first question might include *Boléro*, Rimsky-Korsakov's *Scheherazade*, or *An American in Paris*. You might decide in the case of the Ravel just to give the snare drummer a solo bow and have the others stand as a group, a plan you have to tell the orchestra at rehearsal. Don't be surprised at how many people think that they actually have a solo. For the Rimsky, clearly the violin gets first call. Then you can either do the same as the *Boléro* or single them out individually. What I do is glance at each section and try to remember who, if any, played. In the case of the Gershwin, certainly the trumpet gets up, but you can decide if you wish to acknowledge the tuba, solo violin and saxophones.

And if you forget? Usually it will hit you by the time you get back to the dressing room, when it is too late to do anything. Perhaps members of the orchestra will make a remark while you are basking in the applause. If there is an opportunity, mention the situation to the personnel manager, who can relay your message to a particular musician. Once in a while the offended player will come to ask you if he or she did something wrong. Tell the musician that the playing was wonderful and you simply did not remember in all the commotion onstage.

Imagine that you have conducted a fine performance of, say, *Petroushka*. The orchestra was brilliant, colors well illuminated, but at the end, one of the trumpets completely blew it, pun intended. Now what?

Actually, this is quite easy to solve, albeit uncomfortable. The consequences of not publicly recognizing that person are greater than the alternative. The musician is acutely aware that the solo did not go well, as do the others onstage. Even most of the audience may have noticed that there were problems. Such is the human condition, and unless you have a real grudge against the person, and are willing to risk all manner of trouble, you must beckon the player to rise. Sometimes the musician may refuse, but that is rarely the case. Take the high road and be as gracious as possible.

It is perhaps a good thing that conductors do not have this worry in the opera pit.

8. Do the social aspects of a music director become tiring?

Some conductors love the social dance. Others abhor it, especially as practiced in the States. I have always felt that this is an integral function of the music director's job. Yes, it can be difficult, especially on the heels of a demanding program, but meeting and greeting is an imperative if you are trying to raise money for your orchestra.

This is where some conductors balk. They feel that their duty is to conduct and make music, but they have no desire to do much of anything else. This would seem to go against traditions that stem back almost two hundred years. Glad-handing and the basic practice of social grace have always come with performances. The green room may not have been in existence per se until recent times, but conductors have always met with members of the public.

Attending all the dinners, galas and other events are an inevitable element of, at least, the American music director's milieu. You can control it, to some extent. Polite declining of some invitations is acceptable, but you had better have a good explanation ready. These patrons are funding your post. They provide the opportunity to attain what you have dreamed of. For that, we must show gratitude.

9. How do you deal with the critics?

Sometimes this is phrased, "Do you read what they write about you?" The latter, at least for me, is a resounding yes!

This is very important for the music director. While he or she may be the musical head of the organization, the critic is the individual to whom many people turn, either to validate or repudiate what concertgoers believe took place. The critic can indeed influence whether you will keep your job. In the case of readers who did not attend a performance, the journalist is the sole professional whose opinion may be considered irrefutable. Many in the audience do not fully form their opinion until they have read about it either the next day or later.

Reviews are quoted widely in every aspect of the arts. They can affect fundraising over a period of time. A bad review can close down a multimillion-dollar Broadway show. A good one can launch a career.

At this period in my life, I tend to view things from the perspective of the people writing for the newspapers, magazines, or these days, online outlets. Back when major cities had competing publications, you had a variety of writers to choose from. Now, with only a few exceptions, each city has only one major broadsheet. In that sense, the critics might seem to have a little more power. Those newspapers that still employ full-time music journalists have increased competition from the Internet. Today, literally, anyone can become a critic.

The responsibility of the reporter is to do exactly that, report. At the same time, he or she must render a subjective judgment about what has transpired. The opinion should be well informed and thought out. It must take into account the reaction of the audience, even if the commentator did not share that feeling. Most important, the journalist must state all the facts correctly. On more than one occasion during my tenure with the National Symphony, I notified the *Washington Post* ombudsman that the critic had made numerous misstatements regarding a particular composer. Normally I do not weigh in on this heavily, but under these circumstances, the public was not properly prepared and the writer needed to be taken to task.

Does it hurt when someone writes unfavorably about you? Sometimes, but not always. Most artists are highly critical of their own work. No writer, or for that matter audience member, can know how the creator or re-creator truly feels about what they have done. We are our own worst, or possibly best, critics. So in that sense, we tend to hurt ourselves more than anyone else.

My uncle Victor had a good philosophy when it came to the press reaction. He said, "If they say it was good and it was, they are right. If they say it was bad and it was not, they are wrong. If they say it was bad and they were right, ignore it. And if they say it was good and it was not, take it!"

As to performers who claim to skip looking at the reviews, there is this cautionary tale from my friend, pianist Jeffrey Siegel.

He was soloist in a series of concerts with the Pittsburgh Symphony. His concerto was Brahms' Second. As there were three performances, he had decided not to read the papers so as not to be concerned through the course of the remaining two performances. The first took place on a Thursday evening with another for the Friday matinee.

As he was about to step onstage in the afternoon, the first cellist approached him and said, "Jeffrey. Never mind what they wrote today. We enjoyed working with you."

You just can't win.

10. What would you do if you were not a conductor?

It took me such a long time to settle on this road that it is tough to even imagine doing anything else. I have loved it all. The opportunity to make great, and sometimes not-so-great, music. Collaborating with artists who share the same passion for the art. The feeling of growth and getting closer to the musical truth has been exhilarating. Such a privileged life is more than anyone could possibly wish for or deserve.

If push came to shove, I would either be a teacher or a baseball broadcaster.

Bonus Question: How much do you get paid?

Zubin Mehta has the all-time best answer for this: "I don't know, but whatever it is, it isn't enough."

Codetta

The beginnings and endings of all human undertakings are untidy.

—JOHN GALSWORTHY

No doubt I have left a lot of unanswered questions. The conducting profession is so complex that no one volume can possibly tell all. It is also a world in flux. So to end this tome, I have opted to put down random thoughts, in no particular order.

At this point, there is a quest to uncover the great new podium genius. Youth would seem to be the order of the day. We all have to start somewhere and the infusion of fresh blood on the rostrum is welcome, but simultaneously, some worry that experience will be sacrificed for the glamour of youth. Learning the repertoire takes time and effort. The ability to look good cannot substitute for substance in the long run. I sincerely wish all the kids on the block well. In time they will become the venerable ones. But that comes later.

One of my colleagues recounts the story of his debut with the Philadelphia Orchestra. The work in question was the Second Symphony by Schumann. When they got to the Scherzo, he was having trouble coordinating a particular passage.

He said to the orchestra, "I don't understand. I have never had any trouble in this place before."

A violinist in the seconds responded, "Funny. Neither have we."

The role of the conductor in music education cannot be overemphasized. Even with no previous concert-going experience, a young person realizes the authority of the person on the podium. The maestro seems to command respect and exude leadership. But along with actual conducting, the ability to communicate verbally with musicians and non-musicians must be top-notch.

I developed my own speaking skills and styles from work in radio. It is not sufficient to assume that you can stand up and automatically deliver a cogent message. Whether or not you are scripted or speak extemporaneously, this role is crucial in the development and education of our young people.

Clearly the master of communication was Bernstein. It is said that although he appeared to improvise as he went along, he had scrupulously studied his texts and worked tirelessly on projecting the meaning. My advice is to practice by recording yourself while listening over headsets at the same time. Develop the ability to make speech simple and clear. Do not speak too quickly. When it actually comes to getting up in front of the public, learn as much as possible about projecting your voice. Always speak to the person in the back of the room and never let the last word of a sentence drop off.

You can never conduct enough Haydn or Schubert.

There is a lot of talk about the demise of the symphony orchestra in the twenty-first century, as well as how to "reinvent" the institution. While change is inevitable, what we do is a product of almost three hundred years of accumulated musical wisdom. Letting it go is unthinkable.

With the explosion of interest in classical music to be found in South America, Korea, Japan and China, it is not possible to even imagine our art form disappearing. Lang Lang told me that China has more than 40 million piano students. Many of these young people come to study in the Western hemisphere. They will either return home or settle in their adopted country. Few will become professional musicians. What they will become is our audience, steeped in traditions and demanding quality from those who present our art.

Gimmicks such as onstage screens, interactive cell phones and fancy symphonic productions are passing fads. Journalists and alleged experts may speak of the orchestra as needing to modernize, but the public decides cultural taste that lasts. Right now, my money is on maintaining more or less the same traditions with a few ventures down new paths.

For reasons unknown, you never sneeze while conducting.

Prior to walking onstage for a performance of Beethoven's Fifth, Sir Alexander Gibson facetiously asked the head stagehand in Saint Louis, "Leroy, should I conduct this piece with the score or from memory?"

The response?

"Maestro, I could conduct this piece from memory!"

Some think it is a trick. Others are amazed that anyone can do it. A few dismiss it as a showy gimmick. There is an axiom that says, "Have the score in your head but do not have your head in the score."

Only a handful of conductors have photographic memory and the ability to physically write out every detail of the score if challenged to do so. The rest of us who conduct without the music rely almost exclusively on auditory and physical memory. You can only marvel at conductors such as Dimitri Mitropoulos, Lorin Maazel and Seiji Ozawa, genuinely able to memorize all the details of essentially any work.

After a performance of the *Meistersinger* Prelude, I asked Sir Georg Solti why he still used the music after what must have been the three-hundredth performance of this piece.

"You never know what you might discover."

Point taken.

In my mind it is imperative that every conductor, no, every musician, try to write a piece of music. Understanding the creative process is critical to unlocking the secrets of every composer. The piece does not have to be good, but the effort is worthwhile.

My own skills in this area are limited, but every so often I will sit down and jot notes on paper. Recently, this has taken the form of arrangements for piano and strings written for middle and high school level musicians. Originally planned for my son, Daniel, to play with his string ensemble, the project grew into a couple of volumes of holiday songs. Amazingly, they have been published and young pianists are playing them. There are few satisfactions as wonderful as seeing your name attached to a successful educational project.

There are only three scores you need to study to learn how to orchestrate: Beethoven's *Eroica*, the complete *Nutcracker* and Ravel's *L'enfant et les sortilèges*.

It is not necessary to know how to play all the instruments of the orchestra, but you do need an understanding of how they work, their ranges and how they sound when combined with any other instrument. My suggestion is to learn the rudiments of string playing by studying one instrument for a few months. The overwhelming majority of your instructions to an orchestra will be directed at these musicians, so firsthand knowledge about string mechanics provides a good foundation.

The most underrated composer, at least the composer whose works should be heard and played more frequently, is Paul Hindemith. Any symphony's marketing department head will tell you that his music does not sell to the public, but when it is presented, listeners always enjoy it. Perhaps some of those charged with promoting the works do not know how to really do their jobs.

The single best self-deprecatory remark from a conductor came from Henry Mancini. He was in New York, recording a few commercials, when he decided to make some changes. It went something like this.

"Flutes. In bar nine could we switch to alto flutes? Trumpets and trombones, in measure seventeen I think Harmon mutes with stems out will sound better. Violins, when you get to bar twenty-five, play the next eight measures an octave higher. In the last bar, can we take out the cymbal crash and do it on suspended cymbal with a hard stick instead. Clarinets, that last B-flat sounds too squeaky. Leave it out. In the saxes, give me a lip gliss in bar seventy-two.

"Okay, shall we do a take or should I just go f**k myself?"

The two orchestras of Radio France rehearse in adjacent rooms. Once, I was working with the Philharmonique and Kurt Masur was with his Orchestre national de France, both of us rehearsing the same day at the same time.

One program contained music by Gershwin, Bernstein and Ives. The other had Schumann, Schubert, Spohr and Brahms. Anybody stopping by would have been surprised to find that I was leading the German program and Maestro Masur was handling the American repertoire.

Speaking of France, a late addition to my activities has been to assume the directorship of the Orchestre national de Lyon. Coupled with Detroit this gives me two bases of operation and helps cut down on travel during the course of a season. Lyon is lovely and the orchestra plays with great enthusiasm. It is hoped that this partnership produces some spectacular results. My cardiologist is not thrilled with this appointment.

The pianists Emanuel Ax and Yefim Bronfman, along with violinist Gil Shaham, have one thing in common. Each of them says, "I apologize in advance," before walking onstage.

Believe in yourself. If you have the talent and persevere, you will succeed. The path is filled with stones and pebbles. Each will help you understand your strengths and weaknesses.

Conducting is a noble profession. As with any re-creative artist, it is our responsibility to be honest with ourselves and with the music that we serve. A bit of ego is not a terrible thing and once in a while we can afford to pat ourselves on the back. Just not too often.

Acknowledgments

While virtually everyone who made this book possible is mentioned in the text, there are a few who assisted directly in bringing the project to fruition. I am indebted to the following:

The team at Amadeus Press, who believed in the content and encouraged me to keep writing.

Vanessa Weeks Page, who did the editing and made the words come to life.

The librarians of the Detroit Symphony Orchestra, who worked tirelessly to make the orchestral excerpts as clear as possible.

The family of Ernest Fleischmann, who kindly granted permission to quote from one of his speeches.

My brother, Fred Zlotkin, who is the family historian and provided me with dates and places.

Jacqueline McTee, who made sure that syntax and tense were not opposed to each other.

The numerous friends and colleagues who encouraged me to write many of the stories and ideas contained in the book.

And finally, my wife, Cindy, who was supportive even through those times when sitting at my computer took me away from her.

Music Excerpt Sources

Beethoven, Ludwig van. *Ludwig van Beethovens Werke, Serie 1: Symphonien, No. 5.* Leipzig: Breitkopf & Härtel, 1862.

———. *Ludwig van Beethovens Werke, Serie 1: Symphonien, No. 9.* Leipzig: Breitkopf & Härtel, 1863.

———. *Ludwig van Beethovens Werke, Serie 9: Für Pianoforte und Orchester, No. 69.* Leipzig: Breitkopf & Härtel, 1862–90.

———. Symphony No. 9. Edited by Gustav Mahler. N.p., n.d. Library of the Detroit Symphony Orchestra.

———. Symphony No. 9 (excerpts). Modern transcriptions of Richard Wagner's and Richard Strauss' alterations. Library of the National Symphony Orchestra (Washington DC).

———. Symphony No. 9, with alterations by George Szell. N.p.: Breitkopf & Härtel, n.d. Library of the Cleveland Orchestra.

———. Symphony No. 9, with alterations by Leonard Bernstein. N.p.: Breitkopf & Härtel, n.d. Library of the New York Philharmonic.

Brahms, Johannes. *Johannes Brahms: Sämtliche Werke, Band 1.* Leipzig: Breitkopf & Härtel, 1926–27.

Debussy, Claude. *Three Great Orchestral Works in Full Score.* New York: Dover Publications, 1983.

Dvořák, Antonín. *Symphonies Nos. 8 and 9 ("New World") in Full Score.* Mineola, NY: Dover Publications, 1984.

Mahler, Gustav. *Symphonie No. 1.* Vienna: Universal Edition, 1906.

Mozart, Wolfgang Amadeus. *Wolfgang Amadeus Mozarts Werke, Serie 8: Symphonien.* Leipzig: Breitkopf & Härtel, 1880.

Rimsky-Korsakov, Nikolai. *Scheherazade.* Moscow: Muzgiz, n.d. (1931).

Strauss, Johann II. *An der schönen blauen Donau: Walzer Op. 314.* Detroit: Luck's Music Library, n.d. (after 1960).

Index

Page references in italics indicate photographs or reproduced music examples.